DOGMATIC THEOLOGY
VIII

THE SACRAMENTS

A DOGMATIC TREATISE

BY

THE RT. REV. MSGR. JOSEPH POHLE, Ph.D., D.D.

FORMERLY PROFESSOR OF DOGMATIC THEOLOGY AT ST. JOSEPH'S
SEMINARY, LEEDS (ENGLAND). LATER PROFESSOR OF
APOLOGETICS AT THE CATHOLIC UNIVERSITY
OF AMERICA

ADAPTED AND EDITED

BY

ARTHUR PREUSS

VOLUME I

The Sacraments in General.   Baptism. Confirmation.

THIRD, REVISED EDITION

———

B. HERDER BOOK CO.
17 SOUTH BROADWAY, ST. LOUIS, MO.
AND
68 GREAT RUSSELL ST., LONDON, W. C.
1919

BECKTOLD
PRINTING & BOOK MFG. CO.
ST. LOUIS, MO.

TABLE OF CONTENTS

TABLE OF CONTENTS

INTRODUCTION

The justification of the sinner, with which we have dealt in a previous treatise,[1] is ordinarily not a purely internal and invisible process or series of acts, but requires the instrumentality of external visible signs instituted by Jesus Christ, which either confer grace [2] or augment [3] it.

Such visible means of grace are called Sacraments.[4]

The source and well-spring of all grace under the present dispensation is the Sacrifice of the Cross, from which redemptive power flows into the souls of men through·the Sacraments and the Mass. This consideration led St. Thomas to regard the Passion of Our Divine Saviour as the foundation-stone of the dogmatic treatise on the Sacraments. The importance of this treatise, from both the theoretical and the practical point of view, is in turn evident from the fact that the

1 *Grace, Actual and Habitual*, St. Louis, Mo., 1915.

2 In this sense justification is called *iustificatio prima.*

3 In this sense it is called *iustificatio secunda.*

4 Prayer and sacrifice are also means of grace, but in a different sense, and are therefore treated elsewhere — prayer in moral and ascetic theology, sacrifice partly in Soteriology (cfr. Pohle-Preuss, *Soteriology*, pp. 111 sqq.) and partly in the dogmatic treatise on the Holy Eucharist, Part III, "The Holy Eucharist as a Sacrifice."

grace of the Atonement cannot in the present economy effect justification in the individual soul without the use of the Sacraments, *in re,* or at least *in voto.*

Following the example of the Tridentine Council,[5] modern theologians are wont to introduce the treatise on the Sacraments with an explanation of the nature, operation, and requisites of Sacraments in general.[6] Besides obviating the need of constant repetition, this introduction serves to show that the Sacraments are closely connected by a common bond and together constitute an organic unit.

The present volume contains, besides this general introduction *De Sacramentis in Genere,* the special treatises on Baptism and Confirmation. The next volume will be devoted entirely to the Holy Eucharist, the following one to Penance, while a fourth will deal with Extreme Unction, Holy Orders, and Matrimony.

5 *Concilium Trident.,* Sess. VII, quoted in Denzinger-Bannwart's *Enchiridion,* 11th ed., n. 844 sqq., Freiburg 1911.

6 " *De Sacramentis in genere;* " in German, " *Allgemeine Sakramentenlehre.* "

PART I

THE SACRAMENTS IN GENERAL

CHAPTER I

DEFINITION, DIVISION, AND NUMBER

In this Chapter we shall first define the term "Sacrament," then show how it has been applied to various rites in the Old and the New Testament, and finally demonstrate that under the New Law there are seven Sacraments, neither more nor less.

GENERAL READINGS: — Peter Lombard, *Liber Sent.,* IV, dist. 1 sqq.— St. Thomas, *Summa Theologica,* 3a, qu. 60 sqq., and his commentators, notably the Salmanticenses, *Cursus Theol.,* Vol. XVIII (ed. Paris 1880) ; Billuart, *De Sacramentis in Communi* (ed. Lequette, Paris, Vol. VI, pp. 97 sqq.), etc.—*Suarez, *De Sacramentis* (ed. Vivès, Paris 1856 sqq.).— Bellarmine, *Controvers. de Sacrament. in Genere* (ed. Fèvre, Vol. III, pp. 325 sqq., Paris 1870).— Allen, *De Sacramentis in Genere,* etc., Antwerp 1576.—*M. Cano, *Relectio de Sacramentis in Genere* (ed. Rome 1890).—*De Lugo, *Disputationes de Sacramentis in Genere* (ed. Fournials, Vol. III, Paris 1892). This last-mentioned treatise is especially thorough and valuable.

Among later writers: Drouvenius, *De Re Sacramentaria contra Perduellos Haereticos,* Venice 1737; *Tournely, *Prael. Theol. de Sacramentis,* Paris 1739; N. Muszka, S. J., *De Sacramentis Novae Legis,* Vienna 1758.

Among modern authors: Bautz, Einig, Heinrich-Huppert,

Hurter, Simar, Hunter, Wilhelm-Scannell, *et al.*, in their respective treatises on the Sacraments, and in addition to these the following:

Merlin, *Traité Historique et Dogmatique sur les Paroles ou Formes des Sept Sacrements de l'Eglise*, Paris 1844 (Migne, *Theol. Cursus Completus*, Vol. XXI).— Besson, *Les Sacrements ou la Grâce de l'Homme-Dieu*, Paris 1879.— Katschthaler, *Theol. Dogmatica Cath. Specialis*, Vol. IV, Ratisbon 1884.—*Franzelin, *De Sacramentis in Genere*, 4th ed., Rome 1888.—*De Augustinis, *De Re Sacramentaria*, Vol. I, 2nd ed., Rome 1889.— Billot, *De Ecclesiae Sacramentis*, Vol. I, 4th ed., Rome 1907.— P. Schanz, *Die Lehre von den Sakramenten der kath. Kirche*, Freiburg 1893. — Oswald, *Die dogmatische Lehre von den hl. Sakramenten*, Vol. I, 5th ed., Münster 1894.—*Chr. Pesch, *Praelectiones Dogmaticae*, Vol.VI, 3rd ed., Freiburg 1908.— G. B. Tepe, *Institutiones Theologicae*, Vol. IV, Paris 1896.— J. B. Sasse, *De Sacramentis Ecclesiae*, Vol. I, Freiburg 1897.— Heinrich-Gutberlet, *Dogmatische Theologie*, Vol. IX, Mainz 1901.— H. Lahousse, S. J., *De Sacramentis in Genere*, etc., Bruges 1900.— A. Paquet, *De Sacramentis*, Vol. I, Quebec 1900.— Scheeben-Atzberger, *Dogmatik*, Vol. IV, Part 2, Freiburg 1901.— N. Gihr, *Die hl. Sakramente der kath. Kirche*, Vol. I, 2nd ed., Freiburg 1902.— G. van Noort, *De Sacramentis*, Vol. I, 2nd ed., Amsterdam 1910.— P. Pourrat, *La Théologie Sacramentaire*, 4th ed., Paris 1910 (English tr., *Theology of the Sacraments*, 2nd ed., St. Louis 1914).— D. J. Kennedy, art. "Sacraments," in the *Catholic Encyclopedia*, Vol. XIII.— W. Humphrey, S. J., *The One Mediator*, London 1890.— A. Devine, C. P., *The Sacraments Explained*, 3rd ed., London 1905.— B. J. Otten, S. J., *A Manual of the History of Dogmas*, Vol. I, pp. 338 sqq.; Vol. II, pp. 272 sqq.

Non-Catholic authors worth consulting are: Hahn, *Die Lehre von den Sakramenten in ihrer geschichtlichen Entwicklung innerhalb der abendländischen Kirche bis zum Konzil von Trient*, Breslau 1864, and Alex. Maltzew, *Die Sakramente der orthodox-katholischen Kirche des Morgenlandes*, Berlin 1898.

---

*) The asterisk before an author's name indicates that his treatment of the subject is especially clear and thorough. As St. Thomas is invariably the best guide, the omission of the asterisk before his name never means that we consider his work inferior to that of other writers. There are vast stretches of theology which he scarcely touched.

SECTION I

EXPLANATION OF THE TERM "SACRAMENT"

1. Derivation and History of the Term.—
"Sacrament" is a word of Latin origin. It is derived from *sacrare*[1] and denotes a thing which
produces holiness—a means of sanctification.

The concept *sacramentum* was enriched by the
inclusion in it of the Greek μυστήριον, (from μύω, to
shut the mouth or eyes), and thus came to denote
a thing both sacred and mysterious.[2]

Such sacred and mysterious things were: (a)
venerable objects, as the truths of religion,[3]
and especially (b) signs directing men to God, as,
for instance, the types employed in the Old Testament.[4]

This usage was adopted by the Fathers[5] and retained by the early Schoolmen,[6] even after the
term "Sacrament" had come to be technically restricted to "a definite number of sensible signs
of sanctification, given to man by Christ, who has

[1] As *testamentum* from *testari,*
linimentum from *linire,* etc.
[2] *Res sacra et arcana.*
[3] Cfr. Eph. I, 9, III, 3 sqq.; Col.
I, 27; 1 Tim. III, 16.
[4] Cfr. Tertullian, *Contra Marcion.,* V, 4.
[5] *E. g.,* St. Augustine.
[6] *E. g.,* Hugh of St. Victor.

annexed to the due use of these signs the power of working that which they signify." [7]

The usage mentioned was common alike to profane and ecclesiastical literature. Thus, in the early days of Rome, when a lawsuit was brought, the parties were often bound to deposit a sum of money with the priests, and that portion of it forfeited by the loser was called *sacramentum, i. e. res sacra,* and employed to provide sacrifices for the gods. The Romans used the word *sacramentum* also to denote a solemn engagement, especially a soldier's military oath of allegiance. Tertullian no doubt had this particular usage in mind when he referred to the baptismal vow as a *sacramentum* in the sense of a sacred obligation entered into under the sanction of an oath. [8]   Since whatever is sacred has reference to the Deity, and the Deity is of its very nature mysterious, the term *sacramentum* gradually came to include the various meanings of the Greek word μυστήριον. Hence the indiscriminate use of *sacramentum* and *mysterium* in the Vulgate [9] and the ancient liturgies. St. Augustine read in his Itala Bible: *"Si sciero omnia sacramenta"* (1 Cor. XIII, 2), where our Vulgate has: *"Si noverim mysteria omnia."*

---

7 Cfr. S. J. Hunter, S. J., *Outlines of Dogmatic Theology*, Vol. III, pp. 167 sq.

8 *De Idol.*, c. 6, 19.

9 *E. g.*, Tob. XII, 7: "*Sacramentum regis abscondere bonum est.*"

The words *sacramenta* and *mysteria* were further applied indiscriminately to symbols or signs representative of the "holy mysteries," that is to say, all sacred usages and ceremonies, even such as were not sacramental rites in the technical sense. Thus St. Augustine in his sermons speaks of the "Sacrament of the Lord's Prayer." [10] In the Eleusinian Mysteries the term μυστήρια was applied both to doctrines and rites. [11]

From this vague and indefinite usage it follows that not every rite called *sacramentum* in the primitive Church was necessarily a Sacrament in the later and more precise sense of the term. To understand what is meant in each case we must carefully attend to the context. Thus, for instance, it would be a mistake to attempt to prove from St. Paul's phrase *"magnum sacramentum,"* that he regarded Matrimony as a Sacrament. The Apostle simply meant to say that it is a great mystery. [12] Similarly the Fathers and early ecclesiastical writers employ the term Sacrament very loosely, as may be gathered from the fact

10 *Serm.*, 228, n. 3: *"Sermonem ad altare Dei debemus hodie infantibus de sacramento altaris. Tractavimus ad eos de sacramento symboli, quod credere debeant, tractavimus de sacramento orationis dominicae, quomodo petant, et de sacramento fontis et baptismi."*

11 The rite of initiation, Phallic worship, etc. On the mysteries of the Mithraic cult, which the Ro-

mans got from Persia, see Blötzer, "*Das heidnische Mysterienwesen zur Zeit der Entstehung des Christentums,*" in the *Stimmen aus Maria-Laach,* 1906, 1907. On the mysteries of Eleusis cfr. P. Foucart, *Les Mystères d'Eleusis,* Paris 1914.

12 For further information on this point cfr. the dogmatic treatise on Matrimony.

that Tertullian [13] refers to the Gnostic systems as *"sacramenta haereticarum idearum,"* while St. Augustine repeatedly applies the term to the external worship of God and to sacrifice in general.[14] It was reserved for the Schoolmen, notably Peter Lombard and St. Thomas, to define the term Sacrament, and to restrict its use to certain rites.[15]

2. DEFINITION OF A SACRAMENT IN THE RESTRICTED SENSE OF THE TERM.—Generally speaking, a Sacrament is, as we have seen, "a symbol of a sacred and mysterious thing." Now, as there exists a vast number of such symbols that are not Sacraments in the technical sense, it is necessary to eliminate from the formal definition of the term all those symbols which do not refer to man's personal sanctification. Only the visible signs of internal sanctification are called Sacraments in the proper sense.[16] To distinguish the Sacraments of the Old Testament from the far more excellent and effective ones of the New, we must add, as a characteristic mark of the

13 *Contra Marcion.,* I, 13.

14 *Ad Marcellin.,* ep. 138, n. 7: " *Signa, quum ad res divinas pertinent, sacramenta vocantur."*— *Contra Faust.,* XIX, 11: " *In nullum nomen religionis seu verum seu falsum coagulari homines possunt, nisi aliquo signaculorum vel sacramentorum visibilium consortio colligentur."—De Civ. Dei,* X, 5: " *Sacrificium visibile invisibilis sa-*

crificii sacramentum, i. e. sacrum signum est."

15 Cfr. Pourrat, *La Théologie Sacramentaire,* pp. 1–46, Paris 1910. (English ed., *Theology of the Sacraments,* 2nd edition, pp. 1–47, St. Louis 1914).

16 Petrus Lomb., *Sent.,* IV, dist. 1: " *Sacramentum est invisibilis gratiae* [*sanctificantis*] *visibilis forma."*

latter, that they not only signify but actually confer grace. Hence Peter Lombard's famous definition: *"Sacramentum proprie id dicitur quod ita est signum gratiae Dei et invisibilis gratiae forma, ut ipsius imaginem gerat et causa existat,"* or, more concisely, *"Sacramentum est signum efficax gratiae sanctificantis,"*—a Sacrament is an efficacious sign of sanctifying grace.

a) The note of "personal sanctification" eliminates a multitude of signs or symbols which were formerly included in the term Sacrament, *e. g.,* such Old Testament types as the passage of the Israelites through the Red Sea, the brazen serpent, the manna, and in general all those signs, rites, symbols, and ceremonies which had for their chief purpose the glorification of God rather than the sanctification of man, for example, the sacrifices of the Old Law, the Mass, the physical universe as a manifestation of the Creator's greatness, and so forth.[17] Similarly, the dove as a symbol of the Holy Ghost, the Bible, images of the saints, the sign of the cross, are indeed *signa rei sacrae,* but not Sacraments, because they signify or symbolize something else than the sanctification of the soul. Even among the sensible signs of interior sanctification, only those are truly Sacraments that were permanently instituted for this purpose by God Himself. Such was, for instance, circumcision under the Old Law, such is Baptism under the New. By this criterion we must eliminate merely transient rites, as the communication of the Holy Spirit by breathing, etc.[18] To exclude

17 Cfr. Ps. XVIII, 1.   18 Cfr. John XX, 22.

from the definition of a Sacrament a number of rites or
signs that are merely sacramentals, it is necessary to
emphasize with De Lugo [19] that a true sacrament not only
signifies but actually causes interior sanctification.   In the
complete and perfect sense this is true only of the seven
Sacraments of the New Law.

b) As there were undoubtedly true Sacraments, though of an inferior order, under the Old
Law, we must find some note by which to distinguish the Sacraments of the Christian dispensation from those of the Ancient Covenant, and
elaborate a generic definition applicable to both
classes.

The existence of Sacraments under the Old Law may
be deduced from the constant belief of the Fathers [20]
and Scholastics,[21] and especially from the positive teaching of the Church.   The Council of Trent defines: " If
anyone saith that these Sacraments of the New Law do
not differ from the Sacraments of the Old Law, save that
the ceremonies are different, and different the outward
rites, let him be anathema." [22]   It is not easy to formulate
a generic definition that will fully answer the requirements laid down.   According to the exposition of doctrine drawn up by Eugene IV for the Armenian delegates
at the Council of Florence, A. D. 1439, the essential difference between the Sacraments of the Old and those of the
New Testament consists in this that the former merely

---

19 *De Sacramentis,* disp. 1, sect. 2.
20 Cfr.   St.   Augustine, *Contra
Faust.,* XIX, 11.
21 Cfr.   St.   Thomas, *Summa
Theol.,* 1a 2ae, qu. 102, art. 5.
22 Sessio VII, can. 2: *" Si quis*

*dixerit, ea ipsa Novae Legis sa-
cramenta a sacramentis antiquae
Legis non differre nisi quia caeri-
moniae sunt aliae et ritus alii, anathema sit."* (Denzinger-Bannwart,
n. 845).

symbolize, or prophetically typify, sanctifying grace, whereas the latter " contain " and actually " confer " it.[23] In other words, the distinguishing characteristic of the Sacraments of the New Law is the *efficacia signi,* that of the Sacraments of the Old Law, the *inefficacia signi.* But if the Sacraments of the Ancient Covenant were inefficacious signs,— if they did not somehow truly effect or convey grace, how can they be called Sacraments? Holy Scripture makes a distinction between a twofold sanctity, the legal " sanctity of the flesh," [24] and the theological " sanctity of the spirit." [25] The Sacraments of the Old Law foreshadowed but did not of themselves (*ex opere operato*) confer "theological sanctity," *i. e.* sanctifying grace, but they actually conferred "legal sanctity," and in so far at least were endowed with the necessary causality or *efficacia signi.* They were efficacious signs of legal sanctity in the present, and inefficacious signs of theological sanctity for the future, and consequently types or models of the Sacraments of the New Testament. To exercise this twofold function they had been instituted by God Himself as a permanent institution, to last till the coming of the Messias. This distinction enables us to formulate an adequate generic definition as follows: "A Sacrament is a visible sign of sanctity, instituted by God, the efficaciousness of which is determined by the particular economy of grace to which it belongs." [26]

---

23 " *Novae Legis sacramenta multum a sacramentis differunt antiquae Legis; illa enim non causabant gratiam, sed eam solum per passionem Christi dandam esse figurabant, haec vero nostra et continent gratiam et ipsam digne suscipientibus conferunt.*" (Denzinger-Bannwart, n. 695).

24 *Sanctitas legalis seu carnis.*

25 *Sanctitas theologica seu gratia sanctificans.*

26 On the question whether this definition applies in exactly the same sense or only analogically to the Sacraments of both Testaments, see Bellarmine, *De Sacramentis,* I, 12.

3. Theological Discussion of the Definition.—The important part played by the word
"sign" in both the specific and the generic definition of a Sacrament, makes it necessary to explain the meaning of that term.

a) A sign (*signum*, σημεῖον) is some thing, the knowledge of which leads to the knowledge of some other
thing.   There are here two distinct elements.   The material element is " some thing known; " the formal element, the aptitude of the material to convey " the knowledge of some other thing as yet unknown."

" A sign," says St. Augustine, " is a thing which, over
and above the impression it makes on the senses, causes
something else to come into the mind as a consequence
of itself; as when we see a footprint, we conclude that
an animal, whose footprint this is, has passed by; and
when we see smoke, we know that there is fire beneath." [27]
For the purposes of the present treatise we may disregard
visible signs of visible things [28] and invisible signs of
invisible things,[29] and concentrate our attention on the visible signs of invisible things.

b) Signs may be divided according to the point of
view from which they are regarded.

a) Between a sign and the thing it signifies there must
be some connection.   This connection may either arise
from the nature of the two, independently of any free-will
act, or it may be purely conventional.   Thus it is owing to

---

27 *De Doctrina Christ.*, II, 1:
" *Signum est res praeter speciem,
quam ingerit sensibus, aliud aliquid
ex se faciens in cogitationem venire,
sicut vestigio viso transiisse animal
cuius vestigium est cogitamus et
fumo viso ignem subesse cognoscimus.*"

28 Such as foot-prints, images of
saints, etc.

29 *E. g.*, peace of mind as an in-
dication of the state of grace, the
sacramental character conferred by
Baptism, etc.

the very nature of things that there should be fire where there is smoke, and *vice versa;* smoke is therefore the natural sign of fire. A purely conventional sign bears no innate relation to the nature of things, but originates in an arbitrary act of one person, which is subsequently recognized by others.

To which of these two classes do the Sacraments belong? They are not purely natural signs of invisible grace because their signification is owing to a free act of God. Nor can they be regarded as purely conventional or arbitrary signs because between the sacramental rite and its effects there is a striking similarity, which results in a sort of affinity between the symbol and the thing symbolized. In other words, the Sacraments are arbitrary but at the same time deeply significant signs of grace. It was this observation which led St. Augustine to say: "If the Sacraments did not possess some kind of resemblance to the things which they signify, they would not be Sacraments." [30]

Cardinal Bellarmine [31] divides signs, according to their origin, into three classes: (1) Those which signify some thing by nature, regardless of any act of the free-will (*e. g.* footprints, photographs); (2) those which originate entirely in the free-will of the inventor and are strictly conventional (*e. g.* signals, the ringing of a bell); (3) those which involve what may be called an obvious symbolism (*e. g.* the sign of the cross). It is to this last-mentioned category that the Sacraments belong. Being naturally adapted to symbolize interior grace, they have been chosen to perform this office and formally instituted for this purpose by Christ. Thus the external

---

30 *Ep.*, 98, 9 (*ad Bonifac.*): "*Si sacramenta quandam similitudinem earum rerum, quarum sacramenta* *sunt, non haberent, omnino non essent sacramenta.*"

31 *De Sacramentis,* I, 9.

ablution in Baptism fitly symbolizes the cleansing of the soul from sin; Holy Communion under the species of bread and wine is an apt symbol of the spiritual nourishing of the soul, and so forth.

β) Another classification, important for our purpose, is that into speculative and practical signs. A speculative sign merely symbolizes that which it signifies (*e. g.* the national flag, an image), while a practical sign both symbolizes and effects it. Thus the act of handing over the keys of a fortress to the general of an invading army not only symbolizes the surrender of the stronghold, but actually puts it into effect. From what has been said about the essential distinction between the Sacraments of the Old and those of the New Testament, it is evident that the Sacraments are not merely speculative but practical signs. This is true of the " weak and needy elements " of the Old Covenant,[32] and, in a still higher sense, of the Sacraments of the New Testament.

γ) Signs may also be divided with respect to past, present, or future events. A sign that refers to some past event is called in Scholastic terminology *signum rememorativum.* To this category belong paintings representing battles, commemoratory medals, etc. A sign that refers to some present happening is called *signum demonstrativum.* Such is, for example, the hoisting of a flag to signify the presence of a ruler. A sign that points to some future occurrence is called *signum prognosticum* (*e. g.* the blowing of a whistle to announce the impending arrival or departure of a train). The sacramental signs of the New Testament belong to all three of these categories. They recall the Passion of Our Lord Jesus Christ, they symbolize sanctifying grace as here and now present in the soul, and they foretell the future glory

32 Gal. IV, 9.

of the elect. This teaching of St. Thomas Aquinas [33] and of practically all other Catholic theologians has been adopted into the Roman Catechism.[34] Its truth can be clearly demonstrated from Scripture. Of Baptism, St. Paul teaches: (1) that " we are baptized in Jesus Christ, in his death " ; [35] (2) that by virtue of this Sacrament " we walk in newness of life; " [36] and (3) that Baptism makes us like Christ, as in death, so also in the resurrection.[37] Holy Communion " shows the death of the Lord " in the past,[38] confers spiritual life in the present,[39] and guarantees resurrection " in the last day." [40]

For the other five Sacraments this threefold signification cannot be proved with the same convincingness, but it is virtually included in the indisputable Scriptural truth that the present reception of any one of them postulates as its meritorious cause the Passion of Christ, which is an event of the past, and carries within itself as a reward the future glory of Heaven. Note, however, that the sacramental signs are always primarily *signa demonstrativa* and only secondarily *signa rememorativa* and *prognostica*. This is owing to the fact that the Sacraments by their very nature must produce that which they signify, *i. e.* sanctifying grace here and now present in the soul, because it is sanctifying grace that they actually effect, whereas they merely signify the Passion of Christ and the glory of Heaven, the former as an indispensable requisite, the latter as a promise and a guaranty.

δ) In this connection the Fathers and Catholic theologians are wont to enlarge on a truth of great speculative

33 *Summa Theologica*, 3a, qu. 60, art. 3.
34 *Cat. Rom.*, P. II, cap. 1, n. 12.
35 Rom. VI, 3.
36 Rom. VI, 4.
37 Rom. VI, 5.
38 Cfr. 1 Cor. XI, 26.
39 Cfr. John VI, 57.
40 John VI, 55.

importance with reference to the intrinsic relation between the Sacraments of the Old and those of the New
Testament and between the latter and the glory of
Heaven or eternal beatitude. As the ancient Synagogue
was merely a type foreshadowing the Church, they say, so
the New Covenant is but a type prefiguring the
Heavenly Jerusalem, where we shall behold God as He
is, without sign or symbol. This idea is intimated by St.
Paul when he says in his Epistle to the Hebrews: " For
the law having a shadow of the good things to come, not
the very image of things." [41] In other words, the New
Testament, too, is but a " shadow " and an " image " of
"things " which shall not be unveiled to our eyes until
we are in Heaven. St. Ambrose succinctly expresses
this thought as follows: " A shadow in the law, an image
in the Gospel, truth in Heaven." [42] The relation of the
two Testaments with their respective Sacraments to the
beatific vision of God in Heaven has been beautifully
described by St. Bruno of Asti, who says: " The first
tabernacle, therefore, is the Synagogue; the second, the
Church; the third, Heaven. . . . The first was in a
shadow and an image, the second is in an image and in
truth, and the third [will be] in the truth alone. In the
first, life is foreshadowed; in the second it is given; in the
third it is possessed." [43] This teaching was adopted by
the Scholastics. " There is a threefold state for men,"
says St. Thomas; " the first is that of the Old Law, . . .

[41] Heb. X, 1: " Umbram (σκιάν)
enim habens lex futurorum bonorum
[scil. N. T.], non ipsam imaginem
rerum (οὐκ αὐτὴν τὴν εἰκόνα τῶν
πραγμάτων)."

[42] In Ps., 38, n. 25: " Umbra in
Lege, imago vero in Evangelio,
veritas in coelestibus."

[43] Hom., 34: " Primum igitur
tabernaculum est Synagoga, secundum Ecclesia, tertium coelum. . . .
Primum in umbra fuit et figura,
secundum in figura est et veritate,
tertium [erit] in veritate sola. In
primo ostenditur vita, in secundo
datur, in tertio possidetur." St.
Bruno of Asti was Bishop of Segni
and died A. D. 1123.

the second that of the New Law, . . . the third follows not in this, but in the future life, *i. e.* in the fatherland. But as the first of these states is figurative and imperfect with regard to the state of the Gospel, so this latter is figurative and imperfect with regard to the state of our eternal home, by which it will be supplanted." [44]

ε) There is a final though less important distinction between sensible and insensible signs. The former are in some manner perceptible by the senses, while the latter can be recognized only by immaterial beings. Sensible signs are, *e. g.*, peace of mind, as indicative of the state of sanctifying grace, the sacramental character imprinted by Baptism, etc. The sacramental signs are all sensible. When a sick man is anointed with holy oil, this can be seen with the eyes; when absolution is pronounced in the tribunal of Penance, this can be heard with the ears; when a person receives Holy Communion, he can perceive the Sacrament with several senses simultaneously.

Ockam [45] held that, absolutely speaking, God might have attached sacramental efficacy to a purely spiritual and immaterial sign, such as "contemplative prayer" or "meditation on the Passion,"—a view combated by Bellarmine for the convincing reason that a Sacrament, by its very definition, is connected with an external rite, *i. e.* a sensible sign of some kind. [46]

---

[44] *Summa Theol.*, 1a 2ae, qu. 106, art. 4, ad 1: "*Triplex est hominum status. Primus quidem Veteris Legis, . . . secundus Novae Legis, . . . tertius status succedit non in hac vita, sed in futura, scil. in patria. Sed sicut primus status est figuralis et imperfectus respectu Evangelii, ita hic status est figuralis et imperfectus respectu status patriae, quo veniente iste status evacuatur.*" Cfr. Franzelin, *De Sacramentis in Genere*, 4th ed., thes.

2; N. Gihr, *Die hl. Sakramente der katholischen Kirche*, Vol. I, 2nd ed., pp. 27 sqq., Freiburg 1902.

[45] *Comment. in Quatuor Libros Sent.*, IV, dist. 1.

[46] Bellarmine, *De Sacramentis*, I, 9. On the subject of this entire Section the student may profitably consult C. Oriou, *Étude Historique sur la Notion du Sacrement depuis la Fin du Ier Siècle jusqu'au Concile de Trente*, Montauban 1899.

SECTION 2

CHRISTIAN AND OTHER SACRAMENTS

Catholic theologians distinguish four different states through which the human race has successively passed: (1) The state of original justice in Paradise; (2) the state of the law of nature; (3) the state of the Mosaic Law, and (4) the state of the New Covenant. Each of these states has its own peculiar means of grace.

1. THE QUASI-SACRAMENTS OF PARADISE.— Whether there were true Sacraments in the state of original innocence enjoyed by our first parents in Paradise, is a disputed question. The majority of theologians, following St. Thomas, take the negative, while a respectable minority maintain the positive side.

The Angelic Doctor argues that mankind required no means of sanctification in a state which was of itself holy. "In the state of innocence," he says, "man needed no sacraments, whether as remedies against sin or as means of perfecting the soul." [1]

Bellelli and others contend that the Tree of Life [2] and Marriage [3] might properly be called Sacraments. These

---

[1] *Summa Theol.*, 3a, qu. 61, art. 2: "*In statu innocentiae homo sacramentis non indigebat, non solum inquantum sacramenta ordinantur ad remedium peccati, sed etiam inquantum ipsa ordinantur ad animae perfectionem.*"

[2] "*Sacramentum arboris vitae.*"

[3] "*Sacramentum matrimonii.*"

writers appeal in support of their view to St. Augustine, who ascribes to the Tree of Life the miraculous immortality of the body as well as the communication of supernatural wisdom,[4] and describes the union of Adam and Eve as a pattern of the mystic union between Christ and His Church.[5]   But there is no conclusive proof that St. Augustine regarded these two institutions as Sacraments in the technical sense of the term.   The element of personal sanctification, so essential to the notion of a Sacrament, is not sufficiently evident in either, and, besides, the great Bishop of Hippo probably used the word "Sacrament" in its wider meaning of *signum rei sacrae.*[6]

As for St. Thomas, he did not deny that the marriage of our first parents in Paradise was a true type of Christ's union with His Church.   "Matrimony," he says, "was instituted in the state of innocence, not as a Sacrament, but for a function of nature.   In regard to what followed, however, it foreshadowed something in relation to Christ and the Church, just as everything else foreshadowed Christ."[7]

2. THE STATE OF THE LAW OF NATURE.—The *status legis naturae,* (not to be confounded with the *status naturae purae*),[8] comprises that long

---

[4] Cfr. St. Augustine, *De Genesi ad Lit.,* VIII, 6: "*Illud quoque addo, quamquam corporalem cibum, talem tamen illam arborem praestitisse, quâ corpus hominis sanitate stabili firmaretur, non sicut ex alio cibo, sed nonnullâ inspiratione salubritatis occultâ.*"— *Ibid.,* XI, 40: "[*Arbor vitae*] *sacramentum visibile invisibilis sapientiae.*"

[5] *L. c.,* VIII, 4.

[6] *V. supra,* Sect. I, No. 1.

[7] *Summa Theol.,* 3a, qu. 61, art. 2: "*Matrimonium fuit institutum in statu innocentiae non secundum quod est sacramentum, sed secundum quod est officium naturae. In consequenti tamen aliquid significabat futurum circa Christum et Ecclesiam, sicut et omnia alia quae in figura Christi praecesserunt.*"

[8] On the *status naturae purae* see

interval between the fall of our first parents and the enactment of the Mosaic dispensation, during which men were subject to no other law than that of nature, "written in their hearts." [9]   The state of the law of nature, under the influence of the redemptive grace of Christ promised in the Protogospel, was a supernatural state, and may be divided into two epochs.   The first of these, from Adam to Abraham, had a "Sacrament of Nature;" [10] the second, from Abraham to Moses, possessed a true Sacrament of regeneration in the rite of circumcision.[11]

a) It is theologically certain, and admitted by all Catholic divines, that from Adam to Moses mankind possessed a Sacrament of Nature.

α) To deny this would be to except the infants born during that epoch from the divine will to save, which, as we have demonstrated in our treatise on Grace, is universal.[12]   As God wills to save all men without exception, there must have been some means by which the infants of the pre-Mosaic period could be cleansed of original sin. The Fathers were firmly convinced of the existence of such a *sacramentum naturae*.   St. Augustine repeatedly insists on its necessity.[13]   Suarez states the position of the Schoolmen thus: "It is impious and repugnant to the universal tradition and sentiment of the Church, to hold

Pohle-Preuss, *God the Author of Nature and the Supernatural*, pp. 226 sqq., 2nd ed., St. Louis 1916.

9 Rom. II, 15.

10 " *Sacramentum naturae.*"

11 " *Sacramentum circumcisionis.*"

12 Pohle-Preuss, *Grace, Actual and Habitual*, pp. 153 sqq.

13 Cfr., e. g., Contra Iulian., V, 11, 45: " *Nec tamen credendum est, et ante datam circumcisionem famulos Dei, quandoquidem eis in-*

that, under the natural law and under the law of Moses, infants were without a remedy against original sin, and that consequently all who died before attaining to the use of reason, were damned." [14]

β) The exact character of this *sacramentum naturae* is a matter of conjecture. All that can be said with any degree of certainty is: (1) As a medium of regeneration, the Sacrament of Nature must have been based in some way on belief in the future Redeemer, because "there is no other name under heaven given to men whereby we must be saved." [15] (2) This faith in the Messias most probably found expression in a prayer and was symbolized by a visible sign. [16] (3) As no one but God can cleanse the soul of original sin, the "Natural Sacrament" of the pre-Abrahamic period must have been instituted by Him, at least in substance, though He may have left the determination of its form and the selection of the grace-conferring symbols to the free choice of men. St. Thomas' view of the matter may be gathered from the following passage in the *Summa:* "It is probable that believing parents offered up some prayer to God for their children, especially if these were in any danger, or bestowed on them some blessing, as a seal of faith; just as the adults offered prayers and sacrifices for themselves." [17] These three requisites are suf-

---

erat mediatoris fides, nullo sacramento eius opitulatos fuisse parvulis suis; quamvis quid illud esset, aliquâ necessariâ causa Scriptura latere voluit." Other Patristic passages bearing on this subject will be found in Vasquez's *Comment. in Quatuor Libros Sent.*, III, disp. 165, cap. 1.

14 *De Sacramentis*, disp. 10, sect. 1: "Tam in lege naturae quam Moysis omnes infantes fuisse relictos sine remedio peccati ori-

ginalis atque adeo omnes, qui mortui sunt ante usum rationis, damnatos fuisse, impium est sentire et contra communem ecclesiae traditionem et sensum." Cfr. De Lugo, *De Sacramentis*, disp. 3, sect. 2.

15 Acts IV, 12.

16 This is the common opinion of theologians, including St. Thomas (*Summa Theol.*, 3a, qu. 61, art. 3), against Bonaventure and Vasquez.

17 *Summa Theol.*, 3a, qu. 70,

ficient to constitute a Sacrament in the generic sense of the term.

It is much more difficult, nay practically impossible, to decide whether, in the state of the natural law, there were also Sacraments for adult persons. The Thomists [18] think there were several, while other theologians [19] reject this assumption on the ground that for the state of the natural law God provided only what was absolutely necessary, and Sacraments were not necessary because adults could obtain forgiveness of their sins by an act of perfect contrition.

It is to be noted that for the heathen and the female children of the Israelites the economy of grace which existed in the *status legis naturae* remained in force even after the proclamation of the law of circumcision.[20]

b) At the time of Abraham, long before the promulgation of the Mosaic law, circumcision became the ordinary means of spiritual regeneration. This rite has all the characteristics of a true Sacrament.

a) God promulgated the law in these words: " This is my covenant which you shall observe, between me and you, and thy seed after thee: all the male kind of you shall be circumcised; and you shall circumcise the flesh of your foreskin, that it may be for a sign of the cove-

---

art. 4: *" Probabile est quod parentes fideles pro parvulis natis et maxime in periculo existentibus aliquas Deo preces funderent vel aliquam benedictionem eis adhi-berent, quod erat aliquod signaculum fidei, sicut adulti pro seipsis preces et sacrificia offerebant."*

18 *E. g.*, Gonet, basing on St. Thomas, *Summa Theol.*, 3a, qu. 65, art. 1, ad 7.

19 Notably Suarez, Vasquez, and De Lugo.

20 On the probable nature of the *Sacramentum naturae*, cfr. Franze-lin, *De Sacramentis in Genere*, thes. 3, and De Augustinis, *De Re Sacramentaria*, Vol. 1, 2nd ed., pp. 17 sqq., Rome 1889.

nant between me and you. An infant of eight days old shall be circumcised among you. . . . The male whose flesh of his foreskin shall not be circumcised, that soul shall be destroyed out of his people, because he hath broken my covenant." [21] Here circumcision is plainly made a *conditio sine qua non* of salvation. As no one can be saved unless he is cleansed of original sin, circumcision was obviously an instrument of regeneration. This is the opinion of St. Thomas,[22] and though it is disputed by Vasquez, Tournely, and Bellarmine,[23] Suarez rightly maintains that the teaching of the Angelic Doctor on this head cannot be denied " without a certain degree of temerity," especially in view of Pope Innocent III's declaration against the Cathari, that " Original sin was forgiven and the danger of damnation avoided by the mystery of the circumcision." [24]

The rite of circumcision was truly sacramental: an external sign, accompanied by internal grace, instituted by God for the remission of sin. The Fathers and Scholastics could not have regarded circumcision as the type of Baptism, had they not believed it to be a real Sacrament.[25]

β) In what manner did circumcision remit original sin?

21 Gen. XVII, 10 sqq.: " *Hoc est pactum meum, quod observabitis inter me et vos et semen tuum post te: circumcidetur ex vobis omne masculinum et circumcidetis carnem praeputii vestri, ut sit in signum foederis inter me et vos. Infans octo dierum circumcidetur in vobis . . . Masculus, cuius praeputii caro circumcisa non fuerit, delebitur anima illa de populo suo, quia pactum meum irritum fecit.*"

22 Cfr. *Summa Theol.*, 3a, qu. 70, art. 4: " *Ab omnibus communiter ponitur, quod in circumcisione peccatum originale remittebatur.*"

23 *De Sacramentis*, II, 17.

24 *Decret.*, L. III, tit. 42, c. 3, " *Maiores:*" " *Originalis culpa remittebatur per circumcisionis mysterium et damnationis periculum vitabatur.*"

25 Cfr. Col. II, 11: " *circumcisio Christi.*" See St. Augustine, *De Anima*, II, 11, 15: " *Circumcisio fuit illius temporis sacramentum, quod figurabat nostri temporis baptismum.*" For a more extended argument see De Augustinis, *De Re Sacramentaria*, Vol. I, 2nd ed., pp. 29 sqq., and Hugo Weiss, *Die messianischen Vorbilder im Alten Testament*, pp. 58 sqq., Freiburg 1905.

In adults, no doubt, through the instrumentality of justifying faith (*fides formata*), and consequently " by the work of the worker" (*ex opere operantis*). But how about infants? This question is intimately connected with another, on which theologians disagree, *viz.*: How do circumcision and Baptism differ in regard to their mode of operation? It will prove helpful to review the varying opinions on these two points.

(1) The Scotists contend that circumcision wiped out original sin " by the work wrought " (*ex opere operato*),[26] but that it was not on the same level with Baptism because it did not confer an equal measure of holiness nor an immediate claim to Heaven.[27]   In support of this contention, Scotus and his followers appeal to the authority of St. Augustine, who says that circumcision supplied the place of Baptism among the Jews,[28] and they also

[26] " There is a famous phrase which is employed to express concisely the Catholic doctrine: the Sacraments are said to work ' by the work wrought.' This is opposed to the doctrine that their effect comes about ' by the work of the worker ' — *ex opere operato, ex opere operantis.* Some half-learned Latin grammarians maintain that the first phrase ought to be translated, ' by the work that works.' These critics forget that every word means that which it is intended to mean by him who uses it; and even on their narrow ground of Latin grammar they are wrong, for there are plenty of cases where the participle of a deponent verb is used passively, as may be seen in any good dictionary. (See *dominor, ulciscor,* etc.). This very word *operatum* is so employed by Lactantius (*De Instit. Divin.,* vii, 27; *P. L.,* 6, 819), and by St. Ambrose (*De Incarn.,* c. 9, n. 95; *P.*

L., 16, 841), so that the theological use does not involve a blunder in an elementary point of grammar. The phrase . . . *opus operatum* seems to have been first used by Peter of Poitou, a writer of the twelfth century (*Sent.,* p. 5, c. 6; *P. L.,* 211, 1235); . . . it made its way into the common language of theology, partly through the influence of Pope Innocent III, who saw how aptly it expressed the Catholic doctrine (*De Myst. Missae,* III, 5; *P. L.,* 217, 844), and finally received the sanction of the Council of Trent." (S. J. Hunter, S. J., *Outlines of Dogmatic Theology,* Vol. III, pp. 191 sq.)

[27] Cfr. Scotus, *Comment. in Quatuor Libros Sent.,* IV, dist. 1, qu. 6, and Mastrius, *De Sacramentis,* disp. 1, qu. 2, art. 2.

[28] *Contra Lit. Petil.,* II, 72: " Certe antiquus populus Dei circumcisionem pro baptismo habuit."

quote Pope Innocent III's declaration that original sin
was remitted by the mystery of the circumcision.[29]   But
the Scotist view is incompatible with St. Paul's repeated
assertion of the futility and inefficacy of all " works of
the law," [30] and moreover contradicts the positive teaching of the Fathers that the Sacraments of the Ancient
Covenant had no power to forgive sins.[31]

(2) Bellarmine, Vasquez, Tournely, and a few others
go to the opposite extreme, saying that circumcision was
merely an external sign of Israel's covenant with Jehovah
and a mark distinguishing the Chosen People from the
gentiles.   We have already criticized this theory because
it suggests,— or at least does not absolutely exclude,— the
implication that the circumcised infants remained in the
state of mortal sin.   This assumption is refuted by the
same arguments which speak in favor of a *sacramentum
naturae* for the pre-Mosaic period.[32]

(3) A third group endeavors to reconcile the two ex-
tremes just mentioned by saying that the remission of
original sin depended somehow on the rite of circumcision, though that rite was by no means the cause but
merely an occasion or a *conditio sine qua non* of justifica-

[29] *Decret.*, L. III, tit. 42, c. 3,
"*Maiores:*" "*Etsi originalis culpa
remittebatur per circumcisionis mysterium et damnationis periculum
vitabatur, non tamen perveniebatur
ad regnum coelorum, quod usque ad
mortem Christi fuit omnibus obsera-
tum.*"

[30] Cfr. Rom. III, 20; IV, 15;
VII, 6; Gal. III, 11 sqq.; IV, 9;
V, 2; 1 Cor. VII, 19; 2 Cor. III,
7 sq.; Heb. VII, 18.

[31] A number of Patristic texts
in proof of this assertion will be
found in De Augustinis, *De Re*

Sacrament., Vol. I, 2nd ed., pp. 57
sqq.

[32] *V. supra*, pp. 20 sqq. Pope Innocent III says in the above-quoted
Cap. "*Maiores*" (reproduced in Denzinger-Bannwart, n. 410): "*Absit
enim, ut universi parvuli pereant,
quorum quotidie tanta multitudo
moritur, quin et ipsis misericors
Deus, qui neminem vult perire, aliquod remedium procuraverit ad salutem.*" For a detailed statement see
Suarez, *De Sacramentis*, disp. 5,
sect. 1; J. B. Sasse, *De Sacramentis
Ecclesiae*, Vol. I, pp. 85 sqq., Freiburg 1897.

tion. From this point of view it is clearly a sophism to argue, as the Scotists do: "The remission of original sin is effected either *ex opere operato* or *ex opere operantis;* it is not effected *ex opere operantis* because infants are incapable of justifying faith; consequently, it must be effected *ex opere operato.*" For, unless we take the phrase *ex opere operato* merely as the counterpart of *opus operans,* as De Lugo does,[33] it is possible to insert between the two a middle term, explaining the rite of circumcision merely as a "sign of faith," to which regeneration is outwardly attached but which lacks the intrinsic power of effecting it. Or, to express the idea differently: Circumcision did not, like Baptism, wipe out original sin causally, as a *signum demonstrativum,* but merely incidentally, as a *signum prognosticum.* This theory, which is held by St. Thomas and the majority of Catholic theologians, bears all the earmarks of truth. It takes into account St. Paul's teaching of the inefficacy of all the Old Testament ceremonies, and at the same time agrees with the universal teaching of the Fathers and the conciliary definitions of Florence and Trent.[34]

3. THE SACRAMENTS OF THE MOSAIC LAW.—
The fact that circumcision was an essential con-

[33] *De Sacramentis,* disp. 5, sect. 4, n. 59. Billuart suggested the term *opus operatum passive* for *opus operans* (*De Sacram.,* diss. 3, art. 6).

[34] St. Thomas, *Summa Theol.,* 3a, qu. 70, art. 4: "*In circumcisione conferebatur gratia quantum ad omnes gratiae effectus, aliter tamen quam in baptismo. Nam in baptismo confertur gratia ex virtute ipsius baptismi, quam habet inquantum est instrumentum passionis Christi iam perfectae; in circum-*cisione autem conferebatur gratia non ex virtute circumcisionis, sed ex virtute fidei passionis Christi, cuius signum erat circumcisio, ita scil. quod homo, qui accipiebat circumcisionem, profitebatur se suscipere talem fidem vel adultus pro se vel alius pro parvulis. Unde et Apostolus dicit (Rom. IV, 11) quod Abraham ' accepit signum circumcisionis signaculum iustitiae fidei,' quia scil. iustitia erat ex fide significatâ, non ex circumcisione significante." For a fuller explanation of

stituent of the law given to the Israelites on Mount Sinai shows that the Mosaic code had at least one Sacrament. The teaching of the Fathers and councils permits us to infer that it had more than one.

The existence of several Sacraments is quite in accordance with the spirit and character of the Mosaic economy. Being a special covenant of Yahweh with His Chosen People, and a type foreshadowing the " good things to come," the Mosaic Law not only needed to be more fully equipped with means of grace than the purely natural law, but also to foreshadow more clearly the future Messianic dispensation. Its ceremonies and precepts were calculated to keep awake the desire for the promised " truth and reality " and to presage and prepare the " liberty of the children of God." [35]

But the Mosaic Sacraments were far inferior in character and efficacy to those of the Christian dispensation, of which they were merely an intimation and a " shadow ; " [36] and hence what we have said about circumcision [37] applies to all the Sacraments of the Old Testament.

How many there were, it is impossible to ascertain. St. Thomas, with special reference to their character as types and patterns of the Sacraments of the New Testament, divides them into four categories: (a) Circumcision as the first and most necessary, and a pattern of Baptism; (b) Sacraments designed for the preservation and perfection of righteousness and to serve

the theory discussed above see De Augustinis, *De Re Sacrament.*, Vol. I, pp. 51 sqq.

[35] Cfr. St. Thomas, *Summa Theol.*, 3a, qu. 61, art. 3.
[36] *V. supra*, pp. 16 sq.
[37] *V. supra*, No. 2, pp. 19 sqq.

as figures of the Holy Eucharist, *e. g.,* the eating of the
Paschal lamb,[38] the consumption of the loaves of proposition,[39] and the so-called Eucharistic sacrifices, which
were at the same time types of the Mass; (c) Sacraments
instituted for the expiation of sins and the cure of legal
uncleanness, such as the various purifications prescribed
for the laity, the washing of hands and feet imposed on
the Levites,[40] etc.   These were types of the Sacrament of
Penance.   (d) A fourth and last group had for its object the perpetuation of the Levitic priesthood and consisted of certain consecratory rites [41] which typified the
Sacrament of Holy Orders.[42]

The only Christian Sacraments which have no counter-
parts in the Mosaic Law are Confirmation, Extreme Unction, and Matrimony.   The reason is explained by St.
Thomas as follows: " It is impossible that there should
have been in the Old Law a Sacrament corresponding
to Confirmation, which is the Sacrament of the fulness
of grace, because the time of that fulness had not yet ar-
rived, and the law had not brought anything to perfection
(Heb. VII, 19).   The same must be said of the Sacrament of Extreme Unction, which is a sort of immediate
preparation for man's entrance into the state of glory;
for this was not open in the Old Testament, as the
price had not yet been paid.   Matrimony existed in the
Old Testament as a function of nature, but not as a
Sacrament of Christ's union with His Church, which at
that time had not yet been consummated.   It was for
this reason, too, that a husband under the Old Law could

38 Ex. XII, 26.

39 Lev. XXIV, 9.

40 Cfr. Lev. XII sqq.; Numb.
XIX sqq.

41 Cfr. Ex. XXIX; XXX, 30; Lev.
VIII.

42 On the controverted question
whether the rite of consecration was
administered only to Aaron and
the first generation of Jewish priests,
or to all, see P. Scholz, *Die hl.
Altertümer des Volkes Israel,* Vol.

give his wife a bill of divorce, which is repugnant to the nature of a Sacrament." [43]

4. THE SACRAMENTS OF THE NEW LAW.—The sanctity demanded by the New Law requires more perfect Sacraments than those available under the Mosaic dispensation.

Christ, in whom godhead and manhood are so intimately united, is as it were a living Sacrament — the personal and visible embodiment of uncreated grace. Similarly His Church, as the mystical image of the Hypostatic Union, is the visible medium of supernatural life, and therefore preëminently a sacramental institution. [44]

Another *a priori* argument for the existence of Sacraments in the Christian economy is based on the nature of man as a compound of spirit and body, needing sensible signs for the communication of the higher spiritual life. "The state of the New Law," says St. Thomas, "is between the state of the Old Law, whose figures are fulfilled in the New, and the state of glory, in which all truth will be openly and perfectly revealed; wherefore

I, p. 52, Ratisbon 1868; P. Schegg, *Biblische Archäologie*, p. 550, Freiburg 1888.

43 *Summa Theol.*, 1a 2ae, qu. 102, art. 5, ad 3: "*Sacramento confirmationis, quod est sacramentum plenitudinis gratiae, non potest respondere in Vetere Lege aliquod sacramentum, quia nondum advenerat tempus plenitudinis, eo quod ' neminem ad perfectum adduxit lex' (Heb. VII, 19). Similiter autem et sacramento extremae unctionis, quod est quaedam immediata praeparatio ad introitum gloriae, cuius aditus nondum patebat in Vetere Lege, pretio nondum soluto. Matrimonium autem fuit quidem in Vetere Lege, prout erat in officium naturae, non autem prout est sacramentum coniunctionis Christi et Ecclesiae, quae nondum erat facta; unde et in Vetere Lege dabatur libellus repudii, quod est contra sacramenti rationem.*" On the Sacraments of the Mosaic Law the student may profitably consult Schmalzl, *Die Sakramente des Alten Testamentes im allgemeinen nach der Lehre des hl. Thomas*, Eichstätt 1883.

44 On this point see Scheeben,

then there will be no Sacraments. But now, so long as we know 'through a glass in a dark manner' (1 Cor. XIII, 12), we need sensible signs in order to reach spiritual things, and this is the province of the Sacraments." [45]

A third argument for the necessity of Sacraments in the New Testament may be deduced from the circumstance that sin, through concupiscence, affects both soul and body, and the remedy must consequently be applicable to both; that is to say, it must be partly spiritual and partly material. [46]

In asserting the existence of so-called parallels to the Christian Sacraments in the ethnic religions of antiquity, e. g. the cult of Mithras, the science of comparative religion merely furnishes another proof that the use of visible signs as pledges of invisible sanctification corresponds to a deep-rooted need of human nature.

The Roman Catechism gives seven distinct reasons for the fitness of Sacraments under the Christian dispensation. They are: (1) the need of visible signs, owing to the peculiar constitution of human nature, which makes the spiritual soul dependent on the senses; (2) the consoling assurance to be derived from the use of concrete pledges guaranteeing God's fidelity to His promises; (3) the need of healing medicines to recover or preserve the health of the soul; (4) the desire of belonging to a visible society, knit, as it were, into one body by the bond of

---

Die Mysterien des Christentums, 3rd ed., p. 536, Freiburg 1912.

[45] *Summa Theol.,* 3a, qu. 61, art. 4, ad 1: " *Status Novae Legis medius est inter statum Veteris Legis, cuius figurae implentur Novâ Lege, et inter statum gloriae, in qua omnis nude et perfecte manifestabitur veritas, et ideo tunc nulla* erunt sacramenta. Nunc autem, quamdiu per speculum et in aenigmate cognoscimus (1 Cor. XIII, 12), oportet nos per aliqua sensibilia signa in spiritualia devenire, quod pertinet ad rationem sacramentorum."

[46] Cfr. St. Thomas, *Summa Theologica,* 3a, qu. 61, art. 1.

visible signs; (5) the necessity of an external profession of faith to distinguish Christians from infidels; (6) the advantage of having sacred mysteries to excite and exercise the faith; and (7) the repression of pride and the exercise of humility involved in availing oneself of sensible elements in obedience to God.[47]

While it is perfectly legitimate to infer the fitness of Christian Sacraments from these *a priori* considerations, this fact does not dispense us from proving their actual existence from Revelation.

47 *Cat. Rom.*, P. II, c. 1, n. 9. On the Sacraments of the New Law cfr. N. Gihr, *Die hl. Sakramente der kath. Kirche,* Vol. I, 2nd ed., pp. 34 sqq., Freiburg 1902.

SECTION 3

THE SEVEN SACRAMENTS OF THE NEW TESTAMENT

1. HERETICAL ERRORS VS. THE TEACHING OF THE CHURCH.—After considerable wavering, Protestants finally adopted two Sacraments and two only, *viz.,* Baptism and the Lord's Supper. Against this heretical error the Tridentine Council defined: "If anyone saith that the Sacraments of the New Law . . . are more or less than seven, to wit: Baptism, Confirmation, the Eucharist, Penance, Extreme Unction, Order, and Matrimony, or even that any one of these seven is not truly and properly a Sacrament, let him be anathema." [1]   Hence it is of faith that there are seven Sacraments.

Luther at first retained this dogma.   But in 1520 he declared that there are but three Sacraments, Baptism, Penance, and the Eucharist; [2] in 1523 he reduced the number to two,— Baptism and the Lord's Supper.

---

[1] Sess. VII, can. 1: "*Si quis dixerit, sacramenta novae legis esse plura vel pauciora quam septem, vid. baptismum, confirmationem, Eucharistiam, poenitentiam, extremam unctionem, ordinem et matrimonium, aut etiam aliquod horum septem non esse vere et proprie sa-* cramentum, anathema sit." (Denzinger-Bannwart, n. 844).

[2] *De Captiv. Babyl.*: "*Principio neganda mihi sunt septem sacramenta et tantum tria pro tempore ponenda: baptismus, poenitentia, panis.*"

Melanchthon was equally inconsistent. After asserting in the first edition of his *Loci Theologici* (1522), that there are two Sacraments, Baptism and the Lord's Supper, he later, in his *Apologia* (A. D. 1530), added "Absolution" and "Ordination."

Zwingli and Calvin invented the two-sacrament theory, which has come to be generally accepted among modern Protestants.[3]

That there are exactly seven Sacraments, neither more nor less, can be demonstrated by a twofold method: first, by going through the several rites which the Council enumerates, proving that each of these answers the description of a Sacrament, and then showing that the same cannot be said of any other ceremonies. Second, by positively demonstrating that the Church has always believed in just seven Sacraments, neither more nor less. For pedagogical reasons we shall employ the latter method.

The belief of the Church may be demonstrated both theologically and historically.

2. THE THEOLOGICAL ARGUMENT.—For several centuries before the Protestant Reformation, the belief in seven Sacraments was universal throughout the Church. Now, universal belief in a doctrine of so great a theoretical and practical importance is certain proof of its Apostolic origin. Consequently, the belief in seven Sacraments is not a human invention but part and

---

3 Cfr. Bellarmine, *De Sacram.*, II, 23; Winer-Ewald, *Komparative Darstellung des Lehrbegriffes der verschiedenen christlichen Kirchenparteien*, 4th ed., pp. 171 sqq., Leipzig 1882. The Anglo-Catholic school in the Anglican Church believes in seven Sacraments, though the Thirty-nine Articles teach only two — Baptism and the Eucharist. (Cfr. the *New Schaff-Herzog Encyclopedia of Religious Knowledge*, Vol. X, p. 144).

parcel of the deposit of faith handed down by the Apostles.

a) The minor premise of this syllogism is based on the infallibility of the Church, which in turn is guaranteed by the abiding presence of the Holy Ghost and our Saviour's promise to remain with her unto the consummation of the world. Had the Catholic Church ever, even for a moment, deviated from the truth, she would no longer be the Church of Christ.

St. Augustine enunciates this truth in the following words: "Whatever is held by the whole Church, and was not introduced by any council, but has always been maintained, is rightly held to rest on the authority of the Apostles." [4]

b) The major premise asserts an historical fact which is easily demonstrable from contemporary documents.

α) There is some doubt as to who first drew up our present list of Sacraments. For a while this list was believed to be the work of Radulphus Ardens, who flourished towards the end of the eleventh century, but this assumption has been rendered improbable by the researches of Grabmann. [5] Most probably the first traces of "the Tridentine Seven" will yet be discovered in the hitherto inedited *Libri Sententiarum* of the schools of William of Champeaux (d. 1120) and Anselm of Laon (d. 1118). St. Otto, Bishop of Bamberg (ca. 1127), is reported by his biographer Herbord (d. 1168) to have left to his

4 St. Augustine, *De Baptismo*, IV, 24: "*Quod universa tenet Ecclesia nec conciliis institutum, sed semper retentum est, nonnisi auctoritate apostolicâ traditum rectissime creditur.*"

5 *Geschichte der scholastischen Methode*, Vol. I, p. 250, Freiburg 1909.

faithful flock a set of catechetical instructions, in which he speaks of "the seven Sacraments of the Church" and enumerates them just as we have them to-day, though in a somewhat different order.[6] At about the same time the learned Bishop Gregory of Bergamo (1133–1146), in a treatise composed against Berengarius, gives the number of Sacraments instituted by our Lord Jesus Christ as seven.[7] About the year 1150, Master Roland, later Pope Alexander III, enumerates seven Sacraments in his Book of Sentences.[8] The same number occurs in the statutes of Bishop Richard Poore, A. D. 1217, in the *Statuta Edita* 1222 of Archbishop Stephen Langton of Canterbury,[9] and in the decrees of the provincial councils of Oxford (1222), Clairvaux (1268), London (1272), and Cologne (1280). The synodal constitutions of Odo of Paris, A. D. 1197, give a detailed explanation of only six Sacraments, but the existence of a seventh (Holy Orders) is plainly demanded by the context.[10] Of still greater importance are the doctrinal decisions of various popes and councils, such as the profession of faith prescribed by Innocent III for the Waldenses (A. D. 1210).[11]

6 Migne, *P. L.*, CLXXIII, 1358 sqq.: "*Discessurus a vobis trado vobis, quae tradita sunt nobis a Domino, arrham fidei sanctae inter vos et Deum, septem scil. sacramenta Ecclesiae, quasi septem significativa dona Spiritus Sancti. Ista igitur septem sacramenta, quae iterum vestri causa enumerare libet, i. e. baptismum, confirmationem, infirmorum unctionem, Eucharistiam, lapsorum reconciliationem, coniugium et ordines, per nos humiles suos paranymphos coelestis Sponsus in arrham vestrae dilectionis vobis Ecclesiae ac sponsae suae transmittere dignatus est.*" Cfr. Bolland., *Acta Sanctorum*, t. I, 2 Iul., pp. 396 sqq.;

Pertz, *Monum. Germ. Hist., Script.*, XX, 732.

7 "*Scire debemus, ea solum esse Ecclesiae sacramenta a Servatore nostro Iesu instituta, quae in medicinam nobis tributa fuere, et haec numero adimplentur septenario.*" (Cfr. the Innsbruck *Zeitschrift für kath. Theologie*, 1878, p. 800).

8 Cfr. Gietl, *Die Sentenzen Rolands, nachmals Papstes Alexander III., zum erstenmal herausgegeben*, pp. 154 sqq., Freiburg 1891.

9 Cfr. Mansi, *Concil.*, XXII, 1173.

10 Cfr. the Mayence *Katholik*, 1910, II, pp. 481 sq.

11 Quoted in Denzinger-Bannwart's *Enchiridion*, n. 424: "*Ap-*

At the Council of Lyons, A. D. 1274, the Greek Emperor Michael Palæologus submitted to Pope Gregory X a profession of faith, in which he acknowledged that " the Holy Roman Church holds and teaches that there are seven Sacraments, namely Baptism, etc." [12] The Council of Constance (1418), by order of Martin V,[13] drew up a list of questions to be addressed to the followers of Wiclif and Hus, of which numbers 15 to 22 refer to the seven Sacraments as we have them.[14] The Council of Florence (A. D. 1439), in its *Decretum pro Armenis,* declares that " there are seven Sacraments of the New Law, *viz.:* Baptism, Confirmation, the Eucharist, Penance, Extreme Unction, Holy Orders, and Matrimony." [15]

β) The official teaching of the Church was explained and scientifically defended by the Scholastic theologians of the twelfth century, not merely as a theoretical opinion, but as a dogma of the faith practically applied in every-day life. Hugh of St. Victor (1097–1141), in his treatise *De Caerimoniis, Sacramentis, Officiis et Observationibus Ecclesiasticis,*[16] enumerates the seven Sacraments and describes them one by one. Peter Lombard, who flourished at about the same time,[17] begins his treatise on the subject with these words: " Now let us enter upon the Sacraments of the New Law, which are: Baptism, Confirmation, the Blessing of Bread or Eucharist,

---

probamus ergo baptismum infantium, . . . confirmationem ab episcopo factam, etc."

12 *Ibid.,* n. 465: *" Tenet etiam et docet Sancta Romana Ecclesia, septem esse ecclesiastica sacramenta, unum scil. baptisma, etc."*

13 See the Bull *" Inter Cunctas."*

14 Cfr. Denzinger-Bannwart, n. 665 sqq.

15 *" Novae legis septem sunt sacramenta, vid. baptismus, confirma-*

tio, Eucharistia, poenitentia, extrema unctio, ordo et matrimonium." (Denzinger-Bannwart, n. 695). On the enumeration and proper sequence of the Sacraments see Krawutzky, *Zählung und Ordnung der Sakramente,* Breslau 1865.

16 The authorship of this treatise, however, is not quite certain; some ascribe it to Robert Pulleyn.

17 Died A. D. 1164.

Penance, Extreme Unction, Order, and Matrimony." [18]
The fact that up to the middle of the thirteenth century
various writers, mostly commentators on the Canon Law
of the Church, differed in giving the number of the Sacraments, was due partly to the prevailing vagueness in the
use of the term " Sacrament," and partly to the compila-
tory character of their writings.[19] The great Scholastics, headed by St. Bonaventure and St. Thomas of
Aquin, unhesitatingly accepted the teaching of Peter
Lombard and were at pains to show the congruity of
the septenary number as afterwards defined by the Council of Trent. Thus Dominicus Soto writes: " There is
no question as to the certainty of the number [seven],
since that is settled by ecclesiastical tradition and usage;
but we shall inquire into its congruity." [20]

This brief survey shows that the Tridentine
definition was simply the solemn confirmation of
a doctrine which had been in undisputed possession for at least four centuries before the Protestant Reformation.

3. THE HISTORICAL ARGUMENT.—Any dogmatic truth that has been constantly held by the
universal Church, rests on the authority of the
Apostles, and consequently, of Christ.[21] Now, it

18 *Sent.*, IV, dist. 2, n. 2: " *Iam
ad sacramenta novae legis acceda-
mus, quae sunt: baptismus, confirmatio, panis benedictio, i. e. Eucharistia, poenitentia, unctio extrema, ordo, coniugium.*"

19 Cfr. the *Katholik*, 1909, II, pp.
182 sqq.

20 *Comment. in Sent.*, IV, dist. 1,
qu. 6, art. 1: " *Non quaeritur de*

*numeri certitudine; illa siquidem
Ecclesiae traditione et usu citra dis-
putationem constantissima est; sed
de eius convenientiâ.*"

21 Cfr. Tertullian, *De Praescr.*, c.
28: " *Ceterum quod apud multos
unum invenitur, non est erratum,
sed traditum.*" *V.* St. Augustine,
supra, p. 34, note 4.

can be shown that the Church has at all times believed in and administered the seven Sacraments
as we have them to-day, and that even the heretical sects which broke loose from Catholic unity
in the early centuries, held the same doctrine regarding the number of the Sacraments as that
later defined by the Council of Trent.

a) It is an historical fact that "the Tridentine
Seven" was in undisputed possession at the time
of St. Otto of Bamberg, A. D. 1127.[22]

While the followers of Wiclif and Hus attacked the
Catholic teaching with regard to the requisites of validity, claiming that a Sacrament cannot be validly administered by one who is in the state of mortal sin, they
never denied that there are seven Sacraments, neither
more nor less.

b) Going three centuries further back we
come to the Greek schism of Photius, A. D. 869.

Though this learned heretic was constantly seeking
for pretexts to justify the secession of the Greek Church
from Rome, he never once accused the Latins of having
abolished any of the traditional Sacraments or introduced
new ones. Both Churches were so perfectly at one in
their belief on this point, even after the schism, that
no essential difference of opinion came to light in the
repeated efforts for reunion made at Lyons (A. D. 1274)
and Florence (A. D. 1439). Though the reunion
patched up at Florence came to a bad end, the schismatic
Greeks continued to believe in seven Sacraments, as the

22 *V. supra,* No. 1, pp. 32 sq.

Lutherans found to their sorrow when they tried to
" convert " them.   Jeremias, Patriarch of Constantinople,
in 1573, politely but firmly rejected the overtures of
Martin Crusius and Jacob Andreä, of the theological
faculty of Tübingen, and in a long letter refuted the
Lutheran innovations point for point.   He said *inter alia:*
" We solemnly affirm that the holy Fathers have handed
down to us . . . seven divine Sacraments, *viz.:* Baptism,
Anointment with Sacred Chrism, Holy Communion,
Order, Matrimony, Penance, and the Oil of the last
Unction, . . . neither more nor less. . . . And all these
means of our salvation have been handed down to us
by Christ Himself, our Lord God, and His Apostles." [23]
When, in 1581, the Tübingen divines again appealed to
Jeremias, he bluntly told them to cease their fruitless
efforts.[24]   Half a century later an attempt was made
by a traitor to force the Protestant heresy on the Greek
Church.   Cyril Lucar, a Greek priest, who had espoused Calvinism and somehow managed to intrigue
his way into the patriarchal see of Constantinople, in
a Calvinistic confession of faith which he drew up in
Latin, in 1629, and subsequently translated into Greek,
asserted that there are but two Sacraments.   The Greek
Church at once took alarm, and Cyril was sent into
exile (1634).   In 1637 he purchased his return by bribery

23 *V.* Arnaud, *Perpetuité de la
Foi,* t. V, l. 1, c. 3: " *Dicimus
praeclare nobis sanctos tradidisse
Patres,* . . . *septem divina sacramenta esse, baptismum scil., sacri
chrismatis unctionem, sacram com-
munionem, ordinem, matrimonium,
poenitentiam et extremae unctionis
oleum,* . . . *non plura nec pauciora
esse.* . . . *Et haec quidem omnia
salutis nostrae remedia ipse Iesus
Christus Deus et Dominus noster*

tradidit et sancti eius Apostoli."
24 " *Rogamus itaque vos, ne
posthac labores nobis exhibeatis
neque de iisdem scribatis et scripta
mittatis.*"   For further particulars
concerning this remarkable corres-
pondence between the Lutheran divines of Tübingen and the Patriarch
of Constantinople, see Schelstrate,
*Acta Orient. Ecclesiae contra Lu-
theri Haeresim,* I, 151 sqq., 202 sqq.,
246 sqq., Rome 1739.

and succeeded in having himself reinstated. Thereupon
the indignation of both clergy and people against the man
who dared to set his private opinion above the common belief of the faithful could no longer be restrained.
The unworthy Patriarch was condemned by a council
at Constantinople (A. D. 1638), and, being moreover
suspected of favoring an invasion of the Turkish Empire by the Cossacks, was strangled by order of the Sultan
and his body cast into the sea. His "Confession of
Faith" was condemned and anathema passed upon him by
a synod assembled at Constantinople in September, 1638.[25]

Four years later, at a council held under the presidency
of Parthenius, who was a cordial hater of Rome, there
was adopted a *Confessio Fidei Orthodoxae* drawn up by
Peter Mogilas, metropolitan of Kieff, in which the Latin
doctrine as to the number of Sacraments held a prominent
place. This important symbol in the following year received the official signatures of all four Oriental patri-
archs and of numerous bishops, and was solemnly approved by a council held at Jerusalem in 1672.

These official declarations find their practical confirmation in the liturgical books of the Orthodox Church,
both ancient and modern,[26] and are not denied even by
such radical schismatic theologians as Simon of Thessalonica (d. 1429), Gabriel of Philadelphia, Meletius Syri-
gus, Coresius, and his pupil Georgios Protosynkellos.
Only a few years ago the Orthodox Provost Maltzew, of
the Russian embassy in Berlin, wrote: "While the
Roman Church and all the heterodox Oriental churches
are in perfect agreement with the Orthodox Catholic

25 Cfr. Alzog-Pabisch-Byrne, *Man-
ual of Universal Church History*,
Vol. III, 5th ed., pp. 465 sqq.,
Cincinnati 1899.

26 Cfr. Goar, *Euchologium sive
Rituale Graecorum*, Paris 1647.

Church of the East in regard to the doctrine that there are seven Sacraments, the sects based on the Protestant Reformation admit but two, and interpret even these in a different sense from the Orthodox Church." [27]

In view of the origin of the Greek schism and the great animosity existing between the two churches, it is impossible to assume that the doctrine of the seven Sacraments was borrowed by the West from the East, or *vice versa;* both churches must have derived it from a common source before the Orient severed its connection with the Latin Church. In other words, the Church of Christ had her seven Sacraments long before the time of Photius. [28]

c). Another step takes us back to that agitated period when the Nestorians and the Monophysites broke away from Catholic unity.

α) Did these ancient heretics hold any other doctrine as to the number of Sacraments than that defined at Trent? No. Their liturgical books contain the Catholic dogma in all its purity, and thus furnish clear and indisputable evidence that it antedates the fifth century, when these sects separated from the Church.

β) This argument loses nothing of its force by the curious circumstance that, in the course of ecclesiastical history, a few individual writers belonging to these sects have rejected one or the other Sacrament and substi-

27 Maltzcw, *Die Sakramente der orthodox-katholischen Kirche des Morgenlandes*, p. C, Berlin 1898.

28 The rites of the Copts, Syrians, and Armenians have been collected and published by Denzinger, *Ritus Orientalium*, 2 vols., Würzburg 1863 sqq. The administration of the Sacraments among the Nestorians and Monophysites may be studied in Assemani's *Bibliotheca Orient.*, vols. II and III. Much valuable material is also furnished by Arnaud in his great work *Perpetuité de la Foi*, vol. III, l. 8, c. 18 sqq.

tuted in its place some ceremony or rite which the Church
has never acknowledged as sacramentary. The very fact
that these innovators never deviated from the number
seven, proves that there were seven Sacraments, neither
more nor less, from the beginning. The Greek monks
Job and Damascene of Thessalonica, *e. g.*, after arbitrarily
adding the monastic habit [29] to the list of Sacraments, restored the traditional number seven by contracting Penance and Extreme Unction into one (Job) or striking
Penance entirely from the list (Damascene). Equally
characteristic is the procedure of Vartanus, a thirteenth-
century Armenian of Monophysitic proclivities, who substituted the "burial service" [30] to fill the vacancy he
had created in the roster of Sacraments by fusing Penance
with Extreme Unction. These authors got their new
"Sacraments" from a misunderstood passage in the writings of Dionysius the Pseudo-Areopagite, where the four
"consecratory" Sacraments — Baptism, Confirmation, the
Eucharist, and Holy Orders — are immediately followed
by the rite for the blessing of altars, the monastic habit,
benediction, and the funeral service.

It is not so easy to explain how the Nestorian Ebed
Jesu (d. 1318) came to deny the Sacraments of Matrimony and Extreme Unction and to replace them by the
Sign of the Cross [31] and the "Holy Ferment," whatever
that may have meant.[32] Perhaps these and similar
vagaries owed their origin to the ignorance of hermits who
were far removed from the centres of ecclesiastical learning and deprived of even ordinary means of instruction.[33]
The genuine doctrine of these sects and their authentic
practice must be studied in the liturgical books which

---

29 *Habitus sacer s. monasticus,*
καλογορικὴ ἢ τὸ μέγα σχῆμα.
30 *Funus super defunctos.*
31 *Signum vivificae crucis.*

32 *Sacrum fermentum.*
33 On the ignorance of the Copts
cfr. the Bollandist P. Sollerius, S.
J., *Acta Sanctor.*, t. V, pp. 140 sqq.

contain the primitive rites of the Sacraments, as stated under a).[34]

d) If the belief of the Church in regard to such an important dogma as the number of the Sacraments instituted by Christ, had undergone any essential change between the Apostolic age and the time of Nestorius, this change, whether slow or sudden, would necessarily have left its traces in history.

The bishops and the faithful of the first four centuries jealously guarded the purity of the Apostolic deposit, especially in those matters which involved daily practice. The learned and zealous Fathers who did not hesitate to shed their blood in defense of the orthodox faith against the anti-Trinitarian and Christological heresies, would surely have sounded the alarm had anyone tried to tamper with the doctrine of the Sacraments. Even if, for argument's sake, we were to grant that the primitive Church knew but two or three Sacraments, it would have been impossible, aside from her infallibility and indefectibility, for any innovator to introduce a complete set of new sacramental rites without incurring the determined opposition of bishops, priests, and people. Hence we may safely conclude with Father Hunter that "the doctrine now held by all who reject the authority of the Tridentine Council, is certainly not Apostolic nor traditional; it is a novelty no older than the sixteenth century; it is therefore a freshly introduced doctrine, resting on the authority of Luther or some of his con-

---

34 Page 41, *supra*. For further information on this topic see Franzelin, *De Sacram. in Genere*, thes. 20.

temporaries: it is therefore not to be received, unless the teacher produce his credentials as a divine messenger, and this he is unable to do." [35]   The Catholic doctrine that there are seven Sacraments is of Apostolic origin, and hence derived from our Lord and Saviour Jesus Christ.[36]

4. WHY THERE ARE JUST SEVEN SACRAMENTS. —As there are reasons of congruity for the existence of Sacraments under the Christian dispensation,[37] so there are reasons why there should be precisely seven, neither more nor less.

a) The human intellect is not, of course, able to establish this number with mathematical certainty on *a priori* grounds. Absolutely speaking, God had it in His power to institute as many Sacraments as He pleased. But it is easy to see, *a posteriori,* that the septenary admirably corresponds to the practical needs of man's composite nature.   This was admitted even by Goethe, pagan though he was.[38]   We will not enter into useless

35 S. J. Hunter, S. J., *Outlines of Dogmatic Theology,* Vol. III, p. 178.

36 The argument from prescription for the septenary number of the Sacraments is very ably set forth by Card. Bellarmine, *De Sacram.,* II, 23 sqq. The student will also profit by consulting Heinrich-Gutberlet, *Dogmatische Theologie,* Vol. IX, § 500.

37 *V. supra,* pp. 30 sq.

38 See the famous passage in his *Autobiography,* tr. by J. Oxenford, Vol. I, pp. 239 sqq., Philadelphia, 1882: "In moral and religious, as well as in physical and civil matters, man does not like to do anything on the spur of the moment; he needs a sequence from which results habit; what he is to love and to perform, he cannot represent to himself as single or isolated; and, if he is to repeat anything willingly, it must not have become strange to him. If the Protestant worship lacks fulness in general, so let it be investigated in detail, and it will be found that the Protestant has too few sacraments,— nay, indeed, he has only one in which he is himself an actor,— the Lord's Supper; for baptism he sees only when it is performed on others, and is not greatly edified by it. The sacraments are the highest part of

speculations about the " mystic number seven," but merely note that there is a <u>remarkable analogy between the natural life of the body</u> and the supernatural life of the soul, to both of which the Sacraments so wonderfully minister.

religion, the symbols to our senses of an extraordinary divine favor and grace. In the Lord's Supper earthly lips are to receive a divine Being embodied, and partake of a heavenly, under the form of an earthly nourishment. This import is the same in all kinds of Christian churches: whether the sacrament is taken with more or less submission to the mystery, with more or less accommodation as to that which is intelligible, it remains a great, holy thing, which in reality takes the place of the possible or the impossible, the place of that which man can neither attain nor do without. But such a sacrament should not stand alone: no Christian can partake of it with the true joy for which it is given, if the symbolical or sacramental sense is not fostered within him. He must be accustomed to regard the inner religion of the heart and that of the external church as perfectly one, as the great universal sacrament, which again divides itself into so many others, and communicates to these parts its holiness, indestructibility, and eternity.

" Here a youthful pair join hands, not for a passing salutation or for the dance: the priest pronounces his blessing upon them, and the bond is indissoluble. It is not long before this wedded pair bring a likeness to the threshold of the altar: it is purified with holy water, and so incorporated into the church, that it cannot forfeit this benefit but through the most monstrous apostasy. The child in the course of life goes on progress-

ing in earthly things of his own accord, in heavenly things he must be instructed. Does it prove on examination that this has been fully done, he is now received into the bosom of the church as an actual citizen, as a true and voluntary professor, not without outward tokens of the weightiness of this act. Now, only, he is decidedly a Christian, now for the first time he knows his advantages and also his duties. But, in the mean time, a great deal that is strange has happened to him as a man: through instruction and affliction he has come to know how critical appears the state of his inner self, and there will constantly be a question of doctrines and of transgressions; but punishment shall no longer take place. For here, in the infinite confusion in which he must entangle himself, amid the conflict of natural and religious claims, an admirable expedient is given him, in confiding his deeds and misdeeds, his infirmities and doubts, to a worthy man, appointed expressly for that purpose, who knows how to calm, to warn, to strengthen him, to chasten him likewise by symbolical punishments, and at last, by a complete washing away of his guilt, to render him happy, and to give him back, pure and cleansed, the tablet of his manhood. Thus prepared, and purely set at rest by several sacramental acts, which on closer examination branch forth again into minuter sacramental traits, he kneels down to receive the host; and, that the mystery of this high act may be

St. Thomas develops this thought in the third part of the *Summa:*

" The Sacraments of the Church were instituted for a twofold purpose: namely, in order to perfect man in

still enhanced, he sees the chalice only in the distance: it is no common eating and drinking that satisfies, it is a heavenly feast, which makes him thirst after heavenly drink.

" Yet let not the youth believe that this is all he has to do: let not even the man believe it. In earthly relations we are at last accustomed to depend on ourselves; and, even there, knowledge, understanding, and character will not always suffice: in heavenly things, on the contrary, we have never finished learning. The higher feeling within us, which often finds itself not even truly at home, is, besides, oppressed by so much from without, that our own power hardly administers all that is necessary for counsel, consolation, and help. But, to this end, that remedy is instituted for our whole life; and an intelligent, pious man is continually waiting to show the right way to the wanderers, and to relieve the distressed.

" And what has been so well tried through the whole life, is now to show forth all its healing power with tenfold activity at the gate of death. According to a trustful custom, inculcated from youth upwards, the dying man receives with fervor those symbolical, significant assurances; and there, where every earthly warranty fails, he is assured, by a heavenly one, of a blessed existence for all eternity. He feels perfectly convinced that neither a hostile element nor a malignant spirit can hinder him from clothing himself with a glorified

body, so that, in immediate relation with the Godhead, he may partake of the boundless happiness which flows forth from Him.

" Then, in conclusion, that the whole man may be made holy, the feet also are anointed and blessed. They are to feel, even in the event of possible recovery, a repugnance to touching this earthly, hard, impenetrable soil. A wonderful elasticity is to be imparted to them, by which they spurn from under them the clod of earth which hitherto attracted them. And so, through a brilliant cycle of equally holy acts, the beauty of which we have only briefly hinted at, the cradle and the grave, however far asunder they may chance to be, are joined in one continuous circle.

" But all these spiritual wonders spring not, like other fruits, from the natural soil, where they can neither be sown nor planted nor cherished. We must supplicate for them from another region,— a thing which cannot be done by all persons nor at all times. Here we meet the highest of these symbols, derived from pious tradition. We are told that one man may be more favored, blessed, and sanctified from above than another. But, that this may not appear as a natural gift, this great boon, bound up with a heavy duty, must be communicated to others by one authorized person to another; and the greatest good that a man can attain, without his having to obtain it by his own wrestling and grasping, must be preserved and perpetuated on earth by spiritual things pertaining to the worship of God according to the Christian life, and to be a remedy against the defects caused by sin. And in either way it is becoming that there should be seven Sacraments. For spiritual life has a certain conformity with the life of the body: just as other corporeal things have a certain likeness to things spiritual. Now man attains perfection in the corporeal life in two ways: first, in regard to his own person; secondly, in regard to the whole community of the society in which he lives, for man is by nature a social animal. With regard to himself man is perfected in the life of the body in two ways: first, directly (*per se*), *i. e.* by acquiring some vital perfection; secondly, indirectly (*per accidens*), *i. e.* by the removal of hindrances to life, such as ailments or the like. Now the life of the body is perfected directly, in three ways. First, by generation, whereby a man begins to be and to live: and corresponding to this in the spiritual life there is Baptism, which is a spiritual regeneration. . . . Secondly, by growth, whereby a man is brought to perfect size and strength: and corresponding to this in the spiritual life there is Confirmation, in which the Holy Ghost is given to

inheritance. In the very ordination of the priest is comprehended all that is necessary for the effectual solemnizing of those holy acts by which the multitude receive grace, without any other activity being needful on their part than that of faith and implicit confidence. And thus the priest joins the line of his predecessors and successors, in the circle of those anointed with him, representing the highest source of blessings, so much the more gloriously, as it is not he, the priest, whom we reverence, but his office; it is not his nod to which we bow

the knee, but the blessing which he imparts, and which seems the more holy, and to come the more immediately from heaven, because the earthly instrument cannot at all weaken or invalidate it by its own sinful, nay, wicked nature.

" How is this truly spiritual conception shattered to pieces in Protestantism, by part of the above-mentioned symbols being declared apocryphal, and only a few canonical! — and how, by their indifference to one of these, will they prepare us for the high dignity of the others. "

strengthen us. . . . Thirdly, by nourishment, whereby life
and strength are preserved to man: and corresponding to
this in the spiritual life there is the Eucharist. . . .
This would be enough for man if he had an impassible
life, both corporally and spiritually; but since man is lia-
ble at times to both corporal and spiritual infirmity, *i. e.*
sin, he needs a cure for his infirmity. This cure is
twofold. One is the healing that restores health: and
corresponding to this in the spiritual life there is Penance. . . . The other is the restoration of former vigor
by means of suitable diet and exercise: and corresponding to this in the spiritual life there is Extreme Unction,
which removes the remainders of sin and prepares man
for final glory. . . . In regard to the whole community,
man is perfected in two ways. First, by receiving power
to rule the community and to exercise public acts: and corresponding to this in the spiritual life there is the Sacrament of Order. . . . Secondly, in regard to natural propa-
gation. This is accomplished by Matrimony both in the
corporal and in the spiritual life: since it is not only a
Sacrament but also a function of nature.

" We may likewise gather the number of the Sacraments from their being instituted as a remedy against
the defect caused by sin. For Baptism is intended as a
remedy against the absence of spiritual life; Confirmation,
against the infirmity of soul found in those of recent birth;
the Eucharist, against the soul's proneness to sin; Penance, against actual sin committed after Baptism; Extreme Unction, against the remainders of sins,— of those
sins, namely, which are not sufficiently removed by
Penance, whether through negligence or through ignorance; Order, against divisions in the community; Matrimony, as a remedy against concupiscence in the individ-

ual, and against the decrease in numbers that results from death." [39]

This beautiful argument has been as it were officially approved and consecrated by the Church through its embodiment in the *Decretum pro Armenis* (1439) [40] and the Roman Catechism. [41]

b) The Scholastics, from Peter Lombard to Suarez, devoted much ingenuity to demonstrating the intrinsic fitness of the septenary number of the Sacraments. Perhaps the most original conception is that of St. Bonaventure, who argues from the vicissitudes to which every Christian is subject in his capacity as a soldier of Christ. "Baptism," he says, "is [the Sacrament] of those that enter the army; Confirmation, that of the combatants engaged in actual battle; the Eucharist, that of the soldiers regaining strength; Penance, that of the fighters arising from defeat; Extreme Unction, that of the departing; Order, that of the officers charged with training new soldiers; Matrimony, that of the men whose business it is to furnish recruits." [42] He proves the same thesis from the functions of the different Sacraments as remedies for various diseases of the soul: "There are seven different

---

[39] *Summa Theol.*, 3a, qu. 65, art. 1.

[40] Denzinger-Bannwart, n. 695: "*Novae legis septem sunt sacramenta. . . . Horum quinque prima ad spiritualem uniuscuiusque hominis in seipso perfectionem, duo ultima ad totius Ecclesiae regimen multiplicationemque ordinata sunt. Per baptismum enim spiritualiter renascimur; per confirmationem augemur in gratia et roboramur in fide; renati autem et roborati nutrimur divinae Eucharistiae alimoniâ; quodsi per peccatum aegritudinem incurrimus animae, per poenitentiam spiritualiter*

sanamur; spiritualiter etiam et corporaliter, prout animae expedit, per extremam unctionem. Per ordinem vero Ecclesia gubernatur et multiplicatur spiritualiter; per matrimonium corporaliter augetur."

[41] P. II, c. 1, n. 18.

[42] *Breviloquium*, P. VI, cap. 3: "*Baptismus est ingredientium, confirmatio pugnantium, Eucharistia vires resumentium, poenitentia resurgentium, extrema unctio exeuntium, ordo novos milites introducentium, matrimonium novos milites praeparantium.*"

kinds of diseases, three of guilt, *viz.*: original sin, mortal sin, and venial sin; and four of punishment, *viz.*: ignorance, malice, infirmity, and concupiscence. . . . Against each of these special remedies must be applied. . . . Baptism, against original sin; Penance, against mortal sin; Extreme Unction, against venial sin; Order, against ignorance; the Eucharist, against malice; Confirmation, against infirmity; and Matrimony, against concupiscence." [43] Combining the three theological with the four cardinal virtues into a series of seven, the Saint draws a parallel between them and the Sacraments, as follows: "Baptism disposes for faith, Confirmation for hope, the Eucharist for charity, Penance for justice, Extreme Unction for perseverance, which is the complement and sum of fortitude, Holy Orders for prudence, and Matrimony for temperance." [44]

c) To compare the seven Sacraments with the seven capital sins [45] or with the seven gifts of the Holy Ghost, is rather far-fetched. The mythological interpretation of the number seven as the outward embodiment of the "seven eyes of God," *i. e.* the planets, may be explained by the fact that the coryphæi of Scholasticism were ignorant of the apocalyptic and cabalistic juggling at-

---

43 *Ibid.*: "*Morbus est septiformis: triplex culpabilis, scil. culpa originalis, mortalis et venialis, et quadruplex poenalis: scil. ignorantia, malitia, infirmitas et concupiscentia.* . . . *Hinc est quod oportuit adhiberi* . . . *contra originalem baptismum, contra mortalem poenitentiam, contra venialem unctionem extremam; contra ignorantiam ordinem, contra malitiam Eucharistiam, contra infirmitatem confirmationem et contra concupiscentiam matrimonium.*"

44 *Ibid.*: "*Baptismus disponit ad fidem, confirmatio ad spem, Eucharistia ad caritatem; poenitentia ad iustitiam, unctio extrema ad perseverantiam, quae est fortitudinis complementum et summa, ordo ad prudentiam, matrimonium ad temperantiam conservandam.*" Cfr. P. Minges, O.F.M., *Compendium Theol. Dogmat. Specialis*, Vol. II, p. 12, Munich 1901.

45 Cfr. St. Thomas, *Summa Theol.*, 3a, qu. 65, art. 5.

tributed to them by modern writers on the history of comparative religion.[46]

5. CERTAIN PATRISTIC DIFFICULTIES SOLVED. —Though the Sacraments were in use from the beginning, and references to all of them occur in the writings of the Fathers, there is nowhere to be found in Patristic literature an express statement that there are exactly seven, neither more nor less. It may be asked: Why was the work of synthesis left to the Scholastics of the twelfth and thirteenth centuries? Several reasons account for the silence of the Fathers on this head: (1) the conditions of the time, (2) the discipline of the secret, and (3) the fact that sacramental theology developed rather slowly.

a) The silence of the Fathers with regard to the number of the Sacraments proves nothing against the " Tridentine Seven." One may own a lot of precious gems without making an inventory of them. We shall briefly explain the reasons why it never occurred to the writers of the Patristic period to draw up a formal list of the Sacraments.

α) The circumstances of the time were not favorable to the double task of working out a scientific definition and applying it to the various rites in use. " From the

---

46 The analogy between the seven Sacraments and the seven capital sins is very popular among the schismatic Greeks. On the whole subject of this subdivision cfr. Oswald, *Die dogmatische Lehre von den Sakramenten,* Vol. I, 5th ed., § 12, Münster 1884; N. Gihr, *Die Sakramente der kath. Kirche,* Vol. I, 2nd ed., pp. 173 sqq., Freiburg 1902.

beginning the Church has always lived by her Sacraments and has always had faith in their marvelous efficacy, . . . but she did not from the beginning consider them systematically, ranging them under the concept of efficacious symbols of grace. This was a work of synthesis accomplished only later by theological speculation." [47] Hence we need not wonder that Tertullian mentions one class of Sacraments and passes over the others in silence,[48] or that St. Cyril of Jerusalem treats of three or four without adverting to the existence of the rest.[49] The Fathers in each case wrote from a strictly practical point of view, with the intention of satisfying actual needs, such as the instruction of the faithful or catechumens and the refutation of heretics.[50] Usually it is the teaching of the Church on Baptism, Confirmation, and the Eucharist that is briefly summarized for the benefit of neophytes.[51] The general division that naturally suggested itself to the minds of those early writers was that into *sacramenta consecratoria* and *sacramenta medicinalia*. The *sacramenta consecratoria* (Baptism, Confirmation, the Eucharist, and Holy Orders) [52] claimed their main interest. In limiting their attention to this group, the Fathers by no means wished to deny the existence of the *sacramenta medicinalia* (Penance, Extreme Unction, and Matrimony).[53]

β) Another reason why no effort was made in the early days to determine the exact number of the Sacraments,

47 P. Pourrat, *Theology of the Sacraments*, p. 257, St. Louis 1914.
48 *De Resurrect. Carnis*, c. 8.
49 *Catech. Mystag.*
50 Cfr. Pourrat, *op. cit.*, p. 260.
51 St. Ambrose, *De Myst.* and *De Sacram.*
52 Cfr. St. Thomas, *Summa Theol.*, 3a, qu. 63, art. 6.

53 For a more detailed treatment see Pourrat, *La Théologie Sacramentaire*, pp. 232 sqq., 4th ed., Paris 1910 (English translation, pp. 259 sqq.); cfr. also J. Scheeben, *Die Mysterien des Christentums*, 3rd ed., pp. 507 sqq., Freiburg 1912.

was the *disciplina arcani,* which enjoined secrecy with regard to sacramental rites. The sacred mysteries shrank from the broad daylight which at a later age enabled the Scholastics to analyze them minutely in public. The " discipline of the secret " was strictly enforced throughout the Patristic period. Every copy of St. Cyril's *Catecheses* [54] bore a notice requesting the owner not to show it to catechumens and non-Christians generally, nor to allow copies to be made without prefixing a similar warning.[55] In St. Cyril's day the faithful were instructed never to speak of the mysteries of their religion in the presence of outsiders.[56] The phrase *" norunt initiati "* occurs at least fifty times in the writings of St. Chrysostom. Where he speaks of Baptism he remarks: " I should like to express myself freely on this subject, but cannot do so on account of the presence of some who are not initiated." [57] In the West the *disciplina arcani* survived far into the fifth century. St. Augustine says: " Let not the sacraments of the faithful be revealed to the catechumens." [58] Pope Innocent the First refused to divulge the formula of Confirmation.[59]

---

[54] See *apud* Migne, *P. G.,* XXXIII.

[55] " *Catecheses istas illuminatorum iis quidem, qui ad baptismum accedunt et fidelibus qui lavacrum iam susceperunt exhibens, catechumenis et aliis quibuslibet, qui Christiani non sunt, ne dederis; et si harum exemplar transcripseris, per Dominum rogo, hoc monitum praefigas."* (Migne, *l. c.,* 366).

[56] St. Cyril, *Catech.,* 6, n. 29: " *De mysteriis neque apud catechumenos palam verba facimus."* (Migne, *l. c.,* 590).

[57] *Hom. in* 1 *Cor.,* 40, n. 1: " *Volo quidem aperte hoc dicere, sed non possum propter non initiatos."*

(Migne, *P. G.,* LXI, 348). The relevant texts collated by Val. Schmitt, *Die Verheissung der Eucharistie (Joh. Kap.* 6) *bei den Antiochenern, Cyrill von Jerusalem und Johannes Chrysostomus,* pp. 47 sqq., Würzburg 1903.

[58] *Tract. in Ioa.,* 96, n. 3: " *Catechumenis sacramenta fidelium non prodantur."* (Migne, *P. L.,* XXXV, 1857).

[59] *Apud* Denzinger-Bannwart, n. 98: " *Verba vero dicere non possum, ne magis prodere videar quam ad consultationem respondere."* On the discipline of the secret cfr. Schelstrate, *De Disciplina Arcani,* Rome 1685. See also Döllinger,

γ) No doubt the development of the septenary number was impeded by the discipline of the secret. But even after that discipline had been abolished, a long time elapsed before the number became definitively fixed. No progress could be made in this direction until a precise definition had been worked out. "For that definition being the unit of the septenary number of the Sacraments, so long as it did not exist, the number could not be given." [60] The work of synthesis remained for the speculative theologians of a later age. Nor was it an easy matter, because each Sacrament is a complete and independent unit. Thus the Eucharist has no intrinsic connection with Matrimony. Both were in use as efficacious symbols of grace from the very beginning. The double task of working out the generic definition of a Sacrament, and applying it to each of the seven symbols officially in use, proceeded rather slowly. "Sacramental practice antedates the systematic elaboration of a sacramentary theology. This is to be expected, for the latter is but a scientific statement of the former: *lex orandi, lex credendi.*" [61] Sacramental theology was elaborated in the course of a long process of theological speculation, and the Church did not define the septenary number as an article of faith until the Protestant Reformers had expressly denied it.[62]

b) A difficulty arises from the fact that St. Ambrose and St. Bernard apparently regarded the washing of feet on Holy Thursday [63] as a Sac-

---

Lehre von der Eucharistie in den ersten drei Jahrhunderten, pp. 12 sqq., Mainz 1824; Theo. Harnack, *Der christliche Gemeindegottesdienst im apostolischen Zeitalter,* pp. 1 sqq., Erlangen 1854; Probst, *Kirchliche Disziplin in den ersten drei Jahrhun-*

derten, pp. 303 sqq., Tübingen 1873.

60 Pourrat, *Theology of the Sacraments,* p. 257.

61 Pourrat, *l. c.,* p. 259.

62 Cfr. Franzelin, *De Sacram. in Genere,* thes. 19.

63 Cfr. John XIII, 8 sqq.

rament. That this ceremony is not a Sacrament
cannot be convincingly demonstrated except in the
light of ecclesiastical Tradition. The Mennonites
recognize the *lotio pedum* as a true Sacrament.
In rejecting this teaching modern Protestantism
unwittingly employs the Catholic criterion of Tradition.

a) St. Ambrose says in his *De Mysteriis,* VI, 32:
"*Mundus erat Petrus, sed plantam lavare debebat; habe-
bat enim primi parentis de successione peccatum, quando
eum supplantavit serpens et persuasit errorem. Ideo
planta eius abluitur, ut hereditaria peccata tollantur;
nostra enim propria per baptismum relaxantur.*" [64] Does
this mean that the washing of feet is a Sacrament ordained for the forgiveness of sins, like Baptism, or do
the phrases *primi parentis peccatum* and *hereditaria
peccata* merely signify concupiscence (*fomes peccati*)?
Evidently the latter, for St. Ambrose says in another
passage: "*Lavemus et pedes, ut calcanei lubricum* [that
is, concupiscence] *possimus auferre, quo fida statio possit
esse virtutum.*" [65] More light is thrown on the Saint's
meaning by the anonymous author of the six books *De
Sacramentis,* which is probably "not a later imitation
or recension of the *De Mysteriis,* but the same work published indiscreetly and in an imperfect form by some
disciple of Ambrose." [66] We read there, III, 1, 7: "*Qui
lotus est, non indiget nisi ut pedes lavet. Quare hoc?
Quia in baptismate omnis culpa diluitur. Recedit ergo
culpa, sed quia Adam supplantatus est a diabolo et vene-*

---

64 Migne, *P. L.,* XVI, 398.
65 *In Ps.,* 48, n. 9 (Migne, *P. L.,*
XIV, 1159).

66 Bardenhewer-Shahan, *Patrology,* p. 438.

*num [concupiscentia] ei effusum est supra pedes, ideo
lavas pedes, ut in ea parte, in qua insidiatus est serpens,
maius subsidium sanctificationis accedat, quo postea te
supplantare non possit. Lavas ergo pedes, ut laves ve-
nenum serpentis."* [67]   St. Ambrose's special interest in the
ceremony probably grew out of the custom, in vogue at
Milan, of washing the feet of neophytes after Baptism,—
a practice unknown at Rome, as Ambrose himself tells
us.[68] Augustine distinctly asserts that this custom was
peculiar to the Church of Milan and that it was rejected
and discontinued in many places where it had been
adopted.[69] The fact thus reliably attested, that the *lotio
pedum* was merely a local and transient practice, is sufficient proof that it was not a Sacrament, for a true Sacrament is universal both as regards time and place.

β) In the light of this explanation it is easy to understand how St. Bernard of Clairvaux (d. 1153) could refer to the *lotio pedum* as a Sacrament at a time when belief in the septenary number of the Sacraments was already wide-spread. He writes: *" Ut de remissione
quotidianorum minime dubitemus, habemus eius sacramentum, pedum ablutionem. . . . Et unde scimus, quia
ad diluenda peccata quae non sunt ad mortem [i. e. venia-
lia] et a quibus plane cavere non possumus ante mortem,
ablutio ista pertineat? Ex eo plane quod offerenti manus
et caput pariter ad abluendum responsum est: Qui lotus*

---

67 *De Sacram.*, III, 1, 7 (Migne,
P. L., XVI, 433).

68 *De Sacram.*, III, 1, 5. *" Ecclesia Romana hanc consuetudinem
non habet, cuius typum in omnibus
sequimur et formam. . . . In omnibus cupio sequi Ecclesiam Roma-
nam; sed tamen et nos homines sensum habemus, ideo quod alibi rec-*

*tius servatur et nos rectius custodi-
mus."*

69 Cfr. St. Augustine, *Ep.* 55 *ad
Ianuar.*, n. 33: *" Sed ne ad ipsum
sacramentum baptismi videretur [lo-
tio pedum] pertinere, multi hoc in
consuetudine recipere noluerunt;
nonnulli etiam de consuetudine au-
ferri non dubitaverunt."* (Migne,
P. L., XXXIII, 220).

est, etc." [70] In writing thus he cannot have meant to designate the annual ceremony of washing the feet on Holy Thursday as a true Sacrament. What benefit could the faithful derive from a Sacrament that, having been instituted for the remission of " daily sins," was administered only once a year? Clearly St. Bernard employed the term Sacrament in the wider sense in which it was still used in his day. He regarded the *lotio pedum* as a " sacramental." [71]

READINGS:— Besides the current text-books on sacramental theology see Val. Gröne, *Sacramentum oder Begriff und Bedeutung von Sakrament in der alten Kirche bis zur Scholastik,* Berlin 1853.— P. Schanz, *Der Begriff des Sakramentes bei den Vätern,* in the *Theologische Quartalschrift* of Tübingen, 1891.— P. Schmalzl, *Die Sakramente des Alten Testamentes im allgemeinen nach der Lehre des hl. Thomas,* Eichstätt 1883.

On the number of the Sacraments cfr. Hahn, *Doctrinae Romae de Numero Sacramentorum Septenario Rationes Historicae,* Breslau 1859 (Prot.), and against him, Bittner, *De Numero Sacramentorum Septenario,* Breslau 1859.— Jos. Bach, *Die Siebenzahl der Sakramente,* Ratisbon 1864.— B. J. Otten, S. J., *A Manual of the History of Dogmas,* Vol. II, St. Louis 1918, pp. 292 sqq.

70 *Serm. in Coena Domini,* n. 4 (Migne, *P. L.,* CLXXXIII, 271).

71 For a fuller treatment of this subject consult Franzelin, *De Sacram. in Genere,* pp. 289 sqq., and Heinrich-Gutberlet, *Dogmatische Theologie,* Vol. IX, pp. 21 sqq.

CHAPTER II

THE THREE ESSENTIAL CONSTITUENTS OF A SACRAMENT

The three essential constituents of a sacrament are: (1) the visible sign, (2) invisible grace, and (3) divine institution.

SECTION 1

THE VISIBLE SIGN, OR MATTER AND FORM

As a body is composed of two constituents, the one indeterminate and the other determining, so, too, a Sacrament has two elements, matter and form.[1]

Thesis I: The Sacraments of the New Testament consist of two elements, the one indeterminate (res), the other determining (verbum).

This proposition is *fidei proxima*.

Proof. For a full explanation of the concepts involved we must refer the student to that branch of philosophy called Cosmology.[2] Both *res* (the element and its application or use,—technically, *remote* and *proximate* matter) and *verbum* (the word, in the wider sense of any sign indicating consent) are officially defined as essential constituents of a Sacrament in the statement of doctrine drawn up by Eugene IV for the Armenian delegates at the Council of Florence, where we read, *inter alia:* "Every Sacrament requires three constituents:—things for its mat-

1 Cfr. Wilhelm-Scannell, *Manual of Catholic Theology,* Vol. II, pp. 361 sq.

2 See, for instance, Haan, *Philosophia Naturalis.*

ter, words for its form, and the person of the minister conferring the Sacrament with the intention of doing what the Church does; if any one of these be wanting, there is no Sacrament." [3]

As Pope Eugene IV did not intend to issue a dogmatic definition on the subject but merely to give an account of the common teaching and practice of the Western Church,[4] some of the inferences drawn from his statement by Dominicus Soto [5] and other theologians are manifestly strained. We are not dealing here with an article of faith, so far as philosophical terminology is concerned. However, our thesis embodies the teaching of the Church and might be raised to the dignity of a dogma at any time.

a) That a Sacrament must contain an "element" and a "word" can be stringently proved from Holy Scripture only for the Sacrament of Baptism. Eph. V, 26: "By the laver of water in the word of life." [6]

In regard to Confirmation,[7] the Holy Eucharist,[8] and Extreme Unction,[9] this is merely intimated. But Tradition abundantly supplies what is lacking in Biblical teaching. The Fathers insist that both a *res* and a *verbum*

---

3 *Decretum pro Armenis:* " *Omnia sacramenta tribus perficiuntur, vid. rebus tamquam materiâ, verbis tamquam formâ, et personâ ministri conferentis sacramentum cum intentione faciendi, quod facit Ecclesia; quorum si aliquid desit, non perficitur sacramentum.*" (Denzinger-Bannwart, n. 695).

4 Franzelin, *De Traditione,* p. 120.

5 *Comment. in Sent.,* IV, dist. 1, qu. 1, art. 6: " *Fidei est catholicae, sacramenta constare rebus et verbis, quod sine manifesta haeresi negari non potest.*"

6 Eph. V, 26: " *Lavacro aquae in verbo vitae.*"

7 Acts VIII, 15 sqq.

8 Matth. XXVI, 26.

9 James V, 14.

enter into the constitution of a Sacrament. St. Augustine says: "Take away the word, and what is water but water? The word is added to the element, and there is a Sacrament." [10] This teaching has been preserved and handed down by the churches separated from Rome [11] and is confirmed by the authority of the Scholastics. [12]

b) As regards the Sacraments of the Old Testament (circumcision, the eating of the paschal lamb, certain lustrations, etc.), theologians hold that they did not consist of *res et verbum* but merely of *res et actio,* because of St. Paul's reference to the Old Law as " having a shadow of the good things to come, [but] not the very image of the things." [13] The occasional employment of words in connection with these rites was either unessential or of purely human institution. St. Thomas [14] gives three reasons why it is fit that the Sacraments of the New Testament should be superior to those of the Old, not only in interior effect but also with regard to the external rite. (1) The analogy between the Sacraments and the Incarnation. In the Sacraments, "the word is joined to the sensible sign, just as in the mystery of the Incarnation God is united to sensible flesh." (2) The conformity of the Sacraments to their human recipients, who are composed of soul and body. (3) The superior power of signification peculiar to a definite word over indefinite

---

10 *Tract. in Ioa.,* 80, n. 3: " *Detrahe verbum et quid est aqua nisi aqua? Accedit verbum ad elementum et fit sacramentum.*"

11 Cfr. Schelstrate, *Acta Orient. Ecclesiae,* Vol. I, p. 505, Rome 1739; Denzinger, *Ritus Orientalium,* 2 vols., Würzburg 1863-64; Gass, *Symbolik der griechischen Kirche,* p. 233, Berlin 1872.

12 Cfr. St. Thomas, *Summa Theologica,* 3a, qu. 60, art. 6, ad 2:

" *Ex verbis et rebus fit quodammodo unum in sacramentis sicut forma et materia, inquantum scilicet per verba perficitur significatio rerum.*"

13 Heb. X, 1: " *Umbram futurorum bonorum, non ipsam imaginem rerum.*"

14 *Summa Theol.,* 3a, qu. 60, art. 6. Cfr. Gihr, *Die hl. Sakramente der kath. Kirche,* Vol. I, 2nd ed., pp. 50 sqq., Freiburg 1902.

symbolical acts, such as those employed under the Old Law.

Thesis II: The "sensible element" in a Sacrament corresponds, in philosophical parlance, to "matter," the "word" to "form," and the two are related to each other as materia and forma in the Scholastic sense of these terms.

This proposition may be technically qualified as *certa*.

Proof. The use of the terms "matter" and "form" in the theology of the Sacraments can be traced to William of Auxerre (d. 1223).[15] It was adopted by the Church[16] and received official sanction at the Council of Trent.[17] To reject it, therefore, would be foolhardy.

a) The application to the theology of the Sacraments of the famous Aristotelian distinction between matter and form, is most appropriate and illuminating.

As matter and form coalesce into one whole, which is separate and distinct from each of its component parts, so *res* and *verbum* constitute one complete sign, which is neither a mere element nor a mere word.

Again, as matter, being undetermined, is generically de-

---

15 Several of the Fathers (*e. g.* St. Augustine, *De Peccatorum Meritis et Remissione,* I, 34) speak of a *forma* in connection with the Sacraments; however, they mean by it not the mere words of administration, but the entire external rite.

16 Cfr. the *Decretum pro Armenis,*

ut supra, p. 60, n. 3; the Bull "*Inter cunctas*" of Martin V (quoted in Denzinger-Bannwart, n. 672).

17 *Conc. Trident.,* Sess. XVI, cap. 2 and "*De Extrema Unctione,*" Denzinger-Bannwart, n. 895 and 908.

termined by the form, so is the *res* raised to the rank of a sacramental sign by the differentiating power of the *verbum*.

Furthermore, as matter and form intrinsically supplement and perfect each other, so, too, do *res* and *verbum*. However, since *res* and *verbum* do not represent a physical but merely a moral *totum* (*i. e.* one depending on the free choice of Christ), the terms must be taken analogically. The union of *res* and *verbum* in a Sacrament is not, therefore, a physical but a purely moral synthesis, which does not demand that the component parts co-exist. Thus a penitent who confesses his sins may be validly absolved a day later, because the "element" or act of confession, and the "word" which determines it, despite the interval between them, constitute one moral act. The place of the "word" which is to determine the "thing" cannot be taken by some symbolic act, as, *e. g.,* washing a person with water instead of pronouncing the formula of Baptism. There are many ablutions with diverse symbolic meanings, and the action remains indeterminate so long as there is no *forma* in the shape of a determining word.

In some Sacraments, notably Penance and Matrimony, it is not easy to say precisely wherein matter and form consist, but this difficulty has not deterred theologians from insisting that somewhere and somehow both must be present.

An exception is made by the Scotists and Vasquez in favor of the Holy Eucharist, which they regard as a "permanent Sacrament" and the only one not constituted by a union of matter and form. But this theory is untenable in view of the *Decretum pro Armenis,* quoted above. Moreover, the Holy Eucharist demonstrably has both *res* and *verbum,* matter and form.[18]

18 Cfr. Tepe, *Instit. Theol.,* Vol. IV, pp. 15 sqq., Paris 1896.

b) If "element" and "word" are related to each other as matter and form, it follows that every Sacrament must consist of matter and form.

Scotus and his followers admit that all the Sacraments, including the Eucharist, Penance, and Matrimony, grow out of an " element " and a " word," but they deny that each is essentially composed of *res* and *verbum* as matter and form.   And yet the latter proposition follows logically from the former.   That which originates from a union of matter and form, must necessarily consist of matter and form.   Now, the *Decretum pro Armenis* says: " *Omnia sacramenta perficiuntur rebus tamquam materiâ, verbis tamquam formâ*," which is virtually the same as the teaching of the Roman Catechism that matter and form "are parts pertaining to the nature and substance of the Sacraments, and by which each Sacrament is necessarily constituted." [19]   Hence we maintain with St. Thomas that, since a Sacrament is divisible into matter and form as distinct parts of its essence, every Sacrament consists of an element and a word.[20]

Cardinal Lugo holds [21] that, as the *Decretum pro Armenis* mentions the intention of the minister, this enters into the intrinsic constitution of a Sacrament quite as much as matter and form.   But the opinion is untenable. A Sacrament is constituted by matter and form; the

---

19 P. II, cap. 1, n. 15: " *Haec igitur* [*scil. materia et forma*] *sunt partes, quae ad naturam et substantiam sacramentorum pertinent et ex quibus unumquodque sacramentum necessario constituitur.*"

20 *Summa Theol.*, 3a, qu. 90, art.

2: " *Quodlibet sacramentum distinguitur in materiam et formam sicut in partes essentiae. Unde supra dictum est, quod sacramenta consistunt in rebus et verbis.*"

21 *De Sacrament.*, disp. 2, sect. 5.

intentio ministri is merely a condition of valid administration.[22]

[22] On the *materia* and *forma* of the Sacraments the student may consult Franzelin, *De Sacramentis in Genere,* thes. 4; Sasse, *De Sacramentis Ecclesiae,* Vol. I, sect. 3, Freiburg 1897; Heinrich-Gutberlet, *Dogmatische Theologie,* Vol. IX, § 482.

SECTION 2

In this Section we have to consider, not the efficacy of the Sacraments, nor the manner in which they produce their effects (*modus efficiendi*),[1] but these effects themselves.

The Catholic Church teaches: (1) that through the Sacraments "all true justice either begins, or, when already begun, is increased, or having been lost, is repaired;"[2] (2) that three Sacraments, *viz.*: Baptism, Confirmation, and Holy Orders, imprint an indelible mark upon the soul.

ARTICLE 1

EFFECTS COMMON TO ALL THE SACRAMENTS

All the Sacraments confer sanctifying grace, but, in addition, each one confers a special grace peculiar to its object. This is commonly called *gratia sacramentalis*. The amount of sanctifying and special grace bestowed by a Sacrament depends chiefly on the disposition of the recipient.

We shall demonstrate these statements in three distinct theses.

---

[1] *V. infra,* Ch. III, pp. 121 sqq.
[2] *Concilium Trident.,* Sess. VII, Prooem.: "*Per sacramenta omnis vera iustitia vel incipit vel coepta augetur vel amissa reparatur.*"

66

Thesis I: All the Sacraments confer sanctifying grace.

This proposition embodies an article of faith.

Proof.   The Tridentine Council defines: "If anyone saith that grace, as far as God's part is concerned, is not given through the said Sacraments always and to all men, even though they receive them rightly, but [only] sometimes and to some persons, let him be anathema."[3]   Hence all the Sacraments without exception infallibly confer sanctifying grace when they are worthily received.

a) This teaching can be demonstrated from Scripture and Tradition.   Both the Bible and the Fathers designate "regeneration of God" as the principal effect of Baptism.   "Regeneration" is identical with justification,[4] which is produced by the infusion of sanctifying grace.   Consequently, Baptism confers sanctifying grace. What is true of Baptism, must also be true of the other Sacraments, since they are essentially rites of the same nature.[5]   Besides grace, the Sacraments impart the three divine virtues of faith, hope, and charity, the infused moral virtues, and the other concomitants of sanctifying grace.[6]

---

3 *Conc. Trident.*, Sess. VII, can. 7: "*Si quis dixerit, non dari gratiam per huiusmodi sacramenta semper et omnibus, quantum est ex parte Dei, etiamsi rite ea suscipiant, sed aliquando et aliquibus,* *anathema   sit.*" (Denzinger-Bannwart, n. 850).

4 See Pohle-Preuss, *Grace, Actual and Habitual*, pp. 314 sq.

5 *V. supra*, Ch. I, Sect. 2.

6 Cfr. Pohle-Preuss, *op. cit.*, pp. 362 sqq.

The well-known division into Sacraments of the living and Sacraments of the dead is based on the distinction between first and second justification, with which we have dealt in our treatise on Grace.[7]

The Sacraments of the living are: Confirmation, the Holy Eucharist, Extreme Unction, Holy Orders, and Matrimony.   The Sacraments of the dead: Baptism and Penance.   For further information we must refer the reader to the special treatises following this introduction.

b) Although the Sacraments of the living can be worthily received only in the state of grace, theologians have raised the question whether, and under what conditions, these Sacraments may confer the *iustificatio prima,* and thereby, at least indirectly (*per accidens*), produce the same effects as the Sacraments of the dead.

It is certain that the Sacraments of the dead, when conferred on a person already justified by an act of perfect contrition, increase sanctifying grace and consequently effect the *iustificatio secunda.*   Similarly, it is probable that the Sacraments of the living, under certain conditions, restore sanctifying grace, and consequently effect the *iustificatio prima.*   St. Bonaventure and De Lugo deny this proposition, so far as the Holy Eucharist is concerned.   But ranged against them are such eminent older theologians as Suarez, Viva, St. Thomas [8]

---

7 *Op. cit.,* pp. 388 sqq.
8 *Summa Theol.,* 3a, qu. 72, art. 7, ad 2.

and his entire school, and nearly all modern authors.
The controversy cannot be decided from Tradition, but
there is a strong theological argument in favor of the
Thomistic view. The Tridentine Council teaches: " If
anyone saith that the Sacraments of the New Law . . .
do not confer grace on those who do not place an
obstacle thereunto, . . . let him be anathema." [9] Now
it may easily happen that a sinner, believing himself to
be in the state of grace, receives a Sacrament of the living with only imperfect contrition. Are we to assume
that in such a case the Sacrament is utterly ineffective?
There is no obstacle placed in the way of grace, since
the sinner is in good faith and truly sorry for his sins.
Hence, if the Sacrament has any effect at all, it must be
to establish the state of grace. This can be easily
shown of the Sacrament of Extreme Unction. St.
Thomas expressly asserts it of the Sacrament of Confirmation.[10] It is equally true of Holy Orders and Matrimony, where good faith and attrition conjointly preclude
the possibility of sacrilege and remove the *obex*. Is the
Eucharist alone to form an exception, as De Lugo contends? St. Thomas emphatically denies it. " This Sacrament," he says, " can effect the forgiveness of sin in
two ways. First of all, by being received, not actually,
but in desire . . .; secondly, when received by one in
mortal sin of which he is not conscious, and for which
he has no attachment; for possibly he was not sufficiently contrite at first, but by approaching this Sacrament

---

[9] *Conc. Trident.*, Sess. VII, can.
6: " *Si quis dixerit, sacramenta
Novae Legis . . . gratiam ipsam non
ponentibus obicem non conferre,
anathema sit.*" (Denzinger-Bannwart, n. 849).

[10] *Summa Theol.*, 3a, qu. 72,
art. 7, ad 2: " *Si aliquis adultus*

*in peccato existens, cuius conscien-
tiam non habet, vel si etiam non
perfecte contritus [i. e. attritus]
accedat, dummodo non fictus accedat, per gratiam collatam in hoc
sacramento consequetur remissionem
peccatorum.*"

devoutly and reverently, he obtains the grace of charity, which will perfect his [imperfect] contrition, and bring forgiveness of sin." [11]

Thesis II: Besides sanctifying grace, the Sacraments confer each a special, the so-called sacramental grace.

This proposition may be qualified technically as *sententia communis*.

Proof. a) The existence of a special sacramental grace can be shown in three ways.

α) If the Sacraments produced no other effect than sanctifying grace, there would be no need of having seven of them. Yet the Church teaches that all seven are necessary unto salvation, though not for every individual. "If anyone saith that the Sacraments of the New Law are not necessary unto salvation, but superfluous, . . . though all are not indeed necessary for every individual, let him be anathema." [12]

β) If the Sacraments really "contain," *i. e.* effect, the grace which they "signify," as the

---

[11] *Summa Theol.*, 3a, qu. 79, art. 3: "*Potest hoc sacramentum operari remissionem peccati dupliciter: uno modo non perceptum actu, sed voto . . .; alio modo etiam perceptum ab eo, qui est in peccato mortali, cuius conscientiam et affectum non habet. Forte enim primo non fuit sufficienter contritus, sed devote et reverenter accedens consequetur per hoc sacramentum gratiam caritatis, quae contritionem [scil. imperfectam] perficiet, et re-*

missionem peccati." Cfr. De Augustinis, *De Re Sacramentaria*, Vol. I, 2nd ed., pp. 275 sqq.; Heinrich-Gutberlet, *Dogmatische Theologie*, Vol. IV, § 493.

[12] *Conc. Trident.*, Sess. VII, can. 4: "*Si quis dixerit, sacramenta Novae Legis non esse ad salutem necessaria, sed superflua, . . . licet omnia singulis necessaria non sint, anathema sit.*" (Denzinger-Bannwart, n. 847).

Council of Trent declares,[13] the different signs must effect different graces, there must be as many different graces as there are signs, and hence the grace of Baptism cannot be identical with the grace of Confirmation,[14] and so forth.

γ) The Church teaches that the Sacraments differ in dignity and worth. "If anyone saith," defines the same Council, "that these seven Sacraments are in such wise equal to each other as that one is not in any way worthier than another, let him be anathema." [15] It would be difficult to conceive this inequality, if there were no difference in effect.[16]

b) Regarding the exact nature of the sacramental grace theologians are at variance.

The majority hold that the sanctifying grace conferred by a Sacrament is of the same order and quality as that obtained by prayer, merit, and perfect charity. Aureolus, Paludanus, Eusebius Amort, and others have tried to explain the difference in the effects of the various Sacraments by assuming the existence of habits specifically distinct from sanctifying grace and its accompanying virtues. However, this assumption is gratuitous, (1) because sanctifying grace with its concomitant theological virtues provides sufficiently for the habitual life of the soul, and (2)

---

13 Cfr. *Conc. Trident.*, Sess. VII, can. 6. ". . . *continent gratiam, quam significant.*"

14 Cfr. Acts VIII, 16 sqq.

15 *Conc. Trident.*, Sess. VII, can. 3: "*Si quis dixerit, haec septem sacramenta esse inter se paria, ut nullâ ratione aliud sit alio dignius, anathema sit.*" (Denzinger-Bannwart, n. 846).

16 For a more detailed treatment of this point cfr. Pesch, *Praelect. Dogmaticae*, Vol. VI, 3rd ed., pp. 54 sqq.

because there is no basis for any such assertion in Revelation.

How, then, are we to conceive the graces peculiar to the different Sacraments?

Billuart [17] and other Thomist theologians contend that sacramental grace consists in some mode of perfection which ordinary grace lacks. Suarez [18] thinks sacramental grace is a claim to those actual graces which correspond to the particular object of a Sacrament. In both hypotheses sanctifying grace is the font and well-spring of the *gratia sacramentalis*. The same grace (justification) is conferred by all the Sacraments, but it exercises a different function in each. In Baptism it effects regeneration, in Confirmation it confers spiritual manhood, in the Holy Eucharist it nourishes the soul, and so forth.[19]

The majority of modern theologians prefer to hold with Suarez that the *gratia sacramentalis* is simply a moral claim to actual graces, which are not conferred all at once, but one by one, as they are needed, though always with reference to the Sacrament of which they are the effects. However, there is nothing to prevent us from meeting Billuart halfway by defining sacramental grace as a permanent disposition or habit.[20]

17 *De Sacramentis*, diss. 3, art. 5.
18 *De Sacramentis*, disp. 7, sect. 3.

19 *Decret. pro Armenis*, in Denzinger-Bannwart, n. 695. Cfr. St. Bonaventure, *Comment. in Sent.*, IV, dist. 1, p. 1, qu. 6: "*Gratia sacramentalis est eadem per essentiam cum gratia virtutum [i. e. sanctificante], licet gratia sacramentalis plures connotet effectus.*"

20 Cfr. Heinrich-Gutberlet, *Dogmat. Theol.*, Vol. IV, pp. 151 sqq.; Gihr, *Die hl. Sakramente der kath. Kirche*, Vol. I, 2nd ed., pp. 93 sqq. This teaching is based on that of St. Thomas; cfr. *Summa Theol.*, 3a, qu. 62, art. 2: "*Sicut igitur virtutes et dona addunt super gratiam communiter dictam quandam perfectionem determinate ordinatam ad proprios actus potentiarum [scil. animae], ita gratia sacramentalis addit super gratiam communiter dictam [i. e. habitualem] et super virtutes et dona quoddam divinum auxilium ad consequendum sacramenti finem.*" See also De Augustinis, *De Re Sacramentaria*, Vol. I, 2nd ed., pp. 278 sqq., and De Lugo, *De Sacramentis*, disp. 4, sect. 3.

Thesis III: The amount of grace conferred by a Sacrament depends on the disposition of the recipient.

This thesis is also *sententia communis*.

Proof. The Tridentine Council, speaking of the justification of adult sinners, teaches: ". . . and we are . . . just, receiving justice within us, each one according to his own measure, which the Holy Ghost distributes to every one as He wills, and according to each one's proper disposition and co-operation." [21]

That is to say, the amount of grace conferred by a Sacrament in each instance depends (1) on the eternal decree of God, who has endowed each Sacrament with a definite measure of grace, and (2) on the disposition and co-operation of the recipient. Note, however, that the Sacraments are efficacious *ex opere operato,* and consequently the disposition of the recipient is not the cause of grace, but merely a condition of a richer outpouring of the same, just as the dryness of a stick of wood is not the cause of its burning, but a condition of its being more rapidly consumed by the flames.[22]

a) The Tridentine teaching is in perfect conformity with the mind of the Fathers.

St. Cyril admonishes his catechumens about to receive Baptism: " Cleanse thine vessel, that it may receive a

---

21 *Conc. Trident.*, Sess. VI, cap. 7: ". . . *iustitiam in nobis recipientes, unusquisque suam secundum mensuram, quam Spiritus Sanctus partitur singulis prout vult, et se-* *cundum propriam cuiusque dispositionem et cooperationem."* (Denzinger-Bannwart, n. 799).

22 Cfr. Franzelin, *De Sacramentis in Genere,* thes. 6.

greater measure of grace.   Forgiveness of sins is granted
to all alike, but the communication of the Holy Ghost is
given to each according to the measure of his faith.   If
thine effort be but slight, thou wilt receive little; but if
thou dost much, thine reward will be great." [23]   It is for
this same reason that the Church constantly exhorts the
faithful to serve God more ardently, in order that they
may receive a richer reward.   St. Thomas voices the
conviction of the Schoolmen when he says: " All children are equally disposed to Baptism, . . . all receive an
equal effect in Baptism; whereas adults . . . are not
equally disposed; for some approach with greater, some
with less, devotion, and therefore some receive a greater,
some a smaller share of the grace of renewal." [24]

b) Revelation does not tell us whether or not
Sacraments of a different order (e. g. Baptism
and the Holy Eucharist), all other things being
equal, confer an equal amount of grace.

Objectively the Holy Eucharist is the most perfect of
the Sacraments, and consequently we may assume that
from the nature of the case and regardless of the disposition of the recipient, it confers a larger share of grace
than the others.   Those theologians who, in addition to the
disposition and co-operation of the recipient mentioned by
the Tridentine Council, postulate other external condi-

[23] *Catech.*, I, cap. 5 (Migne, *P. G.*, XXXIII, 378). Other Pa-tristic texts in Suarez, *De Sacram.*, disp. 7, sect. 5.

[24] *Summa Theol.*, 3a, qu. 69, art. 8: ". . . omnes pueri aequaliter se habent ad baptismum, . . . omnes aequalem effectum percipiunt in bap-tismo. Adulti vero . . . non ae-qualiter se habent ad baptismum. Quidam enim cum maiore, quidam cum minore devotione ad baptismum accedunt, et ideo quidam plus, qui-dam minus de gratia novitatis ac-cipiunt." Cfr. De Augustinis, *De Re Sacrament.*, Vol. I, 2nd ed., pp. 294 sqq.; Tepe, *Inst. Theolog.*, Vol. IV, pp. 50 sqq.

tions, merely voice their private opinion and speak without sufficient warrant. Paludanus [25] engages in guesswork when he says that the amount of grace conferred by Baptism is unequal even in infants, because the number of human beings to be saved and the degree of happiness to be enjoyed by each in Heaven must correspond to the number and beatitude of the Angels. Scotus [26] and Gabriel Biel hold that God increases the amount of grace conferred by the Sacraments in some cases according to His absolute decree of predestination, or by reason of a special application of the merits of Jesus Christ, or in consideration of the personal worthiness of the minister of the Sacrament and those who happen to be present during its administration. Such greater lavishness on the part of God in regard to certain persons is, of course, possible, but there is nothing to show that it actually exists, and if it did, it would most assuredly be a special privilege outside the *lex ordinaria*.[27] Cardinal Cajetan thinks that the amount of grace conferred by a Sacrament may be increased by personal sanctity and prayer on the part of the minister.[28] No doubt it makes a difference who administers a Sacrament, whether he be a pious priest or one imbued with a worldly spirit. A saintly minister by his prayers, merits, and spiritual influence may procure many actual graces for the recipient, thus disposing him better personally and making him more receptive. But there is no warrant for asserting that the amount of sanctifying grace conferred by a Sacrament depends on the worthiness of the minister.

[25] *Comment. in Sent.*, IV, dist. 4, qu. 1.

[26] *Comment. in Sent.*, IV, dist. 4, qu. 7.

[27] This point is more fully elaborated by De Lugo, *De Sacramentis*, disp. 9, sect. 2.

[28] *Comment. in S. Theol.*, III, qu. 64, art. 1.

ARTICLE 2

THE SACRAMENTAL CHARACTER PECULIAR TO BAPTISM, CONFIRMATION, AND HOLY ORDERS

Character [1] in general signifies any mark or trait that distinguishes one person or object from others. In Catholic theology the term is used to designate certain indelible spiritual marks imprinted on the soul by the Sacraments of Baptism, Confirmation, and Holy Orders.

1. THE EXISTENCE OF THE SACRAMENTAL CHARACTER.—That there is such a thing as the sacramental character follows from the dogmatically defined truth that the Sacraments of Baptism, Confirmation, and Holy Orders each impress a special, supernatural, and ineffaceable mark upon the soul of the recipient.

Wiclif claimed that this teaching cannot be substantiated from Revelation.[2] The Protestant Reformers denied the existence of the sacramental character. Chemnitz asserted that the "character" had been invented by Pope Innocent III (d. 1216).

The dogmatic teaching of the Church on this point is beyond cavil. The Council of Florence (A. D. 1439) declared: "Among these Sacraments there are three, *i. e.* Baptism, Confirmation, and Holy Orders, that indelibly imprint upon the soul a character, *i. e.* a kind of spiritual

1 *Signum, figura, χαρακτήρ.*   2 *Trial.,* IV, 15.

mark, distinct from all others, and this is the reason why they are administered but once to the same person. The other four do not imprint a character and can be administered more than once."[3]   This definition was solemnly reiterated by the Council of Trent: "If anyone saith that in the three Sacraments of Baptism, Confirmation, and Holy Orders, there is not imprinted on the soul a character, that is, a certain spiritual and indelible sign, on account of which they cannot be repeated, let him be anathema."[4] Hence it is of faith that there is a sacramental character, and that because of this character the three Sacraments in question cannot be repeated.

a) Though this teaching is not directly demonstrable from Holy Scripture, it enables us to interpret satisfactorily certain passages in the Epistles of St. Paul which would otherwise remain obscure.

Thus, the Apostle says that God " hath sealed us, and given the pledge of the Spirit in our hearts."[5]   And

---

[3] *Decretum pro Armenis:* " *Inter haec sacramenta tria sunt: baptismus, confirmatio et ordo, quae characterem, i. e. spirituale quoddam signum a caeteris distinctivum, imprimunt in anima indelebile, unde in eadem persona non reiterantur; reliqua vero quattuor characterem non imprimunt et reiterationem admittunt.*" (Denzinger-Bannwart, n. 695).

[4] *Conc. Trident.,* Sess. VII, can. **9**: " *Si quis dixerit, in tribus sacramentis, baptismo scil., confirmatione et ordine, non imprimi characterem in anima, hoc est signum quoddam spirituale et indelebile, unde ea iterari non possunt, anathema sit.*" (Denzinger-Bannwart, n. 852).

[5] 2 Cor. I, 21 sq.: "*. . . qui unxit nos Deus: qui et signavit nos (ὁ καὶ σφραγισάμενος ἡμᾶς) et dedit pignus Spiritus in cordibus nostris.*"

again: "In whom [*i. e.* Christ] . . . believing, you
were signed with the holy Spirit of promise."[6] And
again: "Grieve not the holy Spirit of God, whereby
you are sealed unto the day of redemption."[7] St. Paul
here tells his hearers: (1) You are anointed, (2) you
are sealed or signed, and (3) you have received the
pledge of the Spirit. "You are anointed" is manifestly
but another way of saying: You are justified (*gratia
creata*). "You have received the pledge of the Holy
Spirit" means: The Holy Spirit has descended upon
you and dwells in you (*gratia increata*). That the *sig-
natio* implied by the phrase "who hath sealed us" must
refer to the Sacraments, appears (a) from the general
economy of divine grace, in which internal grace is ordinarily communicated through the instrumentality of external signs, and (b) from the expression "*unxit nos*,"
which seems to imply an internal as well as an external
unction; just as "*ablutio*" in the writings of St. Paul implies both external and internal washing.[8] This also explains what the Apostle means when he says that to grieve
the Spirit of God is to break the "seal of the Spirit," by
which we are sealed unto redemption.

Sacred Scripture indicates quite unmistakably that Baptism, Confirmation, and Holy Orders can be received but
once.[9]

Some theologians hold that the "*pignus Spiritus*" does
not refer to the sacramental character, but to the "*signum
fidei*"[10] or to the charisma.[11] But it is a noteworthy fact

6 Eph. I, 13: ". . . *in quo* [*scil.
Christo*] *et credentes signati estis*
(ἐσφραγίσθητε) *Spiritu promissionis
Sancto.*"

7 Eph. IV, 30: "*Nolite contri-
stare Spiritum Sanctum Dei, in quo
signati estis* (ἐσφραγίσθητε) *in
diem redemptionis.*"

8 Cfr. 1 Cor. VI, 11; Hebr. X, 22.

9 For Baptism, cfr. Rom. VI, 10,
Eph. IV, 5, Heb. VI, 4 sq.; for
Confirmation, Acts XIX, 1 sqq.;
for Holy Orders, 2 Tim. I, 6.

10 St. Thomas Aquinas.

11 Estius, Cornely.

that the Church bases her traditional teaching of the character precisely on the Pauline passages which we have quoted. It is from them that the Greeks drew their theory of the baptismal " sphragis," which was all but universally received in the second century.[12]

b) A convincing argument for the existence of the *"character sacramentalis"* can be derived from Tradition. St. Augustine defended it as an essential part of the sacramental system of the Church.

In his Letter to Boniface [13] he refers to the mark imprinted by Baptism as *" character dominicus,"* i. e. a mark belonging to Christ, the Chief Shepherd of the flock and Leader of the Christian army.[14] In his treatise on Baptism against the Donatists he says: " Men put on Christ, sometimes so far as to receive the Sacrament, sometimes so much further as to receive holiness of life. And the first of these may be common to good and bad alike, but the second is peculiar to the good and pious." And again: " But which is worse, not to be baptized at all, or to be twice baptized, it is difficult to decide." [15] Elsewhere St. Augustine compares the baptismal char-

---

12 Cfr. Pourrat, *La Théologie Sacramentaire*, pp. 196 sqq.; English tr., pp. 217 sqq.

13 *Ep.*, 98, n. 5: " *Christianis baptismi sacramentum . . . etiam apud haereticos valet et sufficit ad consecrationem, quamvis ad vitae aeternae participationem non sufficiat; quae consecratio reum quidem facit haereticum extra Domini gregem habentem Dominicum characterem, corrigendum tamen admonet sanâ doctrinâ, non iterum similiter consecrandum.*"

14 Cfr. Pourrat, *Sacramental Theology*, p. 229.

15 *De Baptismo contra Donatistas*, V, 24, 34: " *Induunt homines Christum aliquando usque ad sacramenti perceptionem, aliquando et usque ad vitae sanctificationem. Atque illud primum et bonis et malis potest esse commune, hoc autem alterum proprium est bonorum et piorum."— Op. cit.*, II, 14, 19: " *Quid sit autem perniciosius, utrum omnino non baptizari an rebaptizari, iudicare difficile est.*"

acter to the badge of a soldier and says that the same simile may be applied to Confirmation and Holy Orders.[16] Thus, contrary to Harnack's claim,[17] St. Augustine's theory of the sacramental character is not an artificial makeshift framed for the sake of expediency, but, in the words of Pourrat,[18] "a living development of the sacramental principles laid down by the practice of the early Church, a development quite homogeneous with its starting-point."[19]

St. Ambrose teaches: "Therefore we are sealed with the Holy Spirit, not by nature, but by God, because it is written: 'God hath anointed us and hath also sealed us.' We are sealed with the Spirit, in order that we may possess His splendor and image and grace, which is indeed a spiritual seal."[20]

St. Chrysostom says: "Thus it happens that if you leave the ranks [as a deserter], you can be easily recognized by all; for the Jews employ circumcision as a sign; we, the pledge of the Spirit."[21]

St. Cyril of Jerusalem declares that the angels can tell

---

16 Contra Ep. Parmen., II, 13, 29: "An forte minus haerent sacramenta christiana quam corporalis haec nota [i. e. militum], quum videamus nec apostatas carere baptismate, quibus utique per poenitentiam redeuntibus non restituitur et ideo amitti non posse iudicatur."— Cfr. Contra Lit. Petil., II, 104, 239: "Quod [sacramentum chrismatis] in genere visibilium signaculorum sacrosanctum est, sicut et ipse baptismus; sed potest esse et in hominibus pessimis."— Contra Ep. Parmen., II, 13, 28: "Utrumque [scil. baptismus et ordo] sacramentum est et quadam consecratione utrumque homini datur, illud quum baptizatur, illud quum ordinatur; ideoque in catholica ecclesia utrumque non licet iterari."

17 Dogmengeschichte, Vol. III, 3rd ed., pp. 140 sqq., Freiburg 1896.

18 Op. cit., p. 231.

19 Cfr. Pourrat, op. cit., pp. 226 sqq.

20 De Spiritu Sancto, I, 6, 79: "Sancto igitur Spiritu signati sumus non naturâ, sed a Deo, quia scriptum est: 'Quia unxit nos Deus et qui signavit nos.' Spiritu signamur, ut splendorem atque imaginem eius et gratiam tenere possimus, quod est utique spirituale signaculum."

21 Hom. in 2 Cor., 3, n. 7.

a Christian by the sacramental character imprinted on his soul. " In battle," he writes, " the leaders distribute badges to the combatants, by which friends can recognize and help one another. . . . How is the Angel to recognize thee? How is he to rescue thee from thine enemies, if he does not see thy badge? How canst thou say: I belong to God, if thou dost not wear His sign and badge? " [22]

St. Ephraem Syrus writes: " The Holy Ghost imprints His sign upon His sheep with oil. As a sealing-ring imprints an image on wax, so the secret sign of the Holy Spirit is imprinted by means of oil on a person when he is anointed in Baptism." [23]

c) For a better understanding of the sacramental character it will be well to study the question of its duration and the Scholastic distinction between *sacramentum* and *res*.

a) Does the sacramental character endure in the life beyond? The Tridentine Council has defined that it outlasts mortal sin, *i. e.* the loss of sanctifying grace, whence we must conclude that it lasts at least till death. Theologians regard it as certain that the sacramental character survives after death, especially in the souls of the elect. St. Cyril speaks of " a sign indelible for eternity," [25] and St. Thomas teaches: " The [sacramental] character remains after this life, both in the good as adding to their glory, and in the wicked as increasing their shame, just as the character of the military service remains in the soldiers after the victory, as the boast of the conquerors and the disgrace of the conquered." [26]

22 *Procatech.*, n. 4.
23 Assemani, *Biblioth. Orient.*, I, 95.
24 *Pastor Hermae*, Sim. VIII, 6.

25 *Procatech.*, n. 17: σφραγὶς ἀνεξάλειπτος εἰς τοὺς αἰῶνας.
26 *Summa Theol.*, 3a, qu. 63, art. 5, ad 3: " *Post hanc vitam re-*

The intrinsic reason for this indelibility is that there exists no contrary quality or entity which can destroy the sacramental character. God alone is able to destroy it by direct interposition; but God destroys no positive entity except when compelled by a moral motive, as when grace is destroyed by mortal sin. There is no such motive imaginable in regard to the sacramental character, for it can co-exist with mortal sin, and serves two further good purposes,— to enhance the glory of God and the reward of the elect in Heaven, and to shame the reprobate sinners and make their punishment more severe in hell.[27]

β) The Scholastic distinction between *sacramentum* and *res* arose in the twelfth century and is based on the fact that the sacramental character is a sign, like "matter and form," though invisible, while the latter are visible. The Schoolmen distinguish between "*sacramentum tantum*," *i. e.* the external sign consisting of matter and form; "*res tantum*," *i. e.* the internal grace effected by that sign;[28] and "*res simul et sacramentum*," *i. e.* the character, which is both the result of a sign and itself the sign of something else. In other words: In every sacrament that imprints an indelible mark on the soul, there is (1) something which merely signifies but is not itself signified (*id quod significat et non significatur*), *i. e.* matter and form (*sacramentum tantum*); (2) something which is merely signified but does not itself signify anything (*id quod significatur et non significat*), *i. e.* internal grace (*res tantum*); (3) something which is both signified and itself signifies (*id quod significatur et signi-*

manet character et in bonis ad eorum gloriam et in malis ad eorum ignominiam, sicut etiam militaris character manet in militibus post adeptam victoriam et in his qui vicerunt ad gloriam et in his qui sunt victi in poenam."

27 Cfr. Billuart, *De Sacram.*, diss. 4, art. 2.

28 *V. supra*, pp. 59 sqq. and pp. 66 sqq.

ficat), *i. e.* the sacramental character (*res simul et sacramentum*). Considered as an effect of external grace the sacramental character, like sanctifying grace, is both signified and effected; considered as a spiritual mark, it merely signifies, but does not effect, the presence of sanctifying grace. Naturally (*per se*) the baptismal character postulates the grace of Baptism, the character of Confirmation postulates the grace conferred by that particular Sacrament, and the sacerdotal character imprinted by Holy Orders postulates the grace bestowed by ordination. Without sanctifying grace the sacramental character would be incomplete, crying by its very existence and purpose for the spiritual life.[29]

By way of analogy theologians have applied this distinction to the other sacraments, which do not confer a character, trying to find in them something which could take the part of *res simul et sacramentum*. This was easy enough in the Holy Eucharist. For in this Sacrament the external species may be regarded as *sacramentum tantum* in so far as they merely signify without themselves being signified, while the grace (produced by communion) is merely an effect but no sign, and hence there was no difficulty in designating the body of Our Lord, which both signifies (and effects) the internal grace, and is also signified by the species, as *res simul et sacramentum*. In the Sacrament of Matrimony the marriage bond may be called *res simul et sacramentum,* inasmuch as it is a passive, sign, *qua* sacramental effect, and an active sign, *qua* symbol of Christ's union with His Church. The *sacramentum tantum* of Matrimony is its matter and form, while the *res tantum* coincides with the internal grace conferred by the Sacrament. The problem is somewhat more difficult in the case of Extreme Unction.

29 Cfr. St. Thomas, *Summa Theol.,* 3a, qu. 66, art. 1.

Suarez [30] admits both views, *i. e.* that which regards the "internal anointment" (*viz.:* the strengthening of the soul) and that which considers the "alleviation of the body" as the *res et sacramentum*. Perhaps it will be best to combine these two effects into one. Penance, too, offers a problem to the theologian who tries to apply to it the Scholastic distinction of which we are treating. De Lugo, after a critical examination of various theories, gives it as his opinion that the *res simul et sacramentum* of Penance, viewed in the light of the Tridentine teaching,[31] is the "peace of mind" it effects.[32]

2. IN WHAT THE SACRAMENTAL CHARACTER CONSISTS.

With the possible exception of St. Augustine, the Fathers did not discuss the question: In what does the sacramental character consist? The Scholastics tried to deduce some definite conclusions from Patristic teaching and conciliary definitions, but despite their ingenuity it must be admitted that it is much easier to tell in what the character does *not* consist, than in what it consists.

a) Durandus regarded the sacramental character as a purely logical relation, resulting from a divine ordinance or contract.[33] But since the Tridentine Council has

30 *De Sacram.,* disp. 41, sect. 3.

31 *Conc. Trident.,* Sess. XIV, cap. 3.

32 For a more exhaustive treatment of the topics dealt with in this subdivision see Billot, *De Ecclesiae Sacramentis,* Vol. I, 4th ed., thes. 6, Rome 1907; E. Lingens, *Die innere Schönheit des Christentums,* pp. 122 sqq., Freiburg 1895; Scheeben, *Die Mysterien des Christentums,* 3rd ed., § 83, Freiburg 1912; Heinrich-Gutberlet, *Dogmatische Theologie,* Vol. IV, § 483, Mainz 1901.

33 *Comment. in Sent.,* IV, dist. 4, qu. 1: "*Character non est nisi relatio rationis ex ordinatione vel pactione divina.*"

defined the character to be " a spiritual and indelible sign imprinted on the soul," we are not permitted to treat it as a mere figment of the mind. Nor does this theory sufficiently safeguard the Catholic teaching against certain heresies. There are few heretics who would not be willing to admit, for instance, that Baptism is the ground for a purely logical relation, inasmuch as one who has received this sacrament can never deny that he is " baptized."

Scotus and some of his followers have been accused of holding that the sacramental character is a real relation (*relatio realis*) or " relative form." In matter of fact Scotus himself treated this opinion merely as a hypothesis. His own idea was that the sacramental character is an " absolute form," and this teaching was espoused by his immediate followers. The opinion attributed to Scotus is untenable, because every real relation presupposes a foundation that is real, and consequently cannot be conceived without a *forma absoluta*. St. Thomas demonstrates this as follows : " The relation signified by the word ' sign ' must needs have some foundation. Now the relation implied in this sign which is a ' character,' cannot be founded immediately on the essence of the soul, because then it would belong to every soul naturally, [*i. e.* in that case all souls would have a character ; Billuart]. Consequently, there must be something in the soul on which such a relation is founded ; and this is the character itself. Therefore it need not be in the genus *relation,* as some have held." [34]

34 *Summa Theol.,* 3a, qu. 63, art. 2, ad 3 : " *Relatio quae importatur in nomine signi, oportet quod super aliquid fundetur. Relatio autem huius signi, quod est character, non potest fundari immediate super essentiam animae, quia sic conveniret omni animae naturaliter. Et ideo oportet aliquid poni in anima, super quod fundetur talis relatio, et hoc est essentia characteris. Unde non oportebit quod sit in genere rela-*

b) From what we have said it follows that, like sanctifying grace,[35] the sacramental character must be conceived as a real entity, and consequently is either a substance or an accident. It cannot be a substance, hence it must be an accident, and, since it is effected by a Sacrament and imprinted on the soul, it must be a supernatural accident. Such accidents belong to the category of " quality " ($\pi o \iota \acute{o} \tau \eta s$). Consequently, the sacramental character may be defined as a permanent quality of the soul, and, in this respect, resembles sanctifying grace.

The question, to which of the four Aristotelian species of quality the sacramental character belongs, has given rise to a variety of opinions.[36] Suarez says it is an infused habit and reckons it among the " first species " of quality.[37] Others regard it as a spiritual " figure or form " belonging to the " fourth species." Neither theory is tenable. The sacramental character cannot be a figure or form, nor a habit, because, unlike sanctifying grace, it may be applied to both good and evil purposes. Some theologians [38] are inclined to define the character as a " *passibilis qualitas* " (the third species of quality), because it is a sign or mark distinguishing certain men from others. But since the passible qualities are by nature transient [39] and have their proper place in the material world, this explanation, too, is unsatisfactory. The

tionis, sicut quidam posuerunt." The history of this controversy can be read in Pourrat, *Theology of the Sacraments,* French ed., pp. 223 sqq., English tr., pp. 204 sqq.

35 Cfr. Pohle-Preuss, *Grace, Actual and Habitual,* pp. 328 sqq.

36 Cfr. Lehmen, *Lehrbuch der Philosophie auf aristotelisch-scholastischer Grundlage,* Vol. II, 2nd ed., pp. 398 sqq. Freiburg 1904;

Pohle-Preuss, *Grace, Actual and Habitual,* pp. 332 sq.

37 *De Sacram.,* disp. 6, sect. 3, n. 6.

38 E. g., Pesch, *Praelect. Dogmat.,* Vol. VI, 3rd ed., p. 84.

39 Cfr. St. Thomas, *Summa Theol.,* 3a, qu. 63, art. 3: " *Character non est passio, quia passio cito transit, character autem indelebilis est."*

most acceptable theory is that of St. Thomas, who classes the sacramental character among the second species of quality. The sacramental character, he says, " is not a habit, because no habit is indifferent to acting well or ill, whereas a character is indifferent to either, since some use it well, some ill. Now this cannot occur with a habit, because no one abuses a habit of virtue or uses well an evil habit. It remains, therefore, that the character is a power." [40] Note, however, that the sacramental character does not confer a physical power. Those who are baptized, confirmed, and in Holy Orders can accomplish no more physically than others who have not received these three sacraments. The power which the character confers is, therefore, purely moral, and may be defined as a supernatural faculty ordained unto things pertaining to divine worship, according to the rite of the Christian religion, whether such worship (*cultus*) consist in receiving divine gifts or in bestowing them upon others (Billuart). Thus, God does not bestow the grace of another Sacrament on any one who does not wear the baptismal character, and He does not change bread and wine into the body and blood of Jesus Christ except at the bidding of one who has the sacramental character of Orders.[41]

Does the sacramental character reside in the substance of the soul or in some particular faculty thereof? This question also has given rise to a controversy. The Scotists, in accord with their general teaching, hold that the sacramental character resides in the will, while the Thom-

---

40 L. c.: " [*Character*] *non est habitus, quia nullus habitus est, qui se possit ad bene et male habere. Character autem ad utrumque se habet; utuntur enim eo quidam bene, alii vero male, quod in habiti-* *bus non contingit; nam habitu virtutis nullus utitur male et habitu malitiae nullus bene; ergo relinquitur quod character sit potentia.*"

41 Cfr. Billuart, *De Sacram.*, diss. 4, art. 2.

ists assign it to the intellect. "A character needs to be in the soul's cognitive power, where also is faith," says St. Thomas.[42]   Others [43] teach that the sacramental character resides in the very substance of the soul, because the Tridentine Council employs the phrase, "imprinted in the soul." As it is neither necessary nor advisable to accept St. Thomas' radical distinction between the substance of the soul and its faculties, (in the adoption of which the Angelic Doctor was perhaps unduly influenced by his opposition to Scotism and Nominalism), we shall probably do best if we assign the sacramental character primarily to the substance of the soul and secondarily to its faculties or powers, *i. e.* the intellect and the will. This seems all the more acceptable in view of the fact that the object of the character (which is, to confer the ability to perform religious acts of worship) involves both the intellect and the will.

3. THE OBJECT OF THE SACRAMENTAL CHARACTER.—As God does nothing without a purpose, it is impossible to evade the question: For what purpose was the sacramental character instituted? To avoid useless speculation, we shall limit our discussion to the data furnished by divine Revelation.

a) Recalling the passages previously quoted from St. Augustine,[44] we say that the sacramental character implies on the part of the recipient a sort of "consecration"—in the sense of objective sanctification (*sacer,*

---

[42] *Summa Theol.,* 3a, qu. 63, art. 4, ad 3: "*Oportet quod character sit in cognitiva potentia animae, in qua est fides.*"

[43] Notably Bellarmine, Suarez, and De Lugo.

[44] *V. supra,* p. 79, notes 13, and 15.

ὅσιος), not subjective holiness (*sanctus,* ἅγιος).[45] St. Augustine, compelled by the Donatists to emphasize not only the distinction between, but the actual separability of, grace and character (*sanctificatio* and *consecratio*), insisted that heretics may receive and sinners retain the sacramental character without grace. St. Thomas went a long step farther by defining *consecratio* as *deputatio ad divinum cultum, i. e.* a bestowal of the spiritual power necessary to perform acts of divine worship.[46] This is plainly apparent in the Sacrament of Holy Orders. It is not so apparent in Baptism and Confirmation. But the passive receptivity which these Sacraments confer is really an active power, *viz.:* the power, through Baptism, to receive the other Sacraments, to participate in all the rights and duties of a child of the true Church, and to be a member of the mystic body of Christ; and, through Confirmation, the power of professing the Catholic faith, if necessary at the risk of life, and of serving as a soldier in the army of the Lord. All these functions constitute necessary parts of Christian worship.

b) The very name *character* (χαρακτήρ), and its description as a stamp or seal (*signaculum,* σφραγίς, σφράγισμα), indicate that it may be a threefold sign, *viz.:* (1) *signum distinctivum* or a mark discriminating various objects; (2) *signum obligativum,* denoting a duty; (3)

45 The distinction between these two notions is explained in Pohle-Preuss, *God: His Knowability, Essence, and Attributes,* 2nd ed., pp. 258 sq.

46 Cfr. *Summa Theol.,* 3a, qu. 63, art. 1: "*Sacramenta Novae Legis ad duo ordinantur, vid. ad remedium contra peccatum et ad perficiendam animam in his quae pertinent ad cultum Dei secundum ritum christianae vitae. Quicunque autem ad aliquid certum deputatur, consuevit ad illud consignari, sicut milites, qui adscribebantur ad militiam antiquitus, solebant quibusdam characteribus corporalibus insigniri, eo quod deputabantur ad aliquid corporale. Et ideo quum homines per sacramenta deputentur ad aliquid spirituale pertinens ad cultum Dei, consequens est quod per ea fideles aliquo spirituali charactere insigniantur.*"

signum configurativum, marking similarity. The impress of a seal or stamp produces a triple effect: it renders an object recognizable, it marks the object as part of one's property, and it produces in it a likeness of the owner. The sacramental character exercises all these functions, and in addition to them a fourth, namely, to prepare the soul for grace. In this last-mentioned respect it is called *signum dispositivum.*

a) The sacramental character is, first, a *signum distinctivum* or mark differentiating those who are baptized, confirmed or ordained, from those who have not received these Sacraments. No one can belong to the external organism or body of the Church except he wear the character of Baptism, and no one lacking the character of Holy Orders can perform the functions of a priest. The character conferred by the Sacrament of Confirmation is similar to that of Baptism, only perfected and developed.

Though God and the angels require no sign to enable them to tell whether a man belongs to the true Church or to the priesthood, such a sign is by no means superfluous, since God not only appoints men to office, but also gives them the necessary interior qualification. An office that is to be actually exercised requires a real foundation, and it is this that the sacramental character supplies. But even for us, who are unable to perceive it, the character is not without meaning, because the visible reception of one of the three sacraments in question infallibly guarantees the possession of the invisible character.[47] The sacramental character, therefore, retains its value as a distinc-

47 Cfr. *Summa Theol.,* 3a, qu. 63, art. 1, ad 2: " *Character animae impressus habet rationem signi [distinctivi], inquantum per sensibile sacramentum imprimitur; per hoc enim scitur aliquis esse baptismali charactere insignitus, quod est ablutus aquâ sensibili.*"

tive sign also in the world to come, where it will enhance the happiness of the elect and add to the confusion of the damned.

β) The sacramental character is, secondly, a *signum obligativum*, in so far as it marks a man as the inalienable property of Jesus Christ, unites him indissolubly with the God-man, whose sign and livery he wears, and lays upon him the obligation of performing those acts of divine worship which the Sacrament, by virtue of its character, imposes as an official duty. By Baptism, Confirmation, and Holy Orders respectively, the recipient is officially marked and charged with certain specific duties. Baptism imposes the duties of a subject; Confirmation, those of a soldier; Holy Orders, those of a minister of Jesus Christ.[48]

γ) The sacramental character is, in the third place, a *signum configurativum,* inasmuch as it constitutes the soul an image of God.[49] Not, of course, in the sense in which man is a natural likeness of the Creator; nor in the sense in which he is a supernatural image of God by virtue of sanctifying grace. The sacramental character may be in the soul without grace. St. Thomas Aquinas adopts the technical definition of Peter Lombard: *" Character est distinctio a Charactere aeterno [Christo] impressa animae rationali secundum imaginem consignans trinitatem creatam [animam] Trinitati creanti· et recreanti."* [50] This definition, however, can be accepted only with the reservation that every created effect (and the sacramental character *is* a created effect) in some way reflects the

---

48 Cfr. Farine, *Der sakramentale Charakter,* pp. 18 sqq., Freiburg 1904.

49 Cfr. St. Bonaventure, *Comment. in Sent.,* IV, dist. 6, p. 1, qu.

3: *" Actus characteris, a quo nomen accepit, et principalis est configurare."*

50 *Comment. in Sent.,* IV, dist. 4, qu. 1, art. 2, sol. 2.

image of the Blessed Trinity.[51]   In contradistinction to
sanctifying grace, the supernatural *configuratio* or *as-
similatio* conferred by the sacramental character establishes a proper likeness to Christ, not indeed as if the
soul participated in His Divine Sonship,[52] but in the sense
of sharing in His office of High Priest.   By receiving the
sacramental character, a man is designated, empowered,
and placed under obligation to perform certain acts of
worship which bear a special relation to our Divine
Saviour's sacerdotal office.[53]   Consequently, the sacramental character, considered as a *signum configurativum*,
is not so much the character of the Holy Trinity, as that
of Christ the High Priest.   Hence such Patristic phrases
as: *character dominicus*, στίγμα Χριστοῦ, *i. e.* family mark
of Christ.[54]   It would, however, be a mistake to suppose
that the God-man Himself is a high priest only by virtue of
a character in which He permits those who receive the
sacraments of Baptism, Confirmation, and Holy Orders
to share.   Christ is our natural Mediator by virtue
of the Hypostatic Union, and, consequently, a High Priest
not by grace but by nature.[55]   It is only in the light of
this teaching that 1 Pet. II, 9: "You are a chosen gen-

---

51 Cfr. Pohle-Preuss, *God the Author of Nature and the Supernatural*, pp. 38 sqq.

52 Cfr. Pohle-Preuss, *Grace, Actual and Habitual*, pp. 356 sqq.

53 Cfr. Pohle-Preuss, *Soteriology*,
pp. 111 sqq.

54 Cfr.   St.   Thomas,   *Summa
Theol.*, 3a, qu. 63, art. 3: "*Deputatur quisque fidelis ad recipiendum
vel tradendum aliis ea quae pertinent ad cultum Dei, et ad hoc
proprie deputatur character sacramentalis. Totus autem ritus christianae religionis derivatur a sacerdotio Christi. Et ideo manifestum*

*est quod character sacramentalis
specialiter est character Christi, cuius sacerdotio configurantur fideles
secundum sacramentales characteres,
qui nihil aliud sunt quam quaedam
participationes sacerdotii Christi ab
ipso Christo derivatae.*"

55 Cfr. Pohle-Preuss, *Soteriology*,
pp. 127 sqq. St. Thomas, *Summa
Theol.*, 3a, qu. 63, art. 5: "*Christo
non competit habere characterem,
sed potestas sacerdotii eius comparatur ad characterem, sicut id quod
est plenum et perfectum ad aliquam
sui participationem.*"

eration, a kingly priesthood," can be fully understood.

δ) The sacramental character is, lastly, a *signum dispositivum,* a sign disposing the soul for the reception of, and thereby bestowing a claim to, grace. Grace, as we have shown in a previous treatise,[56] is either sanctifying or actual. The sacramental character, as a *signum dispositivum* for sanctifying grace, must not be conceived as a " physical predisposition " for, or a " preliminary stage " of, that grace (*lumen semiplenum, diminutum*),[57] because it is not a form of sanctification. The connection between character and grace is purely moral, and may be described as a kind of affinity, inasmuch as the sacramental character, in view of its purpose, ought never to exist without sanctifying grace.[58] It is in this light that the Fathers who wrote before St. Augustine regarded the sacramental character, when they said that it has an intrinsic relation to adoptive sonship, the indwelling of the Holy Spirit in the soul of the just, and the beatific vision of God in Heaven. Furthermore, the sacramental character confers a moral claim to all actual graces necessary for the worthy fulfilment of the office or dignity conferred by the respective Sacrament.[59] De Lugo, following the Fathers, enumerates still another effect. The guardian angels, he says, watch with special solicitude over the bearer of this " spiritual seal," while the

---

56 Pohle-Preuss, *Grace, Actual and Habitual.—V. supra* Sect. 2, Art. 1, Theses I and II.

57 It is thus conceived by Alexander of Hales, St. Bonaventure, and the Franciscan school of theologians generally.

58 Cfr. St. Bonaventure, *Comment. in Sent.*, IV, dist. 6, p. 1, qu. 2, ad 3: " *Character significat gratiam, et quod ibi non sit, hoc est ex defectu suscipientis tantum.*"

59 This is the teaching of St. Thomas, *Summa Theol.*, 3a, qu. 63, art. 3, ad 1: " *Character autem directe et propinque disponit animam ad ea quae sunt divini cultus exequenda. Et quia haec idonee non fiunt sine auxilio gratiae, . . . ex consequenti divina largitas recipientibus characterem largitur gratiam, per quam digne impleant ea, ad quae deputantur.*"

demons are constrained to moderate their attacks upon him.[60]

c) It remains to explain why only three of the Sacraments confer the character, while the other four do not.

In declaring that Baptism, Confirmation, and Holy Orders confer the sacramental character, the Council of Trent plainly intimates that the other four Sacraments do not confer it. This is indeed the common teaching, which can also be inferred from the fact that, according to the *Decretum pro Armenis,* the other four Sacraments can be received more than once for the reason that they do *not* imprint the sacramental character.[61] But why do only Baptism, Confirmation, and Holy Orders confer the character?

The sacramental character, as we have seen, is intimately related to Christ's office of High Priest. We know from Soteriology [62] that this office is inseparable from our Lord's other offices of Prophet and King, and that the three interpenetrate and limit each other. Now, as there are three offices of the Redeemer, so there are three offices among those whom He has redeemed. Each of these has its special mark or character. Baptism stamps the recipient a subject of Christ as King; Confirmation marks him as a courageous pupil of Christ in His capacity of Prophet or Teacher; Holy Orders distinguishes him as a minister of the God-man in His capacity of High Priest.

---

60 De Lugo, *De Sacram.,* disp. 6, sect. 3, n. 44.

61 *Decret. pro Armen.:* " *Reliqua vero quattuor characterem non imprimunt et* [*ideo*] *reiterationem admittunt.*" (Denzinger-Bannwart, n. 695).

62 Cfr. Pohle-Preuss, *Soteriology,* p. 158.

The remaining four Sacraments do not thus empower those who receive them to perform acts of public worship. Penance and Extreme Unction are essentially medicinal; the Holy Eucharist, though the most sublime of all the Sacraments, is rather a spiritual food and signifies the mystic union of the soul with Christ; Matrimony elevates to the sphere of grace, and thus sanctifies and ennobles, the natural union between male and female. From a purely philosophical point of view there is no reason why this latter Sacrament should not confer a character. Like Holy Orders, it establishes a state of life and represents an important office in the Church, inasmuch as it supplies those whom she is commissioned to raise to the rank of children of God and citizens of Heaven. Nevertheless, there is not between Matrimony and the three offices of the Redeemer that intimate connection which we have shown to exist between those offices and the Sacraments of Baptism, Confirmation, and Holy Orders. Hence there is no place in the external organization of the Church for such a thing as a sacramental character conferred by Matrimony.[63]

READINGS: — St. Thomas, *Summa Theol.*, 3a, qu. 63, art. 2.— Billuart, *De Sacramentis in Communi*, diss. 3, art. 3-5.—*De Lugo, *De Sacram. in Genere*, disp. 4, sect. 2-3.—*De Augustinis, *De Re Sacramentaria*, Vol. I, 2nd ed., pp. 273 sqq., 294 sqq., Rome 1889.— Tepe, *Instit. Theol.*, Vol. IV, pp. 50 sqq., Paris 1896.— Heinrich-Gutberlet, *Dogmat. Theologie*, Vol. IV, § 492 sq., Mainz 1901.— N. Gihr, *Die hl. Sakramente der kath. Kirche*, Vol. I, 2nd ed., § 14 sq., Freiburg 1902.— De Bellevue, *La Grâce Sacramentelle*, Paris 1900.

On the dogma of the character cfr.: St. Thomas, *Summa Theol.*, 3a, qu. 63, art. 1.— Billuart, *De Sacramentis in Communi*,

63 On the questions dealt with in this subdivision of our treatise cfr. Gihr, *Die hl. Sakramente der kath.* *Kirche*, Vol. I, 2nd ed., pp. 109 sqq., Freiburg 1902.

diss. 4, art. 1–3.— Bellarmine, *De Sacram. in Genere,* l. II, cap. 18–20.— De Lugo, *De Sacram. in Genere,* disp. 6, sect. 1–4.— *Franzelin, *De Sacram. in Genere,* thes. 12 sq., Rome 1888.— De Augustinis, *De Re Sacramentaria,* Vol. I, 2nd ed., pp. 308 sqq.— P. Schanz, *Die Lehre von den hl. Sakramenten,* § 10, Freiburg 1893.—*Lorinser, *De Charactere Sacramentali,* Oppolii 1844. — La Farine *Der sakramentale Charakter,* Freiburg 1904.— O. Laake, *Der sakramentale Charakter,* Münster 1903.— F. Brommer, *Die Lehre vom sakramentalen Charakter in der Scholastik bis Thomas v. Aquin inklusive,* Paderborn 1908.— Garrett Pierse, "The Origin of the Doctrine of the Sacramental Character," in the *Irish Theological Quarterly,* Vol. VI (1911), No. 2, pp. 196– 211.— B. J. Otten, S. J., *A Manual of the History of Dogmas,* Vol. I, St. Louis 1917, pp. 341, 344, 350.

THE SACRAMENTS INSTITUTED BY JESUS CHRIST

External sign and interior grace constitute the two internal causes (*materialis* and *formalis*) of a Sacrament. Its external or efficient cause (*causa efficiens*) is its institution by our Lord and Saviour Jesus Christ.

Christ is the author of the Sacraments in a threefold sense: (1) He has merited their sanctifying power by His passion and death; (2) He has personally instituted them; and (3) He has so determined the matter and form of each that the Church cannot alter their substance, though she is free to institute new ceremonies and sacramentals. We shall demonstrate this in four separate and distinct theses.

Thesis I: Christ Himself instituted all the Sacraments in the sense that He alone, by His passion and death, is their meritorious cause.

This proposition is *de fide*.

Proof. The Tridentine Council teaches: "If anyone saith that the Sacraments of the New Law were not all instituted by Jesus Christ our Lord,

. . . let him be anathema." [1]   Hence the institution of the Sacraments by Christ is an article of faith, at least in this sense that they derive their sanctifying power solely from the merits of the atonement, and, consequently, owe their existence to the human will of our Lord.[2]

a) The principle underlying this thesis, (*viz.:* that in the present economy there is and can be no grace not derived from the merits of Christ), has been sufficiently demonstrated in Soteriology.[3]   If Christ is the meritorious cause of the Sacraments, He must also be their author, inasmuch as against or without His will no grace can be bestowed on those whom He has redeemed.[4]   It follows that Christ is, either immediately or mediately, the author of all the Sacraments.

b) From the speculative point of view the following considerations are pertinent.

α) In regard to the institution of the Sacraments we may distinguish a threefold power: the divine *potestas auctoritatis,* the theandric *potestas excellentiae,* and the purely human *potestas ministerii.* The *potestas auctoritatis* belongs to God alone, the *potestas excellentiae* to Christ in His human capacity, the *potestas ministerii* to His ministers or representatives on earth.

---

[1] " *Si quis dixerit, sacramenta Novae Legis non fuisse omnia a Iesu Christo Domino nostro instituta, . . . anathema sit.*" (Sess. VII, can. 1; Denzinger-Bannwart, n. 844).

[2] *V.* Thesis II, *infra,* pp. 101 sqq.
[3] Cfr. Pohle-Preuss, *Soteriology,* pp. 5 sqq., St. Louis, 1914.
[4] Cfr. Matth. XXVIII, 18 sq.; John XX, 21 sqq.; Rom. VI, 3 sq.; 1 Cor. I, 13; Eph. V, 26.

As regards the *potestas auctoritatis,* evidently no one but God was able to attach internal grace to external signs and thus to institute real sacraments. Hence if such visible means of grace exist, they must owe their existence to Him.

The Sacraments derive their origin from, and owe their institution to, Christ, not only as God, but also as man. He is the natural mediator between God and man both in His divine and in His human nature. The graces which He merited for us, and which He distributes through the Sacraments, were merited in His human nature. Consequently, in the institution of the Sacraments, Christ acted not only with His divine but also with His human will. Although His human activity asserted itself only instrumentally and ministerially, it was most excellent for the reason that His humanity, on account of the Hypostatic Union, must be considered as *instrumentum coniunctum* of the Divinity and on account of its dignity stands out as the *causa ministerialis principalis.* It follows that the Sacraments, while they are truly instrumental causes of interior sanctification, are merely *instrumenta separata,* and their human administrators, though ministerial causes of the distribution of grace, are merely *causae ministeriales subordinatae.* Consequently, the human *potestas ministerii* mentioned above, is as far beneath the *potestas excellentiae* of Christ *qua* man, as the *potestas excellentiae* is inferior to the divine *potestas auctoritatis.*[5]

β) The *potestas excellentiae Christi,* which is so important a factor in the institution of the Sacraments, operates in a fourfold manner.

[5] Cfr. St. Thomas, *Summa Theol.,* 3a, qu. 64, art. 3: " *Et ideo sicut Christus, inquantum Deus, habet potestatem auctoritatis in sacramentis, ita inquantum homo, habet potestatem ministerii principalis sive potestatem excellentiae.*"

(1) The merits of Christ are the sole operative power of all the Sacraments. This truth is the very foundation and corner-stone of the Catholic doctrine of the Sacraments.[6]

(2) Christ's *potestas excellentiae* also manifests itself in the fact that there can be no Sacraments except those administered in His name and by His power. The administration and distribution of graces is entirely subject to Him who has merited and accumulated them.[7]

(3) There can be no Sacrament that does not depend, either mediately or immediately, upon the human will of Christ as its author; for it is as man that Christ is our natural Mediator, the fount of grace, and the High Priest of humanity.[8]

(4) The *potestas excellentiae* also reveals itself in this that Christ, as man, is independent of the Sacraments, inasmuch as He can remit sins and impart graces without their instrumentality,— a prerogative denied to His human representatives.[9]

6 Cfr. St. Thomas, *Summa Theol.*, 3a, qu. 64, art. 5: "*Principalis autem causa efficiens gratiae est ipse Deus, ad quem comparatur humanitas Christi sicut instrumentum coniunctum, sacramentum autem sicut instrumentum separatum. Et ideo oportet quod virtus salutifera a divinitate Christi per eius humanitatem in ipsa sacramenta derivetur. . . . Manifestum est autem ex his quae supra dicta sunt (qu. 48, 49), quod Christus liberavit nos a peccatis nostris praecipue per passionem, non solum sufficienter et meritorie, sed etiam satisfactorie. Similiter etiam per suam passionem initiavit ritum christianae religionis. . . . Unde manifestum est quod sacramenta ecclesiae specialiter habent virtutem ex passione Christi, cuius virtus quo-* dammodo nobis copulatur per susceptionem sacramentorum."

7 Cfr. Acts II, 38, VIII, 12; 1 Cor. I, 12 sq.

8 *V.* Soteriology.

9 Matth. IX, 2 sqq. Cfr. St. Thomas, *Summa Theol.*, 3a, qu. 64, art. 3: "*. . . quae quidem [potestas excellentiae] consistit in quattuor: primo quidem in hoc quod meritum et virtus passionis eius operatur in sacramentis . . .; ideo secundo ad potestatem excellentiae, quam Christus habet in sacramentis, pertinet quod in eius nomine sacramenta sanctificentur. Et quia ex eius institutione sacramenta virtutem obtinent, inde est quod tertio ad excellentiam potestatis Christi pertinet quod ipse, qui dedit virtutem sacramentis, potuit instituere*

Thesis II: The Sacraments of the Christian dispensation have been immediately and personally instituted by Christ.

This proposition may be technically qualified as *propositio certa.*

Proof. After showing that the Sacraments have Christ for their author, we have now to demonstrate that He instituted them immediately and personally, and not through the instrumentality of His Apostles or the Church.

Before the Tridentine Council some theologians held that Christ personally instituted most of the Sacraments, but not all. Hugh of St. Victor, Peter Lombard, and St. Bonaventure, for instance, thought that Confirmation and Extreme Unction were instituted by the Apostles under the inspiration of the Holy Ghost.[10] Alexander of Hales even went so far as to maintain that Confirmation cannot be traced farther back than the Council of Meaux, A. D. 845. This was an egregious historical blunder, as the Council of Meaux passed only disciplinary regulations.[11]

Since the Council of Trent Catholic theologians are so firmly convinced of the immediate institution of the Sac-

---

sacramenta. Et quia causa non dependet ab effectu, sed potius e contrario, ideo quarto ad excellentiam potestatis pertinet quod ipse potuit effectum sacramentorum sine exteriori sacramento conferre." These four reasons in principle establish the institution of all the Sacraments by Christ. Cfr. De Augustinis, *De Re Sacramentaria,* Vol. I, 2nd ed., pp. 125 sqq.; Gihr, *Die hl. Sakramente,* Vol. I, 2nd ed., pp. 124 sq.

10 Cfr. St. Bonaventure, *Comment. in Sent.,* IV, dist. 23, art. 1, qu. 2: *" Et ideo probabilius alii dicunt et Magister videtur hoc sentire, imo aperte dicit, quod Spiritus Sanctus hoc sacramentum [extremae unctionis] per Apostolos instituit, sicut supra dictum est de sacramento confirmationis."*

11 See Labbé, *Concil.,* t. VII, p. 1833.

raments by Christ that some of them [12] teach it as a dogma, while all without exception regard it as *doctrina certa*.[13]

Though the Tridentine Council, out of regard for the authority of such eminent theologians as St. Bonaventure, purposely refrained from defining the immediate institution of the Sacraments by Jesus Christ as an article of faith, its teaching on the subject is quite unmistakable in its implications.

(1) Whenever a personal name is connected with the institution of a rite, the bearer of that name must manifestly have instituted the rite in person. In the Tridentine definition " Jesus " and " Christ " are thus connected with the institution of the Sacraments (*v. supra*, Thesis I). Moreover, the Council itself draws a sharp distinction between the ceremonies ordained by the Church [14] and the Sacraments instituted by Christ.[15]

(2) Wherever it speaks of the institution of those Sacraments that were undoubtedly instituted by our Divine Saviour in person, the Council employs precisely the same terms as in the canon just referred to; [16] consequently, that canon must be understood as inculcating the immediate institution of all the Sacraments by Christ.

(3) Had the Church received from her Divine Founder the power to institute Sacraments, she would also have the power of changing the substance of any Sacrament,

---

12 E. g., Bellarmine, Vasquez, Gonet, against Suarez, Billuart, Tournely, *et al.*

13 Cfr. Suarez, *De Sacramentis,* disp. 12, § 1: " *Christus Dominus immediate ac per se ipsum instituit omnia sacramenta Novae Legis. Conclusio est omnino certa ex definitione Concilii Tridentini (Sess. VII, can. 1): ' Si quis dixerit, sa-cramenta Novae Legis non fuisse omnia a Iesu Christo Domino nostro instituta, anathema sit.' "*

14 Sess. VII, can. 13.

15 Sess. VII, can. 1.

16 Cfr. *Conc. Trid.,* Sess. XIV, cap. 1; Sess. XXII, can. 2; Sess. XXIII, cap. 1; Sess. XXIV, prooem: " *Ipse Christus venerabilium sacramentorum institutor . . .*"

both with regard to matter and form. But this is expressly denied by the Council.[17]

(4) The Council teaches in regard to Extreme Unction, the Sacrament mainly in dispute, that it is " a Sacrament instituted by Christ our Lord and promulgated by the blessed Apostle James," [18]— a phrase which positively excludes the theory that this Sacrament may have been instituted by the Apostles or the Church.

In the light of these considerations the reader will be able to form his own opinion of the contention of Loisy,[19] condemned in the so-called " Syllabus of Pius X," that Christ did not institute a single one of the traditional Sacraments, but that they were all introduced in course of time by the Church.[20]

a) Holy Writ furnishes direct evidence that at least two of the Sacraments were instituted immediately by Christ, namely, Baptism (Matth. XXVIII, 19, John III, 5) and the Holy Eucharist (Matth. XXVI, 26 sqq., *et passim*). Besides these there is good scriptural reason to suppose that our Saviour personally instituted Penance (John XX, 23) and Holy Orders (Luke XXII, 19).

While we have no direct evidence concerning the other three Sacraments, we are justified in assuming that they derive their existence from the same divine origin.

17 Sess. XXI, cap. 2: *" Praeterea declarat, hanc potestatem perpetuo in Ecclesia fuisse, ut in sacramentorum dispensatione, salvâ illorum substantiâ, ea statueret vel mutaret, quae suscipientium utilitati seu ipsorum sacramentorum venerationi pro rerum, temporum et locorum varietate magis expedire iudicaret."*

18 Sess. XIV, can. 1: *" Extremam unctionem esse . . . sacramentum a Christo Domino nostro institutum et a B. Iacobo Apostolo promulgatum."*

19 *Autour d'un Petit Livre,* pp. 220 sqq., Paris 1903.

20 Denzinger-Bannwart, *Enchiridion,* n. 2039 sqq.

Like Baptism, the Eucharist, Penance, and Holy Orders, —Confirmation, Extreme Unction, and Matrimony are veritable pillars of the Catholic religion. All three are plainly mentioned in Holy Scripture [21] and therefore cannot possibly have been instituted in post-Apostolic times. That they are not of Apostolic origin may safely be inferred from the fact that the Apostles never appear as the authors but invariably as the administrators of the Sacraments. Cfr. 1 Cor. IV, 1 : " Let a man so account of us as of the ministers of Christ and the dispensers of the mysteries of God." 1 Cor. III, 4 sq.: " What then is Apollo? and what is Paul? The ministers of him whom you have believed." [22]

b) The Fathers know of no distinction between mediate and immediate institution in respect of the Sacraments.

Pseudo-Ambrose asks : " Who is the author of the Sacraments if not the Lord Jesus? These Sacraments have come from heaven." [23] Special importance attaches, as Vasquez points out,[24] to the testimony of St. Augustine, who says: " In the first place, therefore, I want you to hold . . . that the Lord Jesus Christ . . . subjected us to a light yoke and an easy burden. Hence He bound the society of the new people with Sacraments very few in number, easy of observance, eminent in signification, as, for instance, Baptism consecrated by the name of the

---

21 Confirmation, Acts VIII, 17, XIX, 6; Extreme Unction, Jas. V, 14 sqq.; Matrimony, Eph. V, 25 sqq.

22 1 Cor. IV, 1: " Sic nos existimet homo ut ministros Christi et dispensatores (οἰκονόμους) mysteriorum Dei."— 1 Cor. III, 4 sq.: " Quid igitur est Apollo? quid vero Paulus? Ministri (διάκονοι) eius, cui credidistis."

23 De Sacram., IV, 4, 13: " Sacramentorum auctor quis est nisi Dominus Jesus? De caelo ista sacramenta venerunt."

24 Comment. in S. Th., III, disp. 135, c. 1, n. 9.

Trinity, the communication of His own body and blood, and whatever else is commended in the canonical Scriptures." [25] Baptism and the Holy Eucharist are here ascribed immediately to Christ, together with the other Sacraments commended in the canonical Scriptures, *i. e.* all seven as we know them. Where he speaks of the deeds of our Lord on earth, Augustine says: " In the time of servitude, under the Old Law, the people, bound by fear, were burdened with many sacraments. This was useful for them, that they might desire the grace of God which the prophets had predicted. When it came, the wisdom of God, through the assumption of the man by whom we were called to liberty, instituted a few highly useful Sacraments, which were to bind together the society of the Christian people, that is, of the multitude enjoying freedom under the one God." [26] Augustine is well aware of the fact that Christ might have granted the faculty of instituting Sacraments to His Apostles, yet he says: " [Christ] did not wish this, in order that the hope of the baptized be in Him by whom they acknowledge their Baptism. . . . Therefore, lest there be said to be as many baptisms as [there are] ministers who baptize, having received the power to do so from the Lord, the Lord kept for Himself the power of baptizing, giving

25 St. Augustine, *Ep.* 54 *ad Ianuar.*, c. 1: " *Primo itaque tenere te volo, . . . Dominum nostrum Iesum Christum . . . levi iugo suo nos subdidisse et sarcinae levi. Unde sacramentis numero paucissimis, observatione facillimis, significatione praestantissimis societatem novi populi colligavit, sicuti est baptismus Trinitatis nomine consecratus, communicatio corporis et sanguinis ipsius et si quid aliud in Scripturis canonicis commendatur.*"

26 *De Vera Religione*, c. 17, n. 33: " *Populus timore constrictus tempore servitutis in Vetere Lege multis sacramentis onerabatur. Hoc enim talibus utile erat ad desiderandam gratiam Dei, quae per prophetas ventura canebatur. Quae ubi venit, ab ipsa Dei sapientia homine assumpto, a quo in libertatem vocati sumus, pauca sacramenta saluberrima constituta sunt, quae societatem christiani populi, hoc est sub uno Deo liberae multitudinis continerent.*"

His servants [merely] the ministry." [27] The latter part
of this passage indicates the reason why Christ instituted
the Sacraments immediately and personally. The idea
is more fully developed by St. Thomas.[28]

c) Theologians grant the abstract possibility of a mediate institution of the Sacraments by the Apostles or by
the Church, but they grant it only conditionally, that is in
so far as it does not involve a denial of the doctrine set
forth in our first thesis.[29] Though some [30] are unwilling
to admit that Christ could have imparted His power to
mere men, the common opinion is that, had He so willed,
He could have empowered the Apostles and the Church to
institute Sacraments at His behest. Of course, the distinction between the divine *potestas auctoritatis* and the
theandric *potestas excellentiae* must always be kept in
mind. The former is incommunicable, while the latter
may, to a certain limited extent, be bestowed upon creatures.[31]

27 *Tract. in Ioa.*, V, n. 7: "*Hoc
noluit ideo, ut in illo spes esset baptizatorum, a quo se baptizatos agno-
scerent. . . . Ergo ne tot baptisma-
ta dicerentur, quot essent servi
qui baptizarent acceptâ potestate
a Domino, sibi tenuit Dominus
baptizandi potestatem, servis ministerium dedit.*"

28 *Summa Theol.*, 3a, qu. 64, art.
4. See also Suarez, *De Sacram.*,
disp. 12, sect. 1.

29 *V. supra*, p. 97.

30 *E. g.*, Durandus, Scotus, and
Vasquez.

31 Cfr. St. Thomas, *Summa Theol.*,
3a, qu. 64, art. 4: "*Christus in
sacramentis habuit duplicem potestatem: unam auctoritatis, quae competit ei secundum quod Deus, et talis
potestas nulli creaturae potuit com-
municari, sicut nec divina essentia.
Aliam potestatem habuit excellentiae,*

*quae competit ei secundum quod
homo, et talem potestatem potuit
ministris communicare, dando scil.
eis tantam gratiae plenitudinem, ut
eorum meritum operaretur ad sacramentorum effectus, ut ad invocationem nominum ipsorum sanctifica-
rentur sacramenta, et ut ipsi possent
sacramenta instituere et sine ritu
sacramentorum effectum sacramentorum conferre solo imperio. Potest
enim instrumentum coniunctum [i.
e. humanitas Christi], quando fuerit
fortius, tanto magis virtutem suam
instrumento separato [i. e. ministro]
tribuere, sicut manus baculo.*" To
the objection that such a (hypo-
thetic) plenipotentiary, by the possession of such incredible privileges,
would *eo ipso* be the *caput gratiae*
of humanity, St. Thomas replies with
a distinction: "*Si tamen [Christus]
communicasset, ipse esset caput*"

Thesis III: Christ so determined the matter and form of the Sacraments that they are immutable for all time.

This proposition embodies a *sententia communis*.

Proof. The matter and form of a Sacrament may be determined individually, specifically, or generically.

They are determined individually if everything is minutely regulated in detail, as, for instance, the exact method of pouring out the water and the precise words to be pronounced by the minister in Baptism. The history and practice of the Greek Church furnish ample evidence that our Lord did not thus determine the matter and form of the Sacraments *in individuo*.

By specific determination we understand a designation of matter and form *in infima specie*. Theologians are agreed that Christ specifically determined the matter and form of some of the Sacraments (*e. g.*, Baptism and the Eucharist), but not of all (especially Confirmation and Holy Orders).[32]

Generic determination is a designation of matter and form only *quoad genus*. Some theologians [33] assert that Christ determined the rite of ordination in such a general way, leaving the choice of a specific sign to His Church. This would account for the differences existing in the Eastern and the Western Churches. We admit that this theory enables us to explain more satisfactorily, from the

principaliter, alii vero secundario." (*L. c.*, ad 2). Cfr. De Lugo, *De Sacram.*, disp. 7, sect. 1-2; Franzelin, *De Sacram. in Genere*, thes. 14.

32 For further details on this point we must refer the student to the separate treatises on the Sacraments.

33 *E. g.*, De Lugo (*De Sacram.*, disp. 2, sect. 5).

historic point of view, the differences that have developed
in the administration of other Sacraments (*e. g.,* Confirmation and Penance) in the course of centuries. According to the unanimous teaching of theologians, the
phrase " matter and form " comprises all those elements,
and those elements only, which Christ Himself instituted
either *in specie,* or at least *in genere,* and over these the
Church has no power.

Nevertheless, solid arguments can be adduced
in support of the proposition that Christ Himself
so determined both the matter and the form of
all the Sacraments, not only *in genere,* but likewise *in specie,* that the Church has never made
any essential change in regard thereto, and could
not make such a change if she would.

a) One of these arguments may be formulated as follows: Christ immediately and personally instituted all the
Sacraments.[34] Now every Sacrament consists essentially
of matter and form.[35] Consequently, Christ, who instituted the Sacraments, must have determined their matter
and form. If the Apostles or the Church had determined
the matter or the form of any Sacrament, they would
have mediately instituted that Sacrament. And if it
were true, as some theologians assert, that for the Sacrament of Holy Orders the Church took the specification of
matter and form into her own hands and carried it out differently in the East and in the West, it would have to
be admitted that she has changed the Sacrament essentially. For whoever changes the matter and form of a
Sacrament, changes the Sacrament itself. Moreover, if
the Church had at any time in the past possessed the power

---

34 V. Thesis II, *supra.*   35 *V. supra,* Ch. II, Sect. 1.

to determine the matter and form of a Sacrament, she would have the same power to-day, in accordance with Toletus' principle: *" Cuius est facere, est etiam mutare."* [36] But the Church herself expressly denies that she has any such power. [37] Consequently, the matter and form of all the Sacraments — including Confirmation, Holy Orders, and Matrimony — have been specifically determined by Christ Himself.

Tradition affords no evidence that the Church ever introduced any particular sign as the matter and form of a Sacrament, or that she substituted any new sign for one already in use. Pope Benedict XIV, who firmly held the theory just expounded, boldly challenged his opponents to produce any evidence in support of their claim. " Let them tell us," he says, " where, when, by what council or pope such a change was made," and adds: " The contrary seems to be evident from the Tridentine Council, [38] which declares that Christ gave His Church the power to ordain or change whatsoever she may judge expedient in the dispensation of the Sacraments, their substance remaining untouched; a change of matter and form would touch, not the rite and dispensation, but the substance." [39] Well-nigh the only reason why some theologians incline to the opposite opinion, is the difference existing between the rite of ordination in the Eastern and the Western Church. In the Orient, the matter of this Sacrament is the imposition of hands, in the Occident,

---

36 Toletus, *Comment. in S. Theol.*, III, qu. 64, art. 2.

37 *V. supra.*, p. 103.

38 Sess. XXI, cap. 2.

39 Benedict XIV, *De Synodo Dioecesana*, VIII, 10, 10: " *Dicant enim, ubi, quando, in quo concilio, a quo pontifice facta sit eiusmodi mutatio." " Imo oppositum videtur evinci ex Tridentino, ubi declarat, a Christo relictam esse Ecclesiae potestatem mutandi quae sacramentorum dispensationem respiciunt, salvâ illorum substantiâ; mutatio vero materiae et formae non ad ritum et dispensationem, sed ad substantiam pertinet.*"

the *traditio instrumentorum*. This difference, however, as we shall show in our treatise on Holy Orders, does not affect the essence of the Sacrament.[40]

b) The determination of matter and form is not equally specific in the different Sacraments. In the case of Baptism, for instance, the " ablution," which represents the matter, both proximate and remote, of the Sacrament, may be carried out in three different ways — by immersion, by effusion, or by aspersion, while the words constituting the form may be pronounced either in Latin or in Greek or in the vernacular, and may be indicative or deprecatory. The underlying principle may be briefly stated as follows: The matter of a Sacrament remains within the sphere of its determined species as long as it retains, in the popular estimation, its peculiar properties, while the form remains specifically unchanged as long as the logical and theological sense of the formula is preserved intact. Alterations, additions or omissions which do not run counter to this principle are to be regarded as merely accidental changes. Certain doubtful instances will be treated later in connection with the several Sacraments. It should be noted, however, that the validity of a sacramental form may also depend on the intention of the minister, who has it in his power, either through ignorance or purposely, to corrupt the form. If a mistake is made through ignorance, the Sacrament is valid so long as the wrongly pronounced formula may be morally held to retain the objective sense which Christ wished to connect with it. If the corruption is intentional, the form retains its specific integrity only on condition that its objective sense is not

40 For a more detailed treatment consult De Augustinis, *De Re Sacram.*, Vol. I, 2nd ed., pp. 168 sqq.; Franzelin, *De Sacram. in Gen.*, thes. 5; G. M. Van Rossum, *De Essentia Sacramenti Ordinis*, Rome 1914.

essentially altered or the intention to do what the Church wishes to do is not positively excluded. Should the minister of a Sacrament be led by a desire for novelty purposely to render the meaning of a prescribed form ambiguous, or heretically to exclude the right intention, it is evident that he desires to employ another form than that instituted by Christ, and the Sacrament consequently becomes invalid.

Thesis IV: Though the Church has no right to institute Sacraments, she possesses the power to institute sacramentals.

This proposition may be qualified as "*certa.*"

Proof. In the three preceding theses we have explained what the Church *cannot* do in regard to the Sacraments. The present one defines what she *can* do.

There are two kinds of sacramentals: (1) such as accompany the administration of the Sacraments (*e. g.* the exorcisms pronounced in Baptism, the use of salt, the anointing of the forehead), and (2) such as may be used independently of the Sacraments and have a quasi matter and form of their own (*e. g.* the different ecclesiastical blessings). The former are called sacramental ceremonies, the latter sacramentals in the strict sense of the term.

1. That the Church has power to institute sacramental ceremonies or rites, is clear from the following declaration of the Tridentine Council: "If anyone saith that the received and approved rites of the Catholic Church, wont to be used in the solemn administration of the Sacraments, may be contemned, or without sin be omitted at pleasure by the ministers, or be changed by every pastor

of the churches into other new ones, let him be anathema." [41]

a) In proof of this dogma the Holy Synod adduces the example of St. Paul, who concludes his remarks on the Eucharist with these words: "And the rest I will set in order, when I come." [42] There is abundant Patristic evidence for the antiquity of the sacramental ceremonies employed by the Church. Most of those now in use can be traced far beyond the ninth century, as a glance at the Sacramentary of Gregory the Great and the writings of Rhabanus Maurus, Alcuin, and Isidore shows. In the early days of Christianity different ceremonies were in vogue, as may be gathered from the works of Tertullian. [43]

The theological argument for our thesis rests mainly on the fact that the Church possesses legislative power to ordain whatever she judges fit to beautify her services and promote the salvation of souls. The sacramental ceremonies serve both these purposes by giving visible expression to the ideas that underlie the sacred mysteries of religion, and by stimulating, nourishing, and augmenting the devotion of the faithful. [44]

b) A word regarding the use of the Latin language in the administration of the Sacraments. In the first place, no solid argument can be alleged in favor of the vernacular. Those who are ignorant of Latin lose nothing of the sacramental effect, since the Sacraments produce their

---

[41] Sess. VII, can. 13: "*Si quis dixerit, receptos et approbatos Ecclesiae catholicae ritus in solemni sacramentorum administratione adhiberi consuetos aut contemni aut sine peccato a ministris pro libito omitti aut in novos alios per quemcunque ecclesiarum pastorem mutari posse, anathema sit.*" (Denzinger-Bannwart, n. 856).

[42] 1 Cor. XI, 34: "*Cetera, quum venero, disponam.*"

[43] The argument from tradition is copiously developed by Suarez, *De Sacram.*, disp. 15, sect. 3, n. 3.

[44] Bellarmine says they are as necessary to religion as salt is to meat. (*De Sacram.*, V, 31). Cfr. *Conc. Trident.*, Sess. XXII, cap. 5 (Denzinger-Bannwart, n. 943); *Catech. Rom.*, P. II, cap. 1, n. 18.

effects *ex opere operato,* and the meaning of the accompanying words can be easily explained to the faithful. On the other hand, the substitution of a living tongue for Latin would entail very serious inconveniences. Unity of worship is intimately bound up with unity of language and the adoption of different rituals and liturgies in different vernaculars would, externally at least, split up the Church into an equal number of national churches. Moreover, if the liturgical books were composed in a living tongue, it would be necessary to rewrite them from time to time, and there would naturally be danger lest the doctrine itself should become more and more obscured to the detriment of explicit and well-determined faith. The use of a dead language obviates all these difficulties. There is another point. If Latin were not the language of the Church, the clergy would be exposed to the danger of neglecting this important tongue, which is the key to the Vulgate and the writings of the Western Fathers, and thus more easily become a prey to ignorance and intellectual lethargy, which could not but result in injury to the Church and religion.

2. Sacramentals in the strict sense are rites resembling those of the sacraments but independent of them, instituted by the Church for the supernatural advantage of the faithful.

a) The term itself seems to have been coined by Alexander of Hales.[45] Hugh of St. Victor speaks of the sacramentals as *sacramenta minora* in contradistinction to the *sacramenta maiora s. principalia.* St. Thomas refers to them as *sacra* and again as *sacramentalia.*

Sacramentals differ from Sacraments in three essential respects:

45 *Summa Theol.,* P. 4, qu. 23, n. 5.

(1) Unlike the Sacraments, the sacramentals were not immediately instituted by our Lord, but partly by His Apostles (*e. g.* the sign of the cross) and partly by the Church (*e. g.* the blessing of the baptismal font).

(2) They do not communicate sanctifying grace, but work other inferior though salutary effects.

(3) They produce these effects not *ex opere operato,* but *ex opere operantis.*

They resemble the Sacraments in this that they ordinarily consist of matter and form and produce a spiritual effect in the recipient.

The blessings and exorcisms of the Church have their prototype in Christ.[46]   The ceremony of washing the feet was directly instituted by him, while the other sacramentals derive their justification from the legislative power of the Church.   Harnack shows a woful lack of understanding when he writes: " We must study the theory and practice of the benedictions and sacramentals in connection with indulgences, in order to see how far the Catholic Church has progressed towards Paganism.   The dogmatic teaching in regard to the *benedictio constitutiva* and the *consecratio,* as distinguished from the *benedictio invocativa,* is a veritable insult not only to the Christian but to every spiritual religion. . . . As the Church by the adoption of indulgences, truly, *i. e. in praxi,* created another Sacrament of Penance, so in the sacramentals she created new Sacraments more convenient than the old, because entirely under her control.   In both respects she has legitimized Rabbinism and the theory and practice of the Pharisees and Talmudists." [47]   This is absolutely false. If the sacramentals were mere remnants of Paganism, Phari-

46 Cfr. Matth. X, 8, XIV, 19, XIX, 15; Mark IX, 37, XVI, 17; Luke X, 17.

47 *Dogmengeschichte,* Vol. III, 3rd ed., pp. 604 sq.

seeism, and Talmudism, the same would be true of the Sacraments, whereas their power rests on the divinity of Christ in exactly the same way as that of the sacramentals rests on the divinity of the Church. True, Harnack denies both these premises; but as a historian he ought in fairness to judge the sacramentals not from the rationalistic but from the Catholic point of view. Surely it cannot be affirmed historically that Christ employed a Pagan or Talmudic rite when He exorcised demons or when He blessed bread and wine before the consecration. Why, then, accuse the Church of Paganism when, following the example of her Divine Founder, she blesses persons and objects, calls down a benediction upon the fields, and pronounces exorcisms against evil spirits? That indulgences take the place of the Sacrament of Penance, and that the sacramentals have supplanted the original Sacraments, is an utterly gratuitous assertion. An indulgence is merely a remission of temporal punishment, whereas in the Sacrament of Penance sins are forgiven. The sacramentals derive their efficacy from the disposition of the recipient, and consequently by no means render superfluous the Sacraments, which produce their effects *ex opere operato*. That the spiritual effects of both Sacraments and sacramentals depend on external signs and symbols, far from involving an insult to the Christian religion, responds to a normal postulate of human nature, which is a compound of spirit and matter, in which the spiritual must be attained by means of the senses. The use of the sacramentals remains optional, while to receive certain Sacraments is of strict obligation. The only thing that is forbidden in connection with the sacramentals is contempt and superstitious use. Educated Catholics may not relish all the sacramentals, but they know that the Church, as a kindly mother, supplies all reasonable needs and demands of her children, even those of the weak and simple. In extending her blessings to every province of nature, she constantly reminds us that the earth is still groaning under the curse of sin and that man's true home is not here below. It is a truly magnificent conception that underlies the Catholic doctrine of the sacramentals.[48]

b) As regards the classification of the sacramentals, an attempt has been made to reduce them to six, embodied in the ancient hexameter:

" *Orans, tinctus, edens, confessus, dans, benedicens.*"
Aside from the fact that public prayer (*orans*), the general avowal of faults made in the recitation of the Confiteor (*confessus*), and almsgiving (*dans*) are not sacramentals in the true sense of the term, it is to be remarked that the actual number of sacramentals is by no means limited to the other three rites enumerated above, *viz.:* the use of holy water (*tinctus*), the eating of blessed food (*edens*), and papal, episcopal, and sacerdotal blessings (*benedicens*).

Equally inadequate is the sevenfold division of the sacramentals indicated in the line:

" *Crux, aqua, nomen, edens, ungens, iurans, benedicens.*"

To pronounce the Holy Name of Jesus (*nomen*) is merely an ejaculatory prayer, while the sign of the cross (*crux*), the use of holy water (*aqua*), the eating of blessed food (*edens*), the use of holy oil (*ungens*), exorcisms (*iurans*), and ecclesiastical benedictions (*benedicens*), though true sacramentals, by no means exhaust their number.

---

[48] Cfr. Oswald, *Die dogmatische Lehre von den hl. Sakramenten,* Vol. I, 5th ed., pp. 15 sqq., Münster 1894; Gr. Rippel, *Die Schönheit der kath. Kirche in ihren hl. Zeremo-* *nien,* 23rd ed., Mainz 1898; A. A. Lambing, *The Sacramentals of the Holy Catholic Church,* New York 1892.

A more comprehensive division is that made by St. Thomas, to which Harnack adverts in the passage quoted above. The Angelic Doctor distinguishes consecrations (*consecratio s. benedictio constitutiva*) and benedictions (*benedictio invocativa*). To this has been added as a third species, exorcism (*adiuratio daemonum*). A consecration is a rite by which the Church dedicates a person (*e. g.* an abbot) or an object (*e. g.* an altar) to the service of God. A benediction is an ecclesiastical rite by virtue of which some benefit, either spiritual or corporal, is applied to a designated person. The application may be either immediate (as in the case of the papal blessing) or mediate (as in the use of a blessed object, such as holy water). The term sacramentals is by a well-known figure of speech applied to consecrated or blessed objects, though strictly speaking it belongs only to the act of consecration or benediction, or to the use of consecrated or blessed objects. The exorcisms are partly integral constituents of sacramental ceremonies, and partly direct adjurations of the devil, or of natural objects with a view to withdraw them from the curse of sin and the power of Satan.[49]

c) With regard to the efficacy of the sacramentals we must never lose sight of the fundamental principle that they neither obliterate mortal sin nor infuse sanctifying grace. If they were capable of working these effects, there would be no difference between them and the Sacraments. Theologians argue as to whether the sacramentals may confer other graces *ex opere operato* (as, for example, the forgiveness of venial sins, the remission of temporal punishments) and not merely through the intercession of the Church or the action of the one

[49] Cfr. Rom. VIII, 20 sq.; 1 Cor. V, 5; Acts XXVI, 18.

who uses them. Some writers (*e. g.* Dominicus Soto and
Bellarmine) do not hesitate to attribute such efficacy to
the sacramentals, whereas the majority reject the assumption, and justly so, for three reasons: first, because the
Church is not empowered to institute efficacious signs of
grace; second, because the sacramentals do not produce
their effects infallibly; and third, because the Church in
her rites makes use, not of affirmative, but of deprecatory
expressions, which shows that she looks to the divine
mercy for the effect. Hence the sacramentals derive
their efficacy entirely *ex opere operantis.*[50]   This efficacy
is nevertheless very special in that it owes its power
not to the *opus operans* (*i. e.* the pious acts) of the faithful alone, but also to the *opus operans* (*i. e.* the intercession) of the Church. If this were not so, it might
make no difference whether a Catholic would sprinkle
himself with holy water or with ordinary water,
because in both cases his piety and devotion might
be the same, and there would be no other source of
efficacy. The purely deprecative character of the sacramentals is also revealed by the fact that any priest,
regardless of his personal worthiness, can validly bless
and consecrate; it is the Church that blesses and consecrates through him. This explains the theory of
some theologians that the operation of the sacramentals
lies midway between the *opus operatum* and the *opus
operans,* in regard to which theory it may be well to
remark that the *opus operatum* is simply the *opus
operans* of the Church. These considerations afford a
standard for measuring the mode and extent of the effects
wrought by the sacramentals. Aside from the personal
devotion of the user there can be no effects other than

50 Cfr. St. Thomas, *Summa Theol.*, 3a, qu. 83, art. 3, ad 3.

those for which the Church prays and which are deducible
from her official formularies.

d) The fruits or effects of the sacramentals may be
similarly divided into three categories. Consecration
(*benedictio constitutiva*) results in the effective with-
drawal from profane use of the person or thing upon
which it is bestowed, and its dedication to the purpose
of divine worship (*e. g.,* the tonsure, minor orders, the
blessing of oil, the dedication of a church, an altar, a
vestment). Benediction (*benedictio invocativa*) has four
distinct effects: forgiveness of venial sins, remission of
temporal punishments, bestowal of actual graces and of
material benefits. The forgiveness of sins resulting from
the use of sacramentals is ascribed by St. Thomas to an
implied act of contrition.[51] The remission of temporal
punishments due to sin requires something more, *viz.:* an
ardent love of God elicited during the use of the sacramentals.[52] There is only one exception to this rule, *viz.:*
when indulgences are attached to the use of blessed objects
(*e. g.* rosaries, medals), because an indulgence is a remission of temporal punishments by virtue of the power of
the keys entrusted by Christ to His Church. The bestowal
of actual graces in connection with sacramentals depends
partly on the subjective devotion and receptivity of the
faithful, partly on the effective intercession of the Church.
Lastly, the sacramentals may also bring down upon their
users material benefits (blessing of bread, dwellings, fields,
etc.), provided, of course, that the benefits asked for by the

51 *Summa Theol.,* 3a, qu. 87, art.
3, ad 1: ". . . inquantum inclinant
[*sacramentalia*] animam ad motum
poenitentiae, qui est detestatio peccatorum vel implicite vel explicite."

52 St. Thomas, *l. c.,* ad 3: "Non
autem per quodlibet praedictorum
semper tollitur totus reatus poenae,

quia sic qui esset omnino immunis a
peccato mortali, aspersus aquâ
benedictâ statim evolaret [ad
caelum]; sed reatus poenae remit-
titur per praedicta secundum motum
fervoris in Deum, qui per praedicta
excitatur quandoque magis, quandoque autem minus."

Church do not conflict with the divine economy of grace or the salvation of souls. The effect of exorcisms (*adiuratio daemonum*) consists solely in a moral power enabling man to overcome the attacks and temptations of the devil and to weaken or frustrate his assaults.

READINGS:—*St. Thomas, *Summa Theologica*, 3a, qu. 64, art. 1–4.— Bellarmine, *De Sacramentis*, I, 23.—*De Lugo, *De Sacramentis*, disp. 7, sect. 1–2.—Franzelin, *De Sacramentis in Genere*, thes. 14, Rome 1888.— De Augustinis, *De Re Sacramentaria*, t. I, 2nd ed., pp. 125 sqq., Rome 1889.— W. Humphrey, S.J., *The One Mediator, or Sacrifice and Sacraments*, London 1890.— P. Schanz, *Die Lehre von den Sakramenten der kath. Kirche*, § 8, Freiburg 1893.— Tepe, *Instit. Theologicae*, Vol. IV, pp. 19 sqq., Paris 1896. — B. J. Otten, S. J., *A Manual of the History of Dogmas*, Vol. I, St. Louis 1917, pp. 348 sq.; Vol. II (1918), pp. 295 sqq.

On the sacramentals cfr. Probst, *Kirchliche Benediktionen und ihre Verwaltung*, Tübingen 1857.—IDEM, *Sakramente und Sakramentalien in den drei ersten christlichen Jahrhunderten*, Tübingen 1872.— G. M. Schuler, *Die kirchlichen Sakramentalien*, Bamberg 1867.—*P. Schanz, *Die Wirksamkeit der Sakramentalien*, in the *Theol. Quartalschrift*, Tübingen 1886, pp. 548 sqq.—*Fr. Schmid, *Die Sakramentalien der kath. Kirche in ihrer Eigenart beleuchtet*, Brixen 1896.—*Arendt, S.J., *De Sacramentalibus Disquisitio Scholastico-Dogmatica*, 2nd ed., Rome 1900.—Heinrich-Gutberlet, *Dogmatische Theologie*, Vol. IX, § 481, Mainz 1901.— Ad. Franz, *Die kirchlichen Benediktionen im Mittelalter*, 2 vols., Freiburg 1909.— A. A. Lambing, *The Sacramentals of the Holy Catholic Church*, New York 1892.— H. Leclercq, O.S.B., art. "Sacramentals," in the *Catholic Encyclopedia*, Vol. XIII.

CHAPTER III

THE EFFICACY OF THE SACRAMENTS AND THEIR MANNER OF OPERATION

We have now to explain the efficacy of the Sacraments and the manner in which they produce their effects.

As we have seen, the Sacraments produce internal grace.[1] The question now arises whether they cause this effect *ex opere operato, i. e.* by the work performed, independently of the merits of minister and recipient, and if so, whether they are to be regarded as the physical or as the moral causes of the grace they confer.

The first question involves an article of faith, the second merely a free opinion, on which theologians may and do differ.

[1] *V*. Ch. II, Sect. *2, supra.*

SECTION I

THE EFFICACY OF THE SACRAMENTS EX OPERE OPERATO

1. THE PROTESTANT SACRAMENTAL SYSTEM AND THE DEFINITION OF THE COUNCIL OF TRENT.
—The Protestant Reformers regarded the Sacraments merely as "exhortations designed to excite faith" (Luther) or as "tokens of the truthfulness of the divine promises" (Calvin) or as "mere signs of Christian profession by which the faithful testify that they belong to the Church of Jesus Christ" (Zwingli and the Socinians). The Council of Trent condemned these erroneous opinions and solemnly defined that the Sacraments are means of grace, which produce the grace they "contain" *ex opere operato* in all those who do not place an obstacle.

a) The sacramental system of the Reformers flowed quite logically from their false idea of justification. If justification really consisted in a merely extrinsic application of the merits of Jesus Christ, which cover the sinner and hide his wickedness from the sight of God, and if faith were the only thing whereby man is justified,[2]

2 Cfr. Pohle-Preuss, *Grace, Actual and Habitual*, pp. 285 sqq., St. Louis 1915.

it would be perfectly proper to regard the Sacraments in the sense of Luther as a kind of acted sermons calculated to sustain the faith (*signa paraenetica* or *concionatoria*). Quite consistently, therefore, did the Augsburg Confession " condemn those who hold that the Sacraments work justification *ex opere operato*." [3]

Calvin, in keeping with his theory of " absolute predestination," declared that " the Sacraments are given to us by God as bearers of good tidings are sent by men," and that they merely announce and declare the gifts we owe to the liberality of God, or at most are pledges calculated to make us sure of these gifts.[4]

Zwingli was even more radical. He taught that the Sacraments are merely discriminating labels of Christian profession, separating the followers of Christ from unbelievers. " It would be difficult to go any further," rightly observes Pourrat, " and to lower still more the value of the Sacraments of the New Law." [5] Zwingli's conception of the Sacraments was later adopted by the Socinians.[6]

b) Against these heretical errors the Council of Trent insisted on the objective efficacy of the Sacraments, declaring that the subjective activity of the recipient is merely dispositive in character, and defining the causality of the Sacraments as a true *efficacia ex opere operato*.

3 Art. 13, quoted in Müller, *Die symbolischen Bücher*, p. 42: " *Damnant illos qui docent, quod sacramenta ex opere operato iustificant.*" On the changes in Luther's teaching see Pesch, *Praelect. Dogmat.*, Vol. VI, 3rd ed., p. 46.

4 Calvin, *Instit.*, IV, 14, §12: " *Hoc unicum est sacramentorum officium, ut Dei promissiones oculis nostris spectandas subiiciant et earum nobis sint pignora.*"

5 Pourrat, *Theology of the Sacraments*, p. 181.

6 On the development of the doctrine among Protestants see Herzog's *Realenzyklopädie*, Vol. XVII, 3rd ed., pp. 369 sqq., Leipzig 1906 (condensed in *The New Schaff-Herzog Encyclopedia of Religious Knowledge*, Vol. X, pp. 143 sq., New York 1911).

" If any one saith that the Sacraments of the New Law
do not contain the grace which they signify; or that
they do not confer that grace on those who do not place
an obstacle thereunto; as though they were merely outward signs of grace or justice received through faith,
and certain marks of the Christian profession, whereby
believers are distinguished among men from unbelievers,
let him be anathema." [7]   Therefore, the Sacraments are
more than signs instituted for the purpose of nourishing
the faith.[8]   They infallibly confer grace, not only on the
predestined, but on " all who receive them rightly." [9]
Their efficacy is *ex opere operato, i. e.* derived from the objective value of the rite itself, not from the merits of
minister or subject.[10]

2. The Dogmatic Teaching of the Church Explained and Defended.

—It is an article of
faith, as we have seen, that the Sacraments of
the New Law produce their effects *ex opere
operato;* whence it may be concluded that the

---

[7] *Conc. Trident.*, Sess. VII, can.
6: " *Si quis dixerit, sacramenta
Novae Legis non continere gratiam
quam significant aut gratiam ipsam
non ponentibus obicem* [*i. e. dis-
positis*] *non conferre, quasi signa
tantum externa sint acceptae per
fidem gratiae et iustitiae et notae
quaedam christianae professionis,
quibus apud homines discernuntur
fideles ab infidelibus, anathema sit.*"
(Denzinger-Bannwart, n. 849).

[8] *Conc. Trident.*, Sess. VII, can.
5: " *Si quis dixerit, haec sacramenta propter solam fidem nutrien-
dam instituta fuisse, anathema sit.*"
(Denzinger-Bannwart, n. 848).

[9] *Conc. Trident.*, Sess. VII, can.

7: " *Si quis dixerit, non dari
gratiam per huiusmodi sacramenta
semper et omnibus, quantum est ex
parte Dei, etiamsi rite ea suscipiant,
sed aliquando et aliquibus, anathema sit.*" (Denzinger-Bannwart,
n. 850).

[10] *Conc. Trident.*, Sess. VII, can.
8: " *Si quis dixerit, per ipsa Novae
Legis sacramenta ex opere operato
non conferri gratiam, sed solam
fidem divinae promissionis ad gratiam consequendam sufficere, anathema sit.*" (Denzinger-Bannwart,
n. 851). On the topic of this subdivision cfr. Bellarmine, *De Sacramentis in Genere*, I, 13-17.

formulas employed in their administration are not merely exhortatory, but consecratory. It is also of faith that, in order to receive the Sacraments unto justification, the sinner must receive them "rightly," that is, with the proper disposition. We shall set forth this teaching in three distinct theses.

Thesis I: The Sacraments are really and truly efficient causes, producing their effects ex opere operato, independently of the merits and disposition of the recipient.

This proposition is *de fide*.

Proof. The Council of Trent defines the efficacy of the Sacraments both negatively and positively: negatively, by pointing out that they are not merely outward signs instituted for the sake of nourishing the faith, or marks of Christian profession; positively, by declaring that they "contain the grace which they signify" and confer it "in virtue of the act performed" (*ex opere operato*).

To say that the Sacraments produce their effects independently of the disposition of the recipient, does not mean that they require no moral preparation on his part. On the contrary, we know that such preparation is necessary to enable the Sacraments to produce the full effect required for justification.[11] According to the Tridentine Council, this necessary preparation consists in " not plac-

11 Cfr. Pohle-Preuss, *Grace, Actual and Habitual*, pp. 285 sqq.

ing an obstacle to grace," *i. e.* in removing any previous indisposition opposed to the character of the respective Sacrament.

(1) That the performance of the sacramental rite not merely signifies but actually produces grace, can be shown from both Scripture and Tradition.

a) Sacred Scripture again and again points to the causal relation existing between the sacramental sign and grace. Cfr. John III, 5: "Unless a man be born again of water and the Holy Ghost, he cannot enter into the kingdom of God." [12] An analysis of this text shows that St. John ascribes spiritual rebirth (*i. e.* justification) to the element of Baptism as its instrumental cause; for the particle *"ex"* refers not only to the Holy Ghost, but likewise to the water: *"ex aqua et Spiritu Sancto."* As truly, therefore, as the spiritual rebirth of a man is caused principally by the Holy Ghost, so is it caused instrumentally by the water, and consequently, the water of Baptism exercises a causal influence on justification. In confirmation we may quote Tit. III, 5: "He saved us, by the laver of regeneration, and renovation of the Holy Ghost." [13] The very expression "laver of regeneration" proves the sac-

---

12 Ioa. III, 5: *" Nisi quis renatus fuerit ex aqua et Spiritu Sancto, non potest introire in regnum Dei."*

13 Tit. III, 5: *" Salvos nos fecit per lavacrum regenerationis et renovationis Spiritus Sancti."*

ramental efficacy of the baptismal water, and still more the phrasing of the passage: "He saved us *by* the laver of regeneration."

In other Biblical texts the ablative of instrument is used to denote the same fact. Cfr. Eph. V, 26: ". . . cleansing it, by the laver of water in the word of life," [14] where the Apostle evidently means that a bath of water in the word of life possesses the power of cleansing the interior man, *i. e.* justifying him. Cfr. Acts XXII, 16: "Be baptized, and wash away thy sins." [15] When a physician orders a patient to take a medicinal bath, that he may be cured of disease, the bath becomes a means of regaining health. If Baptism, therefore, effects the forgiveness of sins, the former is related to the latter as a cause to its effect. Cfr. Acts II, 38: ". . . be baptized every one of you in the name of Jesus Christ, for the remission of your sins." [16] Note that those to whom these words were addressed by St. Peter, had already embraced the faith and were sorry for their sins.[17]

A similar argument can be construed for the other Sacraments—Confirmation, Acts VIII, 17; the Holy Eucharist, John VI, 57 sqq.; Penance,

---

[14] Eph. V, 26: "*Mundans lavacro aquae* (τῷ λουτρῷ τοῦ ὕδατος) *in verbo vitae.*"

[15] Act. XXII, 16: "*Baptizare et ablue peccata tua.*"

[16] *Ibid.*, II, 38: "*Baptizetur unusquisque vestrum in nomine Iesu Christi in remissionem peccatorum vestrorum.*"

[17] Cfr. Acts II, 37.

John XX, 22 sq.; Extreme Unction, James V, 14 sq.; Holy Orders, 2 Tim. I, 6.[18]

The Scriptural texts cited by Protestants to show the part faith takes in the process of justification are in no wise incompatible with the efficacy of the Sacraments *ex opere operato*. A careful analysis of these texts shows that they apply either to objective belief, *i. e.* the doctrine of Christ (the Gospel) [19] or to subjective faith, *i. e.* belief in the word of God.[20] In the first-mentioned case faith, *i. e.* the object of faith, justifies in so far as divine revelation puts at man's disposal all the means of justification, including the Sacraments.[21] In regard to texts that fall under the latter category it must be remarked that the subjective faith of justification is either *formata* or *informis, i. e.* a faith vivified by perfect charity or not vivified at all, and therefore dead. The *fides formata* justifies of itself, while the *fides informis* remains inefficacious until it has absorbed the remaining dispositive acts and achieved its consummation in the Sacrament.[22] In both cases we are dealing with a true causality of faith in the matter of justification, though this causality is of a different order than that of the Sacraments. Faith, as such, is merely a dispositive cause of justification,— part of its *causa materialis,*— whereas a Sacrament is a true efficient cause, though, of course, dependent for its efficacy on the disposition of the recipient, as upon a condition, because " wet wood cannot catch fire." [23]

18 For more detailed information on this point we refer the reader to the special treatises on the different Sacraments.

19 Cfr. Rom. I, 16; 1 Cor. XV, 1 sq.; 1 Pet. I, 23 sqq.; Jas. I, 18.

20 Cfr. Heb. XI, 6.

21 Cfr. Matth. XVI, 16 sq.

22 Cfr. Pohle-Preuss, *Grace, Actual and Habitual*, pp. 298 sq.

23 That the fiduciary faith of the Lutherans does not justify, but is an unscriptural figment, has been demonstrated in our treatise on Grace,

b) The Fathers are clear and positive in their teaching on the efficacy of the Sacraments. Their expressions concerning Baptism, which are characteristic of their whole attitude on the subject, may be grouped around several fundamental conceptions.

The Fathers are filled with admiration at the power of the water which, in the Sacrament of Baptism, produces interior holiness. " Is it not wonderful," says Tertullian, " that death should be washed away by bathing? But it is the more to be believed if the wonderfulness be the reason it is *not* believed. For of what kind does it behoove divine works to be, except that they be above all wonder? We also ourselves wonder, but it is because we believe." [24] St. Cyril of Jerusalem says in an address to his neophytes: " Each one of you was asked whether he believes in the name of the Father and of the Son and of the Holy Ghost. You have pronounced the salutary profession, you have been thrice immersed in the water, thereby symbolizing Christ's stay of three days in the tomb. For just as our Saviour spent three days and three nights in the bowels of the earth, so you, in emerging the first time from the water, have imitated the first day, and in being immersed, the night which Christ spent in the earth, . . . and at the same moment you died and were born again; that salutary

---

pp. 286 sqq. For a more detailed treatment we must refer the student to Franzelin, *De Sacramentis in Genere*, thes. 8. Other objections from Holy Scripture are effectively refuted by De Augustinis, *De Re Sacramentaria*, Vol. I, 2nd ed., pp. 84 sqq.

24 *De Bapt.*, c. 2: " *Nonne mirandum est, lavacro dilui mortem? Atqui eo magis credendum, si quia mirandum est, idcirco non creditur. Qualia enim decet esse opera divina nisi super omnem admirationem? Nos quoque ipsi miramur, sed quia credimus.*"

wave became alike your grave and your mother . . . O
new and unheard-of species of things!" [25]

The power thus inherent in the baptismal laver is a
truly divine power unto justification. "You have seen
water," says Pseudo-Ambrose, "but not all water heals;
that water heals which has the grace of Christ. The
element is one thing, the consecration another; the work
is one thing, the operation another. The work is the
water, the operation is of the Holy Ghost. The water
does not heal unless the Spirit descends and consecrates
it." [26] Similarly Cyril of Alexandria: "As water
poured into a kettle, if exposed to intense heat, absorbs
the power thereof, so the material water, through the operation of the [Holy] Spirit, is changed into a divine, un-
speakable virtue and sanctifies all on whom it is found." [27]

The influence of the baptismal water is compared to
that of the maternal womb. Thus St. Chrysostom says:
"What the womb is for the child, that is water for the
faithful Christian; for in water he is shaped and formed.
In the beginning it was said (Gen. I, 20): 'Let the waters bring forth the creeping creature having life.' But
since the Lord descended into the Jordan, the water no
longer brings forth creeping creatures, but rational souls
that bear within themselves the Holy Ghost. . . . What is
formed in the womb, requires time. Not so in the water:
there everything happens in an instant." [28] St. Leo the
Great compares the baptismal font to the virginal womb
of Mary: "The origin which [Christ] took in the womb

25 *Cat. Myst.*, 2, c. 4.

26 *De Sacrament.*, I, 5: "*Vidisti
aquam, sed non aqua omnis sanat;
sed aqua sanat quae habet gratiam
Christi. Aliud est elementum, aliud
consecratio; aliud opus, aliud operatio. Aqua opus est, operatio Spiri-*
*tus Sancti est. Non sanat aqua, nisi
Spiritus descenderit et aquam illam
consecraverit.*"

27 *In Ioa.*, l. II (Migne, *P. G.*,
LXXIII, 243).

28 *Hom. in Ioa.*, 6, n. 1 (Migne,
P. G., LIX, 153).

of the Virgin, He placed in the font of Baptism. He gave
to the water what He had given to His mother. For the
virtue of the Most High and the overshadowing of the
Holy Spirit, which caused Mary to bring forth the
Saviour, also causes the water to regenerate the believing [Christian]." [29]

The efficacy of Baptism does not depend on the personal
merits of the recipient. St. Augustine says: "Baptism
does not consist in the merits of those by whom it is administered, nor in the merits of those to whom it is administered, but in its own sanctity and truth, on account
of Him by whom it has been instituted, [it is] for the
perdition of those who use it badly and for the salvation
of those who use it well." [30] Tertullian attributes a
like efficacy to all the Sacraments. "The flesh is
washed off," he says, "in order that the soul may be
cleansed; the flesh is anointed, in order that the soul may
be consecrated; the flesh is signed, in order that the soul
may be fortified; the flesh is overshadowed by the imposition of hands, in order that the soul may be illuminated
by the Holy Spirit; the flesh is fed with the body and
blood of Christ, in order that the soul may be nourished
by God." [31]

---

[29] Serm. in Nativ. Dom., 5, c. 5:
"Originem quam sumpsit [Christus]
in utero virginis, posuit in fonte baptismatis. Dedit aquae quod dedit
matri. Virtus enim Altissimi et
obumbratio Spiritus Sancti, quae
fecit ut Maria pareret Salvatorem,
eadem facit ut regeneret unda credentem."

[30] Contr. Crescon., IV, 16, 19:
"Non eorum meritis, a quibus mi-
nistratur, nec eorum quibus mini-
stratur, constat baptismus, sed pro-
priâ sanctitate et veritate propter
eum, a quo institutus est, male utentibus ad perniciem, bene utentibus
ad salutem."

[31] De Resurrect. Carn., c. 8:
"Caro abluitur ut anima emaculetur,
caro ungitur ut anima consecretur,
caro signatur ut anima muniatur,
caro manus impositione adumbra-
tur ut et anima Spiritu illuminetur,
caro corpore Christi et sanguine
vescitur ut anima de Deo saginetur."
Cfr. Franzelin, De Sacram. in Genere, thes. 6; Bellarmine, De Sacram., II, 5-7.

c) The theological argument for our thesis is based partly on the practice of infant Baptism and partly on the fact that the Protestant doctrine entails absurd consequences.

α) If infant Baptism (*paedobaptismus*) blots out original sin by the infusion of sanctifying grace, this cannot be except on the supposition that Baptism produces its effects without regard to human merits. Hence the practice of infant Baptism furnishes an argument for the efficacy of the Sacraments *ex opere operato*. And since in the primitive Church Baptism was immediately followed by Confirmation and Communion, the administration of these two Sacraments to infants is likewise an argument to the same effect. That the belief in such efficacy of the Sacraments can be traced back to the Apostolic age, is plain from the statement of Origen [32] that infant Baptism was practiced at that time. The cogency of this inference is admitted by Harnack, who says that a "superstitious idea of Baptism" is found already in Tertullian [33] and Irenaeus,[34] and adds: "This appears also from the practice of infant Communion, which, though first attested by Cyprian, can hardly be of later origin than infant Baptism. Communion seemed equally indispensable with Baptism, and the child had just as much right to that magic celestial food as the adult." [35] This is a plain admission that the Catholic view of the efficacy of the Sacraments, as defined by the Tridentine Council, goes back to the first centuries of the Christian era, which is sufficient evidence that it is true.

β) That the Lutheran system of justification cannot

---

32 *In Epist. ad Rom.*, 5, 9.
33 *De Bapt.*, c. 18.
34 *Adv. Haer.*, II, 22, 4.

35 Harnack *Lehrbuch der Dogmengeschichte*, Vol. I, 3rd ed., p. 438.

consistently admit any Sacraments in the Catholic sense of the term, is convincingly demonstrated by the same Rationalist theologian: "Luther not only did away with the septenary number of the Sacraments,— that is the least thing he did,— but he upset the entire Catholic idea of the Sacraments by triumphantly demonstrating these three propositions: (1) that the Sacraments were instituted for the forgiveness of sins, and for no other purpose; (2) that '*non implentur dum fiunt, sed dum creduntur;*' (3) that they are a peculiar form of the saving Word of God (of the *promissio Dei* fulfilling itself), and consequently derive their power from the historic Christ. Carrying this teaching to its logical conclusions, Luther reduced the Sacraments to two (three), nay, at bottom to one, *viz.:* the Word of God." [36]

The question naturally suggests itself: If this is so, why do Protestants baptize their children? What is the use of Sacraments if they are so immensely inferior to preaching and have no reasonable purpose except perhaps to serve as an object-lesson for the ignorant? They do not even serve that purpose well. "According to this view," says Gutberlet, "the baptismal rite would most effectively fulfil its purpose of awaking the faith, if the preacher proclaimed the divine promise from the pulpit, while the sacristan ostentatiously washed each single *baptizandus* with as large a quantity of water as possible. The congregation would thus receive a more vivid impression of the purification signified by Baptism than if each person submitted to the operation himself. At all events it would not be necessary for each individual to be baptized. The public Baptism of one would lead hundreds and thousands to believe and be justified.

36 *Op. cit.*, Vol. III, 3rd ed., p. 72.

Such absurd conclusions are entailed by a denial of the objective efficacy of the Sacraments, a truth so clearly taught in Holy Scripture." [37]

If the "orthodox" Lutherans nevertheless persist in holding that sins are remitted in infant Baptism (though only in the sense of a mere covering up of the soul and hiding its wickedness from the sight of God), we can not but conclude that at heart they believe in the efficacy of Baptism *ex opere operato,* which Luther so vigorously rejected.

We must now more fully explain the meaning of the technical phrase *ex opere operato.*

(2) The traditional teaching of the Church regarding the efficacy of the Sacraments was, at the beginning of the thirteenth century, couched in the technical formula: *"Sacramenta operantur ex opere operato,"* which was later on officially adopted by the Council of Trent.

a) So far as we know the phrase occurs for the first time in the writings of Peter of Poitiers (d. 1204), who says: "The act of baptizing is not identical with Baptism, because it is an *opus operans,* while Baptism is an *opus operatum.*" [38] It was adopted by Pope Innocent III,[39] William of Auxerre,[40] Alexander of Hales,[41] Albert the Great,[42] and St. Bonaventure,[43] but was not yet in general use when St. Thomas wrote his commentary on

---

[37] *Dogmat. Theol.,* Vol. IV, p. 95.
[38] *Sent.,* P. 5, c. 6: "*Baptizatio . . . est aliud opus quam baptismus, quia est opus operans, sed baptismus est opus operatum.*"
[39] *De Myst. Missae,* III, 5.
[40] *Summa Aurea,* l. IV, art. 2.

[41] *Summa Theol.,* 4a, qu. 3, n. 4, art. 1.
[42] *Comment. in Sent.,* IV, dist. 1, art. 5.
[43] *Comment. in Sent.,* IV, dist. 1, p. 1, art. 1, qu. 5.

the *Liber Sententiarum,* for the Angelic Doctor says:
" By some the sacrament itself is called *opus operatum."* [44]

The grammatical opposition between *opus operans* and
opus operatum shows that in the former phrase *operari* is
used actively, in the latter passively. The use of the past
participle of a deponent verb in a passive sense is often met
with in conversational Latin and in the more elaborate
writings of classical authors, and hence there is no need
to seek for a different explanation, as Möhler did when he
suggested: " *ex opere operato, scilicet a Christo,* instead of
quod operatus est Christus." [45] Needless to say, the
theological sense of the formula is not to be deduced from
grammatical considerations but from the decrees of Trent.
The Tridentine Fathers wished to oppose the objective
character of the Sacraments as effective means of grace,
to the subjectivism of the Reformers, and with this
purpose in view defined the Catholic teaching as follows:
" If any one saith that by the said Sacraments of the
New Law grace is not conferred *ex opere operato,* but
that faith alone in the divine promises [*opus operantis
s. recipientis*] suffices for the obtaining of grace, let him
be anathema." [46] The meaning of the formula *ex opere
operato,* therefore, is plainly this: (1) that it is the correct
use of the sign instituted by Christ which confers the grace
of justification; (2) that the grace conferred is not derived from the merits of either the minister or the
recipient (*ex opere operantis*), though both the free
action of the former and the moral preparation of the
latter (if he be an adult) are required for the validity

44 *Comment. in Sent.,* IV, dist. 1,
art. 4: " *Ipsum sacramentum dicitur a quibusdam opus operatum."*
45 *Symbolism,* §28.
46 *Conc. Trident.,* Sess. VII, can.

8: " *Si quis dixerit, per ipsa Novae
Legis sacramenta ex opere operato
non conferri gratiam, sed solam
fidem* [*ex opere operantis*] . . .
sufficere, anathema sit."

and worthy reception of the Sacrament. To emphasize the last-mentioned requisite the Council adds that the Sacraments " confer grace on those who do not place an obstacle thereunto," and again : " As far as God's part is concerned, grace is . . . given through the . . . Sacraments always and to all men." [47] The free action of the minister is required, because without his combining matter and form with the corresponding intention (*opus operans*), there can be no *opus operatum*. On the other hand, the Sacrament is frustrated in its effects if the subject " places an obstacle " (*obex gratiae*) by not having the right disposition. On this point the teaching of the Council regarding justification [48] applies in full force. It is as necessary to prepare for the worthy reception of a Sacrament as it is to prepare for justification.[49]

b) This explanation is sufficient to disprove both the intentional and unintentional misunderstandings of the formula *ex opere operato* found in many Protestant controversial works, beginning with the Augsburg Confession.[50] The oft-repeated accusation, invented by Calvin and Chemnitz, that Catholics attribute " a magic effect " to the Sacraments, is based on the mistaken assumption that the Church requires neither faith nor a good impulse of the heart for their worthy reception even in the case of lay adults. One expects " a magic effect " only from

47 *Conc. Trident.*, Sess. VII, can. 6 : ". . . *sacramenta conferre gratiam non ponentibus obicem.*"— Can. 7 : ". . . *dari gratiam per sacramenta semper et omnibus, quantum est ex parte Dei.*"

48 Sess. VI, can. 6-7.

49 Cfr. Pohle-Preuss, *Grace, Actual and Habitual*, pp. 272 sqq.

50 Art. 13, n. 18 : " *Damnamus totum populum scholasticorum doctorum qui docent quod sacramenta non ponenti obicem conferant gratiam ex opere operato sine bono motu utentis. Haec simpliciter iudaica opinio est sentire, quod per caeremoniam iustificemur sine bono motu cordis, hoc est, sine fide.*" (Müller, *Die symbol. Bücher*, p. 204).

an inadequate natural agent or from the devil. Why should we look to the baptismal water for magical effects, since we attribute the regeneration of the soul principally to the Holy Ghost? The charge, made in the Augsburg Confession, that the Scholastics believed that the Sacraments confer grace *sine bono motu cordis et sine fide,* is no longer upheld in such a sweeping form by Protestant controversialists, though they still insist that the Schoolmen, from Scotus to Gabriel Biel, regarded every good impulse of the heart as superfluous, until Gropper and Bellarmine, pressed by the Reformers, laid greater stress upon the moral coöperation of the recipient. The simple truth is that the Scholastics, in treating of the Sacraments, assumed the Catholic teaching on justification to be well known, and by no means neglected to insist on the need of a proper preparation. The very passages adduced by our opponents from Scotus and Biel, though badly mutilated, clear these writers of the charge made against them. Scotus, in teaching that " a Sacrament of the New Law confers grace by virtue of the act performed (*ex virtute operis operati*), so that there is not required a good impulse of the heart which would merit grace, but it is sufficient that the recipient place no obstacle," [51] clearly presupposes not only a proper disposition,[52] but the removal of obstacles, *i. e.* due preparation on the part of the recipient. What the " Subtle Doctor " denies is simply and solely that it is by the *bonus motus* required for the worthy reception of a Sacrament that man merits the grace of justification. This is also the plain teaching of

[51] *Comment. in Sent.,* IV, dist. I, qu. 6, n. 10: "*Sacramentum Novae Legis ex virtute operis operati confert gratiam, ita quod non requiritur ibi bonus motus qui mereatur gratiam, sed sufficit quod suscipiens non ponat obicem.*"

[52] *Comment. in Sent.,* IV, dist. I, qu. 4: ". . . *aliqualem displicentiam de peccatis et propositum cavendi de cetero.*"

Gabriel Biel.[53] The Protestant objection against the Schoolmen really strikes at Luther's doctrine that justification is wrought by faith alone. There can surely be no worse preparation for justification than to follow the advice: "*Pecca fortiter, crede fortius.*" [54]

Thesis II: Since the Sacraments produce their effects **ex opere operato,** the words which constitute their "form" have not merely the value of an exhortation but are in a true sense consecratory.

This proposition embodies a theological conclusion.

Proof. Whereas in the Lutheran theory of justification the sacramental form is a mere *verbum concionale, i. e.* purely an exhortation, Catholics regard it as a *verbum consecratorium, i. e.* as sanctifying. The Tridentine Council declares: "If anyone saith that these Sacraments were instituted for the sake of nourishing faith alone, let him be anathema." And: "If anyone saith that the Sacraments of the New Law do not contain the grace which they signify, or that they do not confer that grace on those who do not place an obstacle thereunto, as though they were merely outward signs of grace or justice received

---

[53] For a defense of Biel see Bellarmine, *De Sacram.,* II, 1, and Franzelin, *De Sacram. in Gen.,* thes. 7.

[54] Cfr. Schanz, *Die Lehre von den hl. Sakramenten,* pp. 131 sqq., Freiburg 1893; Heinrich-Gutberlet, *Dogmatische Theologie,* Vol. IV, § 487; J. Mausbach, *Die kath. Moral,* *ihre Methoden, Grundsätze und Aufgaben,* 2nd ed., pp. 135 sqq., Cologne 1902 (English tr., New York 1914); A. Seitz, *Die Heilsnotwendigkeit der Kirche nach der altchristlichen Literatur bis zur Zeit des hl. Augustinus,* pp. 267 sqq., Freiburg 1903.

through faith, and certain marks of the Christian profession, whereby believers are distinguished among men from unbelievers; let him be anathema." [55]

Of course the Catholic Church does not exclude the exhortatory element. It is evident from the significant ceremonies surrounding their administration, that the Sacraments are intended also as means of nourishing the faith and as outward pledges of the divine promise of forgiveness. But this purpose is secondary. The primary object of the Sacraments is practical sanctification, not theoretical instruction. They are above all *signa practica et efficacia gratiae,* and only secondarily *signa theoretica concionalia* in the meaning previously explained.[56] In the light of this explanation it is impossible to accept the Modernist contention that " the Sacraments are designed solely to recall to man's memory the everlasting and beneficent presence of the Creator." [57]

a) If we consider Baptism and the Holy Eucharist,—the only two Sacraments which Protestants have retained,—we find that the words of institution, as spoken by our Divine Saviour, do not contain a "sermon of faith" nor a "divine promise," but are primarily and principally designed to consecrate the natural elements of water, bread, and wine, in such wise that "thing" and "word" become the matter and form of an external sign which symbolizes and effects internal grace.[58]

55 Sess. VII, can. 5 and 6.   57 Denzinger-Bannwart, n. 2041.
56 *V. supra,* p. 14.   58 *V. supra,* Ch. II, Sect. 1.

If the Sacraments had for their main object to nourish the faith or to inspire trust in the divine promises, as Protestants assert, it would be more appropriate, in administering Baptism, to employ the words: " Unless a man be born again of water and the Holy Ghost, he cannot enter into the kingdom of God," [59] and in giving Communion, the text: " He that eateth my flesh, and drinketh my blood, hath everlasting life: and I will raise him up in the last day." [60]   As a matter of fact, if these words were employed, there would be no Sacrament, because the divinely instituted form of Baptism is: " I baptize thee," etc., whilst that of the Consecration runs: " This is my body," etc.   Note, also, that St. Paul draws a sharp distinction between baptizing and preaching the Gospel: " Christ sent me not to baptize, but to preach the gospel." [61]

b) For the teaching of the Fathers, see Thesis I, *supra*.

Harnack says of Luther: " He showed that even the most enlightened among the Fathers had but hazy notions on this, the most important point of all [*i. e.* that the word of God is the only Sacrament].   Augustine has much to say about the sacrament, but very little about the word, and the Scholastics have made the matter still more obscure.   Luther attacks both the magic of the *opus operatum* and the disparity of the salutary effect of the Sacraments according to the disposition of the recipient. . . . He destroys the convenient, yet so important notion of ' vehicles of grace,' and puts into the Sacrament the living Christ, who as *Christus praedi-*

[59] John III, 5.
[60] John VI, 55.
[61] 1 Cor. I, 17: "*Non enim misit me Christus baptizare, sed evangelizare.*" (On St. Paul's teaching see MacRory's Commentary, Dublin 1915).

catus subdues the old man and awakes the new." [62]   If Augustine " says so much about the sacrament and so little about the word," as Harnack alleges, how comes it that he is constantly quoted in support of the Lutheran theory that the sacramental form is purely exhortatory?   But even here it is a mere straw at which our adversaries grasp. St. Augustine teaches: " ' Now you are clean because of the word I have spoken to you.'   Why does He [Christ] not say: You are clean because of the Baptism by which you have been washed?   Why does He say: because of the word which I have spoken to you, unless it be for the reason that the word cleanses also in the water? Take away the word, and what is the water but mere water?   The word is added to the element, and there is a sacrament, which itself is as a visible word.   Whence does this water receive such virtue that it touches the body and cleanses the heart, unless through the operation of the word, not because it is spoken, but because it is believed. For in the very word itself the transient sound is one thing, the virtue that remains, another. . . . This word of faith has such power in the Church of God that through him who believes, offers up, blesses and washes, it cleanses even the smallest infant, although as yet unable to believe with the heart unto justice and to profess the faith with the mouth unto salvation." [63]   The very fact that Augus-

---

[62] *Lehrbuch d. Dogmengeschichte*, Vol. III, 3rd ed., p. 72, Freiburg 1896.

[63] *Tract. in Ioa.*, 20, n. 3: " *Iam vos mundi estis propter verbum quod locutus sum vobis. Quare non ait: Mundi estis propter baptismum quo loti estis, sed ait: Propter verbum quod locutus sum vobis, nisi quia et in aqua verbum mundat? Detrahe verbum et quid est aqua nisi aqua? Accedit ver-bum ad elementum et fit sacramentum etiam ipsum tamquam visibile verbum. Unde ista tanta virtus aquae, ut corpus tangat et cor abluat nisi faciente verbo, non quia dicitur, sed quia creditur? Nam et in ipso verbo aliud est sonus transiens, aliud virtus manens. . . . Hoc verbum fidei tantum valet in Ecclesia Dei, ut per ipsam credentem, offerentem, benedicentem, tingentem etiam tantillum mundet in-*

tine attributes to the " word " in conjunction with water such a wonderful power to cleanse the heart, even in the case of infants who have not yet attained the use of reason, shows that he derives the efficacy of Baptism from the rite performed (*ex opere operato*), not from the word as preached or from the subjective faith of the recipient. Hence, the " word of faith," in the passage quoted, is simply the baptismal formula, which, conjointly with the material element, constitutes the Sacrament, consecrates the *materia,* and at the same time embodies the " objective faith," *i. e.* the baptismal symbol.[64]

Thesis III: The efficacy of the Sacraments ex opere operato by no means excludes, but rather presupposes, a proper diposition on the part of the recipient.

The proof for this thesis will be found in Ch. IV, Sect. 2, *infra.* Cfr. also Thesis I, *supra.* Regarding the influence which the disposition of the recipient exerts on the measure of grace he receives, see Ch. II, Sect. 2, Art 1, Thesis III, *supra.*

fantem, quamvis nondum valentem corde credere ad iustitiam et ore confiteri ad salutem."

64 For a more exhaustive treatment of the argument from Tradition consult Franzelin, *De Sacram. in Gen.,* thes. 9, schol. 2; De Augustinis, *De Re Sacram.,* Vol. I, 2nd ed., pp. 163 sqq.

SECTION 2

WHETHER THE SACRAMENTS ARE PHYSICAL
OR MORAL CAUSES OF GRACE

1. STATE OF THE QUESTION.—The Sacraments, as we have shown, produce their effects *ex opere operato*. But how, in what manner? Is their efficacy physical, or purely moral, or both?

a) A moral cause (*causa moralis*) is one which, through the exercise of some influence operating through the intellect or emotions (a command, counsel, request) determines a rational being to action. The death of our Saviour was such a cause, in so far as it moved God to have mercy on humanity. Let it not be objected that the effective intercession of one person for another, such as that of the crucified Redeemer for us, is a final rather than an efficient cause, because it constitutes a true motive to attain a desired end. Every moral cause operates because of its presence (*quia est*), whereas a final cause operates in order that something else may come into being (*ut sit*). The passion and death of Christ being the "meritorious cause of justification," [1] is certainly not the physical cause of our salvation; but, on the other hand, it is more than a final cause, and consequently, it is the true moral cause of justification.

A physical cause (*causa physica*) is one which by its

---

[1] *Conc. Trident.*, Sess. VII, cap. 7.

action produces an immediate effect, as when a carpenter makes a table.

Both physical and moral causes are either principal (*causa principalis*) or instrumental (*causa instrumentalis*). What a saw is in the hands of a carpenter, that, *mutatis mutandis,* an ambassador is in the hands of his government. Carpenter and government are principal, saw and ambassador instrumental causes.

A cause, no matter whether physical or moral, principal or instrumental, is both really and logically distinct from a condition. A condition, even though it be indispensable (*conditio sine qua non*), is merely something that is required in order that something else may exist, but it has no part in producing its effects. A cause is also distinct from a mere occasion (*occasio, causa occasionalis*), *i. e.* a conjunction which facilitates an effect, but is not necessary to its production.[2]

b) In applying these metaphysical concepts to the Sacraments, we must first of all guard against the false notion (unjustly attributed by Dom. Soto to Alexander of Hales, St. Bonaventure, Duns Scotus, and other Scholastic theologians), that the Sacraments are merely a *conditio sine qua non,* or the occasion, of sanctifying grace.

To say that the Sacraments are merely the condition or occasion of the bestowal of sanctifying grace involves a practical denial of the dogma that they produce their effects *ex opere operato,* and destroys the essential distinction between the Sacraments of the Old and those

2 Cfr. John Rickaby, S. J., *General Metaphysics,* pp. 339 sqq. (Stonyhurst Series).

of the New Law. The principle that the Sacraments are true *signa efficacia* must be so firmly upheld that, if it were demonstrated that as moral causes they would be no more than mere " *conditiones* " or " *occasiones,*" we should prefer to admit that their efficacy is physical, even though this theory involves some difficulties. For this reason it is of the greatest importance to prove that the sacramental signs are at least true moral causes of grace (Thesis I). In the case of some of the Sacraments, their moral operation is perhaps supplemented by a physical influence. This is true especially of the Holy Eucharist.[3] In the case of the other Sacraments it is preferable to assume a purely moral causality, as weighty arguments can be alleged against the theory of physical causation (Thesis II).

Before discussing this difficult problem it is important to establish accurately the state of the question. Assuming, what is self-evident, that the Sacraments as such are merely instruments (*causae instrumentales*) in the hand of God, and that God, as their *causa principalis,* physically produces sanctifying grace in the soul, the fundamental problem at issue may be formulated as follows: Does the external sign receive from God a peculiar supernatural power enabling it physically to produce sanctifying grace in the soul, either by a quality inherent in the rite, as Billuart and the Thomists contended, or by an external stimulation of the *potentia obedientialis* in the soul, as Suarez held? By formulating the question thus we avoid the ambiguity involved in the assertion that the Divine Omnipotence, as embodied and included in the sacramental sign, physically produces grace (Viva), or that the Holy Ghost exerts a physical causality in the applica-

---

3 See the treatise on the Holy Eucharist.

tion of the external sign (Berti). These assertions, correct enough in themselves, do not touch the point at issue. The problem to be decided is *whether or not the sacramental sign as such, i. e. as an instrument distinct from the Divine Omnipotence and from the Holy Ghost, exerts a physical efficacy after the manner of a physical cause.*

2. DOGMATIC THESES.—If it can be shown that the sacramental signs are endowed with a true, though purely moral causality, we may, without trenching on the dogmatic teaching of the Church, set aside the theory that they are physical causes of grace. Taking this ground will enable us to shatter the absurd Protestant contention that the Church attributes a sort of magic efficacy to her Sacraments.

Thesis I: All the Sacraments, as acts of their invisible author and chief minister, Jesus Christ, by virtue of their immanent dignity, move God to the (physical) production of grace, and hence exert at least a moral causality.

This proposition may be technically qualified as *communis.*

Proof. Even those theologians [4] who assert the physical efficacy of the Sacraments, do not deny their moral efficacy. Others [5] content themselves with upholding the moral efficacy of the Sacraments, without fear lest they be thereby de-

[4] Suarez, Gonet, and Gutberlet.

[5] De Lugo (*De Sacram. in Genere,* disp. 4, sect. 4), Franzelin (*De Sacram.,* thes. 10 sq.), Chr. Pesch, Sasse, Tepe, *et al.*

prived of the "mysterious" element in their operation.[6] Indeed, is it not a profound mystery that
God allows Himself to be moved by an external
sign to bestow sanctifying grace?

The moral efficacy of the Sacraments is sufficiently secured by two conditions: first, that the
sign instituted by Christ, according to moral estimation, is considered as filled with the merits
of the passion and death of Christ, and secondly,
that the sacramental act of the human minister
is looked upon as performed by our Divine
Saviour Himself. From these two elements
the sacramental rite receives an objective dignity
which raises it far above its natural meaning, constitutes it the moral cause of the bestowal of
grace, and renders it independent of the spiritual
condition of the minister.

a) The argument from Sacred Scripture may
be formulated as follows: Christ's passion is
the moral, because it is the meritorious cause of
justification.[7] Consequently, and *a fortiori,*
the Sacraments, being a mere application of the
merits of the passion, are only the moral cause
of justification. The Sacraments derive their
efficacy from their immediate relation, not only
to the blood of Christ,[8] but likewise to His sacred

6 This fear is entertained by Atz-
berger and Gihr.

7 Cfr. Rom. V, 10; Eph. I, 7; 1
John I, 7; Apoc. I, 5, etc.

8 Cfr. Col. I, 19 sq.; Heb. IX, 13
sq.; 1 Pet. I, 2, etc.

Person, in whose name and as whose representative the human minister acts,[9] and thus they cannot be merely conditions or occasions of grace.

1 Pet. III, 21, we read: *"Salvos facit baptisma, non carnis depositio sordium, sed conscientiae bonae interrogatio* (ἐπερώτημα) *in Deum per resurrectionem Christi."* Our English Bible renders this text as follows: ". . . Baptism . . . now saveth you also: not the putting away of the filth of the flesh, but the examination of a good conscience towards God by the resurrection of Jesus Christ." Here the water of the Deluge, from which some were rescued according to the body, is opposed to the water of Baptism, through which all faithful Christians are saved according to the spirit, and Baptism is declared to be more than a " putting away of the filth of the flesh," *i. e.* more than a Levitic purification. Whence does Baptism derive its power of spiritual regeneration? First of all from " the resurrection of Jesus Christ," which term is here employed by synecdoche for the entire work of the Redemption.[10] St. Peter goes on to describe Baptism as συνειδήσεως ἀγαθῆς ἐπερώτημα εἰς Θεόν. The Greek word ἐπερώτημα in this connection can only mean " question " (*interrogatio*) or " petition " (*rogatio, petitio*), all other meanings — such as " vow " (*sponsio*) or " treaty " (*pactum*) — being excluded either for exegetical or lexicographical reasons. But the Latin rendering of the Vulgate, *" conscientiae bonae interrogatio,"* which is followed by our English Bible, evidently does not give the right sense. For to think of an examination of the *baptizandus* before Baptism would

9 Cfr. 1 Cor. I, 13, III, 4 sq., IV, 1.

10 Cfr. Pohle-Preuss, *Soteriology*, pp. 101 sqq.

be to confuse an accidental rite with the essence of the Sacrament, which the Apostle means to characterize. Consequently, ἐπερώτημα must here mean [11] a prayer or petition for a good conscience, *i. e.* a purified and regenerated soul.[12] Now prayer and petition belong to the category of moral causes, and consequently Baptism,— and all the other Sacraments *a pari,*— exert a moral efficacy.[13]

b) Tradition asserts the moral causality of the Sacraments wherever it speaks of the sacramental sign as "containing" the merits of Christ, who is the meritorious cause of our salvation, or refers to the human minister as a mere representative of the Redeemer.

In the former case a Sacrament produces its effects in the same way as the Precious Blood of Christ, *i. e.* as a moral cause; in the latter, the rite, conceived as an action, has the same dignity and power before God as if the Redeemer baptized, confirmed, consecrated,[14] absolved, etc., in person, employing the human minister merely as His instrument or agent.[15]

Needless to say, the human minister of a Sacrament must not be identified with its Divine Institutor and principal Administrator. The instrumental cause has its

11 Cfr. Matth. XVI, 1: ἐπερώτη-σαν = rogaverunt.

12 Cfr. John III, 5.

13 On 1 Pet. III, 21, see Hundhausen, *Das erste Pontifikalschreiben des Apostelfürsten Petrus,* Mainz 1873.

14 Cfr. the "*Hoc est corpus meum*" in the Canon of the Mass.

15 Cfr. St. Augustine, *Contr. Lit. Petil.,* III, 49, 50: "*Hic* [*i. e. Christus*] *est qui baptizat in Spiritu Sancto, nec, sicut Petilianus dicit, iam baptizare cessavit, sed adhuc id agit, non ministerio corporis, sed invisibili opere maiestatis.*" Both these momenta are also emphasized by St. Thomas (*v. supra,* p. 100, n.

own peculiar operation, which does not coincide with that of the principal cause. Therefore, all defects, such as moral unworthiness, neglect, faulty pronunciation of the form, etc., are imputable to the minister. If he were to mutilate the baptismal formula in some non-essential point, it would not be true to say: "The Lord has baptized wrongly." Nor would it be right to say with regard to Penance: "Christ confesses through the penitent." But it would be proper to say: "Christ absolves the sinner through the priest." Where the recipient himself has to furnish the matter of a sacrament, as in Confession, the form alone is the work of the human minister, and, in the last resort, of Christ. But even where both matter and form are furnished by the minister, it is not permissible to substitute Christ unconditionally for His minister, though in most cases, as in the administration of Baptism, Confirmation, Holy Orders, and Extreme Unction, this would generally be true. Not so, however, in the case of Matrimony, which is both a human contract and a mystic relation, and consequently limited to human beings, and hence it would be false to say: "Christ enters into the matrimonial state."[16]

c) To this may be added the following metaphysical considerations. The Sacraments derive their dignity from the merits and the ministerial action of Jesus Christ. Not, of course, from any merits acquired after His sacred passion or any new motive arising in His holy will. A Sacrament is merely an application of the exist-

6); cfr. Morgott, *Der Spender der hl. Sakramente nach der Lehre des hl. Thomas,* pp. 2 sqq., Freiburg 1886.

16 For the solution of other difficulties see De Augustinis, *De Re Sacramentaria,* Vol. I, 2nd ed., pp. 245 sqq.

ing merits of the Redeemer; but it is more than a
mere condition or occasion of grace.   It is a true
moral cause.   Let us illustrate our meaning by an
example.   A king grants a general amnesty to
all political offenders.   Though this act of itself
objectively includes all, nevertheless, petitions
submitted by the convicts severally may be a moral
cause of pardon, inasmuch as by these petitions
the king is moved to apply his general will of
showing mercy to each separate individual.
Other examples sometimes adduced by theologians are less appropriate.   Take, e. g., that of
"a man who, on presenting a leaden coin, receives,
by the king's command, a hundred pounds; not
as though the leaden coin, by any operation of its
own, caused him to be given that sum of money,
this being the effect of the mere will of the king."
St. Thomas, who cites this example, justly observes: "If we examine the question properly,
we shall see that according to the above mode
the Sacraments are mere signs; for the leaden
coin is nothing but a sign of the king's command
that this man should receive money." (S. Th.,
3a, qu. 62, art. 1.)   If the simile is really to illustrate the causality of the Sacraments, it must
be changed as follows: Man, in the Sacrament
which he receives, presents a gold coin, which,
on account of its intrinsic value, morally compels his sovereign to be liberal.   Melchior Cano

compares the recipient of a Sacrament to a man who, by submitting a list of the merits of Jesus Christ, compels God to give the promised grace as a *quid pro quo.* This example is somewhat more pertinent but still inadequate. Velasquez's contention that the moral causality of the Sacraments is owing to a merely impetratory influence is altogether unacceptable. The most satisfactory theory is the one we have adopted, *viz.:* that the objective dignity of the Sacraments is due partly to the fact that they embody the effects of the merits of Jesus Christ, and partly to the act of their principal minister, *i. e.* our Lord Himself.

Thesis II: The Sacraments are not physical causes of grace.

This proposition is held as "more probable" by the majority of Catholic theologians.

Proof.   The doctrine enunciated in our thesis is defended by the Scotists without exception, by Cano, Vasquez, De Lugo, Tournely, Franzelin, De Augustinis, Pesch, Tepe, and others, against almost the entire Thomist school and Suarez, Bellarmine, Ysambert, Drouin, Schäzler, Katschthaler, Oswald, Gutberlet, and Gihr. Since the latter group all unhesitatingly admit the moral causality of the Sacraments, whereby the doctrine of their efficacy *ex opere operato* is fully safeguarded, it is not easy to see why they should, in addition, adopt the theory of physical causality, which is both unprovable and unintelligible.

a) It is unprovable.   The Scriptural and Patristic arguments upon which these writers base their contention merely prove the efficacy of the Sacraments but nothing as to the manner in which it is exercised.   We may add, however, that the exaggerations (suggesting physical causality) upon which they lay so much stress may be welcome material in the defence of the real efficacy of the Sacraments,—in the same way as the hyperboles of St. John Chrysostom in regard to the real presence of Christ in the Holy Eucharist are often used in support of that dogma.

That such Biblical phrases as " born again of water," [17] " cleansing it by the laver of water," [18] " He saved us by the laver of regeneration," [19] etc., do not necessarily imply a physical, but may be understood of a moral efficacy, is evidenced by such parallel passages as : " Being born again not of corruptible seed, but incorruptible, by the word of God," [20] " We have redemption through his blood," [21] " Alms is that which purgeth away sins," [22] and so forth.   No doubt many Patristic

17 Ioa. III, 5: " Renatus . . . ex aqua."

18 Eph. V, 26: " Mundans lavacro aquae."

19 Tit. III, 5: " Salvos nos fecit per lavacrum regenerationis."

20 1 Pet. I, 23: " Renati non ex semine corruptibili, sed incorruptibili per verbum Dei vivi."

21 Eph. I, 7: " Habemus redemptionem per sanguinem eius."

22 Tob. XII, 9: " Elemosyna . . . ipsa est, quae purgat peccata."

expressions regarding the efficacy of the Sacraments are derived from physical phenomena, as *e. g.* the comparison of Baptism to water that engenders fish, or to the maternal womb developing a fœtus. But they are employed merely to prove the efficacy of the Sacraments, not to define the nature of that efficacy. Whenever the Fathers speak of physical causality as such, they refer it either to the *totum,* as the synthesis of "omnipotence and sign," or to the divine omnipotence alone, and thereby indirectly admit that the sign, as sign, produces its effects in a purely moral way.[23]

It is claimed that the surprise which the Fathers often betray at the mysterious power of the baptismal water would be inexplicable, had they held the efficacy of Baptism to be merely moral.[24] But the theory of moral causality leaves sufficient room for surprise and mystery. Is not justification through the instrumentality of a visible sign mysterious enough? Does not the fact that God makes His grace dependent on material elements challenge surprise and admiration?

b) The theory of physical causality is unintelligible. In itself, this would not be a sufficient reason for rejecting it; but it justifies us in demanding stringent proofs before admitting a new theological mystery.

Scotus [25] and some of his followers declare that it is impossible for a material element physically to produce

23 For the Patristic texts in proof of this statement see De Augustinis, *De Re Sacrament.,* Vol. I, 2nd ed., pp. 258 sqq.; Chr. Pesch, *Praelect. Dogmat.,* Vol. VI, 3rd ed., pp. 65 sq.

24 Cfr. Billuart, *De Sacram.,* diss. 3, art. 2.

25 *Comment. in Sent.,* IV, dist. 1, qu. 5.

supernatural effects. We would not go as far as that; but we do hold with De Lugo that matters of religious belief should not be unnecessarily rendered obscure or difficult.[26] The two principal arguments against the theory of physical causality are based on the nature of the sacramental rite and the revival of the Sacraments.

a) The whole sacramental sign never exists simultaneously. Either the sacramental form in its physical entity has passed away, as in the reception of the Holy Eucharist, or the matter is no longer present, as in the absolution of a penitent who has confessed his sins the day before he receives absolution. But even where matter and form coëxist, as they do *e. g.* in Baptism, the administration of the Sacrament requires time; that which physically existed at the beginning no longer exists in the end, and *vice versa.* Now it is a philosophical axiom that action supposes being, and consequently, nothing can produce physical effects unless it has a physical existence. Which part, then, of the sign produces the effect? Or does each part produce part of the effect? Is justification divisible? Does it arrive by parts? Clearly, here is a new mystery. To escape the force of this argument, Suarez [27] and others declare that the bestowal of grace is physically bound up with the last word or final syllable of the sacramental form. Why not with the last letter? — or, to be entirely consistent, with the last breath escaping from the mouth of the minister who pronounces the formula? If only a part of the sign is efficacious, what value has the remainder? Or, if it be admitted that what has physically passed away endures morally

---

26 *De Sacram.,* disp. 4, sect. 4, n. 35: "*Non debemus res nostrae fidei absque necessitate difficiliores et obscuriores reddere.*"

27 *De Sacrament.,* disp. 8, sect. 2, n. 15.

and produces moral effects, what reason is there to assume that it is precisely the last word or syllable of the form that becomes the physical instrument of grace? Then, again, there are cases in which the necessary conditions of physical efficacy are entirely absent, as in a marriage contracted by proxy. Who would assert that God causes the consent of a bride residing in New York to produce a physical effect in the soul of her husband in London, or *vice versa?* These and similar consequences entailed by the theory of physical causation provoke the scorn of infidels and help nothing towards clearing up the mysterious action of the Sacraments.[28]

β) The possibility of a revival of the Sacraments (*reviviscentia sacramentorum*) furnishes another convincing argument against the theory of physical causality. This argument may be briefly stated thus: The Sacraments frequently confer grace in an exclusively moral manner, as when Baptism is validly conferred on an unworthy subject and attains its efficacy only after the existing obstacle has been removed (*remoto obice*). If grace can be conferred by a purely moral influence in exceptional cases, why assume that it produces its ordinary effects by physical causation? Baptism, though physically past, effects in its unworthy subject, as soon as he acquires the proper disposition, spiritual regeneration and forgiveness of sins. This cannot be a physical effect, because the cause is no longer present when the effect sets in, as even Suarez admits.[29]

The contention of certain Thomists that the sacramental character is the physical medium of grace, is inadmissible. To produce grace is not the purpose of the

28 Cfr. Vasquez, *Comment. in Sent.*, III, disp. 123, c. 6.
29 *De Sacram.*, disp. 9, sect. 2, n. 20: "*In eo casu sacramentum praeteritum non concurrit per physicam efficientiam ad gratiam praestandam.*"

character, but of the Sacrament itself. Besides, there are Sacraments which, though they confer the sacramental character, are incapable of being revived. Where, for instance, is grace to find its physical medium in Matrimony? There is nothing left but to admit that it is truer and more probable to assume that those Sacraments which do not imprint a character on the soul produce their effects morally, not physically, when the obstacle is removed.[30] But if this be admitted in some cases, why not in all?

c) The attitude of St. Thomas is in dispute. Perhaps the Angel of the Schools, like St. Bonaventure,[31] favored neither opinion. It is safe to assume, however, that he regarded the Sacraments as moral, without denying that they are also physical, causes of grace. There is no contradiction in ascribing to the Sacraments such a twofold causality. If St. Thomas believed in the latter theory, he did not exclude the former, as is evidenced by his declaration that "The Sacraments of the Church derive their power especially from Christ's passion, the virtue of which is in a manner united to us by our receiving the Sacraments."[32] If the passion of our Lord is

30 Cfr. Gonet, *De Sacram.*, disp. 3, art. 3, §2, n. 81: "*Verior et probabilior est solutio ac doctrina aliorum Thomistarum asserentium, sacramenta quae non imprimunt characterem recedente fictione* [*i. e. remoto obice*] *non causare physice, sed moraliter.*"

31 *Comment. in Sent.*, IV, dist. 1,

p. 1, qu. 4: "*Nescio tamen, quae sit verior.*"

32 *Summa Theol.*, 3a, qu. 62, art. 5: "*Sacramenta Ecclesiae specialiter habent virtutem ex passione Christi, cuius virtus nobis quodammodo copulatur per susceptionem sacramentorum.*"

morally efficacious, the same must be true of its concrete embodiment and application through the sacramental sign.[33] In his earlier days St. Thomas held that the sacramental sign, on account of its inability to produce the substance of sanctifying grace,—this being reserved to the Divine Omnipotence,—effects in the soul only a kind of spiritual disposition (*dispositio spiritualis*) or ornament (*ornatus animae*) which, as *res* and *sacramentum,* is on a level with the sacramental character, and imperatively demands the infusion of sanctifying grace.[34] Whether he conceived this *dispositio* or *ornatus* as produced by physical or moral means, is open to debate. However, the fact that the Angelic Doctor does not mention this theory in the *Summa Theologica*[35] seems to prove that he attributed no particular importance to it. At any rate, since its rejection by Cardinal Cajetan, the theory has disappeared from the writings of the Thomists, who vigorously defend the physical causality of the Sacraments. The only reason why we mention it at all is that it has been recently revived by Cardinal Billot,[36] who holds that the Sacraments produce sanctify-

33 This argument is ably developed by Tepe, *Instit. Theol.,* Vol. IV, pp. 47 sq.

34 *Comment. in Sent.,* IV, dist. 1, qu. 1, art. 4. He was followed in this opinion by nearly all pre-Tridentine theologians,— Capreolus, Paludanus, Sylvester of Ferrara, etc.

35 It recurs, however, in his *Quaestiones Disp., De Potentia.*

36 *De Ecclesiae Sacramentis,* Vol. I, 4th ed., pp. 68 sqq., Rome 1907.

ing grace neither morally nor physically, but *efficienter dispositive, i. e.,* by creating in the soul a certain spiritual disposition, of the same kind as that which the ancients called *ornatus.* If this were true, the efficacy of the sacramental rite would be indirect,—an assumption which unduly depreciates the Sacraments. To this should be added the following consideration: The spiritual disposition produced in the soul by the Sacraments, according to Billot, is either a physical quality, or it is not. If it is, there is no essential distinction between those Sacraments that imprint a character and those that do not. If the *dispositio spiritualis* is not a physical quality of the soul, it can hardly be anything more than a moral claim to grace (*titulus gratiae*), and then the efficacy of the Sacraments is purely moral.

Scheeben's curious theory that the Sacraments produce their effects by a sort of "hyper-physical" efficacy, is too obscure to obtain general acceptance.[37]

READINGS:—*C. von Schäzler, *Die Lehre von der Wirksamkeit der Sakramente ex opere operato,* Munich 1860.— Bucceroni, *Commentarius de Sacramentorum Causalitate,* Paris 1889.—G. Reinhold, *Die Streitfrage über die physische oder moralische Wirksamkeit der Sakramente,* Vienna 1899.—*Heinrich-Gutberlet, *Dogmatische Theologie,* Vol. IV, § 485–491, Mainz 1901.— Gihr, *Die*

---

37 On the *ornatus animae* cfr. M. Buchberger, *Die Wirkungen des Bussakramentes nach der Lehre des hl. Thomas,* pp. 150 sqq., Freiburg 1901. For a defence of Billot's teaching see G. Van Noort, *De Sacramentis,* Vol. I, 2nd ed., pp. 48 sqq., Amsterdam 1910.

hl. Sakramente der kath. Kirche, Vol. I, 2nd ed., pp. 63 sqq., Freiburg 1902.— Pourrat, *La Théologie Sacramentaire,* pp. 85–184, Paris 1910 (English tr., *Theology of the Sacraments,* pp. 93–196, St. Louis 1914).— Möhler, *Symbolik,* § 28 sqq., 11th ed., Mainz 1890 (English tr. by J. B. Robertson, 5th ed., pp. 202 sqq., London 1906).— J. B. Röhm, *Konfessionelle Lehrgegensätze,* Vol. III, pp. 539 sqq., Hildesheim 1888.— B. J. Otten, *A Manual of the History of Dogmas,* Vol. II, St. Louis 1918, pp. 276 sqq., 472 sqq.

CHAPTER IV

THE MINISTER OF A SACRAMENT

The primary or principal minister (*minister primarius sive principalis*) of the Sacraments is our Lord and Saviour Jesus Christ.[1] Those whom He employs as His representatives are called secondary or instrumental ministers (*ministri secundarii sive instrumentales*).

---

1 *V. supra*, pp. 146 sqq.

SECTION 1

THE CONDITIONS OF VALID ADMINISTRATION

The conditions of the valid administration of a Sacrament depend partly on the qualification of the minister and partly on his interior disposition. The minister need not be in the state of grace, nor need he have the faith (negative disposition), but he must have the right intention (positive disposition).

ARTICLE 1

THE PERSON OF THE MINISTER

The combination of matter and form into a sacramental sign (*confectio*), and its application to the individual recipient (*administratio*),— two factors which, with the sole exception of the Holy Eucharist, invariably coincide, — require a minister who has the full command of reason. Hence lunatics, children, and others who have not the full use of reason are incapable of administering a Sacrament.[2]

Besides this there are several other requisites of valid administration.

[2] *Decretum pro Armenis:* " *Omnia sacramenta tribus perficiuntur, videlicet rebus tamquam materia, verbis tamquam forma et personâ ministri conferentis sacramentum cum intentione faciendi quod facit Ecclesia: quorum si aliquod desit, non perficitur sacramentum.*" (Denzinger-Bannwart, n. 695).

1. The Minister of a Sacrament Must be in the Wayfaring State.—This condition excludes the angels and the departed.   Christ conferred His powers upon living men,[3] and the Apostles in their turn chose living men for their successors.[4]   "It is those who inhabit the earth, and walk upon it," says St. Chrysostom, "who are called to administer heavenly things, and who have received a power which God has granted neither to the angels nor to the archangels."[5] This truth, so clearly inculcated by Sacred Scripture and Tradition, is entirely consonant with reason; for as the Sacraments are means of grace intended for the living, it is obvious that they must be administered by living agents.

True, certain Saints (e. g. St. Stanislaus Kostka) are said to have received Holy Communion through the medium of angels.   But Holy Communion is, so to speak, a permanent Sacrament, already consummated, and if some privileged Saint received it at the hands of an angel, this does not argue that the consecration of the species took place through the same agency.   Following the lead of St. Augustine,[6] Aquinas teaches: "As God did not bind His power to the Sacraments, so as to be unable to bestow the sacramental effect without conferring the Sacrament; neither did He bind His power to the ministers of the Church, so as to be unable to give angels power to administer the Sacraments."[7]

3 Cfr. Matth. XXVIII, 19; John XX, 22; Luke XXII, 19.

4 Cfr. 1 Cor. IV, 1 sqq.; Eph. IV, 8 sqq.

5 *De Sacerdotio*, III, 5.

6 *Contra Ep. Parmen.*, II, 15.

7 *Summa Theol.*, 3a, qu. 64, art. 7: " *Sicut Deus virtutem suam non*

It is well, however, to exercise great caution in regard to such alleged happenings. Thus the statement of Nicephorus Callistus,[8] that St. Amphilochius was consecrated by an angel, and that his fellow-bishops confirmed the act as valid, is open to serious objections. Such extraordinary reports must be established by incontrovertible evidence, lest the certainty of the sacramental economy be exposed to grave danger. Luther exceeded all bounds by asserting that the devil can validly baptize, consecrate, and absolve,[9]— a possibility which had been denied by St. Thomas Aquinas and Thomas of Argentina.[10]

2. THE MINISTER OF A SACRAMENT MUST BE A DULY QUALIFIED PERSON.—The Tridentine Council teaches against Luther: "If anyone saith that all Christians have power to administer the word and all the Sacraments, let him be anathema."[11]   It follows that, in order to be able to administer at least some of the Sacraments, a person must be specially qualified. Such qualification is imparted by the Sacrament of Holy Orders. The only two exceptions to this rule are Baptism and Matrimony.

The secondary minister in the administration of a Sacrament acts "*in persona Christi*,"[12] as Christ's per-

---

alligavit sacramentis, quin possit sine sacramentis effectum sacramentorum conferre, ita etiam virtutem suam non alligavit Ecclesiae ministris, quin etiam angelis possit virtutem tribuere ministrandi sacramenta."

8 *Hist. Eccles.*, XI, 20.

9 *Von der Winkelmesse und Pfaffenweihe*, 1533.

10 *Comment in Šent.*, IV, dist. 6, qu. 1, art. 1.

11 Sess. VII, can. 10: "*Si quis dixerit, Christianos omnes in verbo et omnibus sacramentis administrandis habere potestatem, anathema sit.*" (Denzinger-Bannwart, n. 853).

12 Cfr. 2 Cor. II, 10.

sonal representative. It stands to reason that not every man is such a special representative of Christ, but only he who has been expressly commissioned. In civil life an ordinary citizen cannot perform official acts unless he is duly authorized. The exception in favor of Baptism and Matrimony is apparent rather than real. The parties to a marriage, by entering into the matrimonial contract, do not become either civil officials or public ministers of Christ; they may be said to represent the person of Christ only in so far as they mutually administer the Sacrament to each other, but not in the full sense in which the term minister is used in regard to the other Sacraments.

The question is even simpler in respect of Baptism. Its solemn administration requires a bishop, priest or deacon; only in cases of urgent necessity can this Sacrament be conferred by a lay person, acting not as a public official of the Church, but merely as a private helper in need. According to Suarez [13] this is true even of priests when they baptize without the prescribed ceremonies in urgent cases. Luther claimed that every Christian is a priest, because St. Peter says: " You are a chosen generation, a kingly priesthood." [14] But 1 Pet. II, 9 by no means proves this contention. The priesthood in which all the faithful share is purely metaphorical, as appears from 1 Pet. II, 5: " Be you also . . . a holy priesthood, to offer up *spiritual* sacrifices." [15] If the term ἱεράτευμα (priesthood) were to be strictly interpreted in this passage, we should also have to take βασίλειον (kingly) in its literal sense, which is manifestly impossible.

13 *De Sacram.*, disp. 16, sect. 4.
14 1 Pet. II, 9: " *Vos autem genus electum, regale sacerdotium* (βασίλειον ἱεράτευμα)."

15 1 Pet. II, 5: ". . . *sacerdotium sanctum* (ἱεράτευμα ἅγιον), *offerre spirituales hostias.*"

3. No One Can Administer a Sacrament to Himself.

—The minister of a Sacrament and its recipient must be separate persons.

This requirement is based (1) on the nature of things, because in most instances it is impossible for the minister to apply the matter and form of a Sacrament to himself; (2) on the divine economy of grace, it having pleased God to make men dependent on one another; and (3) on Christ's positive command to His Apostles and their successors, to dispense the means of grace *to others*. The only exception is the Holy Eucharist, which can be administered and received by the same individual.

ARTICLE 2

REQUISITES OF VALID ADMINISTRATION

As the sacramental sign is the inanimate medium of grace,[16] so the minister is its animate instrument in the hands of Christ. Both together constitute the *instrumentum adaequatum gratiae*. The human minister, being a person, not only exercises an instrumental activity of his own, but is possessed of certain moral qualities. The question arises whether one who is in the state of mortal sin, or has lost the true faith, can validly administer the Sacraments. We will set forth the Catholic teaching on these points in two theses.

Thesis I: The validity of a Sacrament does not depend on the personal worthiness of the minister.

This proposition embodies an article of faith. Proof. The early Donatists asserted that a

16 *V.* Ch. III, *supra.*

minister, in order to confer a Sacrament validly, must be in the state of sanctifying grace. This teaching was revived in the Middle Ages by the Waldenses, the Fraticelli, the Albigenses, the Wiclifites, and the Hussites. Innocent III demanded of the Waldenses a profession of faith in which this error was expressly repudiated.[17] The Council of Constance (A. D. 1418) condemned Wiclif's assertion that a bishop or priest who is in the state of mortal sin can neither baptize nor consecrate nor confer holy Orders.[18] Lastly, the Council of Trent defined: "If anyone saith that a minister, being in mortal sin,— if he observe all the essentials which belong to the effecting or conferring of a Sacrament,—neither effects nor confers the Sacrament, let him be anathema."[19]

Our thesis cannot be proved from Sacred Scripture, but rests wholly on Tradition and reason.

a) The Church has always regarded the administration of a Sacrament in the state of mortal sin as a sacrilege, and insists on the personal sanc-

---

17 *Profess. Fidei Waldensibus ab Innocentio III. Praescripta:* " *Sacramenta, . . . licet a peccatore sacerdote ministrentur, dum Ecclesia eum recipit, in nullo reprobamus.*" (Denzinger-Bannwart, n. 424).

18 " *Si episcopus vel sacerdos existat in peccato mortali, non ordinat, non consecrat, non baptizat.*" (Denzinger-Bannwart, n. 584).

19 Sess. VII, can. 12: " *Si quis dixerit, ministrum in peccato mortali existentem, modo omnia essentialia quae ad sacramentum conficiendum aut conferendum pertinent servaverit, non conficere aut conferre sacramentum, anathema sit.*" (Denzinger-Bannwart, n. 855).

tity of her priesthood;[20] but she has never conditioned the validity of a Sacrament on the moral worthiness of the minister. Her early teaching on the subject is clearly apparent from the writings of St. Optatus of Mileve and St. Augustine against the Donatists.

Aside from certain peculiar views of Tertullian[21] and Origen,[22] the question regarding the moral disposition of the minister arose later than that regarding his orthodoxy, which was hotly debated in the controversy that raged about the question of the rebaptizing of those who had been baptized by heretics.[23]   When bishops and priests began to apostatize in time of persecution, conscientious Catholics quite naturally asked themselves: " Can such unworthy men validly baptize or confer Holy Orders? "   It was this question, in fact, which may be said to have given rise to the Donatist schism.   In the year 311, Bishop Felix of Aptunga, who was (falsely) accused of having delivered the sacred books of the Christians to their enemies, consecrated a certain archdeacon named Cæcilian to the episcopal see of Carthage.   A party of zealots in the last-mentioned city denounced this act as invalid and set up another bishop in the person of one Majorinus, who was soon after succeeded by Donatus the Great.   Optatus, bishop of Mileve, in his work *De Schismate Donatistarum* (written about 370), triumphantly demonstrated that the validity of a Sacrament does not depend on the disposition of the minister.   It remained, however, for St. Augustine to break the backbone of the new heresy.   Starting from the favorite Donatist distinction between " pub-

20 *V. infra*, pp. 188 sq.
21 *De Pudic.*, c. 21.
22 *In Matth.*, t. XII, 14.
23 *V. infra*, Thesis II.

lic" and "private" sinners, he argued as follows: The Sacrament of Baptism is administered either by a private or a public sinner. If by a private sinner, Baptism among the Donatists themselves is uncertain, since they, too, have private sinners among their number. If by a public sinner, the case stands no better, since all guilty of mortal sin, whether public or private, are on a par before God. Consequently, the validity of a Sacrament can not depend on the worthiness of the minister. In matter of fact, there is no Baptism of Donatus or Rogatus, etc., but only the one Baptism of Jesus Christ, which confers grace by reason of its innate power, independently of human merit.[24]

In the East, at about the same time, St. John Chrysostom taught: "It may happen that the rulers of a nation are bad and corrupt, and their subjects good and pious, that the laity live moral lives while the priests are guilty of iniquity. But if grace always required worthy [ministers], there would be no Baptism, no body of Christ [Eucharist], no sacrifice [of the Mass]. Now God is wont to operate through unworthy men, and the grace of Baptism is in no wise stained by the [sinful] life of the priest." [25]

Several Patristic writers exemplify this truth by striking metaphors. Thus St. Gregory of Nazianzus compares a Sacrament to a signet ring and says that the emperor's iron ring has the same power of making a

---

24 Cfr. St. Augustine, *Contra Crescon.*, II, 21, 26: "*Baptizant, quantum attinet ad visibile ministerium, et boni et mali, invisibiliter autem per eos ille baptizat, cuius est et visibile baptisma et invisibilis gratia.*"— IDEM, *Tract. in Ioa.*, V, n. 18: "*Si quos baptizavit ebriosus, quos baptizavit homicida, quos baptizavit adulter, si baptismus Christi erat, Christus baptizavit.*"— A list of St. Augustine's writings against the Donatists can be found in Bardenhewer-Shahan, *Patrology*, pp. 484 sq. Several of the most important of them are translated into English in Dods, *The Works of Aurelius Augustine*, Vol. III, Edinburgh 1872.

25 *Hom. in Ep.* 1 *ad Cor.*, 8, n. 1.

mark as a ring of gold;[26] and St. Augustine calls attention to the fact that the rays of the sun shine upon filth without being contaminated by it.[27]

The same ideas were again brought forward in the conflict with the spiritualistic sects of the Middle Ages.

b) From the philosophical point of view the following considerations are pertinent. As far as mere possibility is concerned, there can be no doubt that Jesus Christ, had He so willed, could have limited the power of conferring His Sacraments to members of the true Church, and made it dependent on the subjective disposition of the minister. However, in His wisdom our Lord preferred to tolerate innumerable sacrileges rather than limit too narrowly the requisites of valid administration. By making the Sacraments independent of the personal merit or demerit of the minister, He safeguarded three important truths: (1) their objective efficacy, depending in no wise on the moral character of the minister; (2) His own priesthood, which cannot be tainted by His representatives; and (3) the certainty to which the faithful have a right in matters pertaining to eternal salvation. If the validity, power, and effect of the Sacraments had been made to depend on the subjective condition of the minister, the doctrine of their objective efficacy *ex opere operato* would have been endangered as well as the important truth that all human ministers are but representatives of the one great High Priest, the God-man Jesus Christ, and the faithful would have had no certainty with regard to the valid reception of Baptism, Confirmation, Holy Orders, etc. Such a state of affairs would have produced insufferable qualms of conscience and brought contempt and disregard upon

26 *Or. de Bapt.*, 40, n. 26.   27 *De Bapt. c. Donat.*, III, 10, 15.

the divinely instituted means of grace.[28]   Nor would it be possible, without this safeguard, to uphold the hierarchical order.   To assure themselves that the Sacraments were validly administered, the laity would pry into the private life of the clergy, and there would arise a system of espionage which would necessarily entail denunciation, calumny, slander, quarrels, and scandals.   The administration of the Sacraments would thus be surrounded by conditions which would make them a source of evil rather than of blessing.

Thesis II: The validity of a Sacrament does not depend on the orthodox belief of the minister.

This thesis is *de fide* in respect of Baptism.

Proof.   It is the formal and solemn teaching of the Tridentine Council that heretics baptize validly if they observe the prescribed form and have the intention of doing what the Church does.   "If anyone saith that the Baptism which is given by heretics in the name of the Father and of the Son and of the Holy Ghost, with the intention of doing what the Church doth, is not true Baptism, let him be anathema." [29]   *A pari,* and because of the established practice of the Church, theologians regard it as *fidei proximum*

---

28 Cfr. St. Bonaventure, *Brevil.,* VI, 5: *" Si sacramenta dispensari solum possent a bonis, nullus esset certus de susceptione sacramenti, et sic oporteret semper iterari et malitia unius praeiudicaret alienae saluti."*

29 Sess. VII, De Bapt., can. 4:

" Si quis dixerit, baptismum qui etiam datur ab haereticis in nomine Patris et Filii et Spiritus Sancti cum intentione faciendi quod facit Ecclesia, non esse verum baptismum, anathema sit."   (Denzinger-Bannwart, n. 860).

that heretics can validly administer all the other Sacraments, with the sole exception of Penance,[30] which cannot, barring cases of urgent necessity, be validly conferred by heretical and schismatic priests;—not on account of their lack of orthodoxy, but because they have no ecclesiastical jurisdiction.

a) With the outbreak of schisms and heresies there naturally arose doubts concerning the validity of Baptism when administered by heretics or, generally, by those outside the fold. As early as 256, Pope Stephen I decided against the practice of rebaptizing heretics, which had been introduced by St. Cyprian and his fellow-bishops in Africa.[31]

Up to the third century it was regarded as an Apostolic rule to recognize Baptism conferred by heretics as valid. About 220, Agrippinus, bishop of Carthage, began to rebaptize converted heretics. The new practice received the sanction of two councils (A. D. 255 and 256), presided over by St. Cyprian.[32] When Pope Stephen had decided against it, Cyprian wrote to Firmilian, bishop of Cæsarea, to ascertain the views of the churches of Asia Minor. These, at a council held in Iconium, sanctioned the African practice, but their

---

30 Maldonatus and Morinus mistakenly except also Confirmation and Holy Orders.

31 " Si qui ergo a quacumque haeresi venient ad vos, nihil innovetur nisi quod traditum est, ut manus illis imponatur in poenitentiam." (Denzinger-Bannwart, n. 46).

32 Cfr. St. Cyprian, Ep., 73, n. 13 (ed. Hartel, II, 787): " Proinde frustra quidam, qui ratione vincuntur, consuetudinem nobis opponunt, quasi consuetudo maior sit veritate aut non id sit in spiritualibus sequendum, quod in melius fuerit a S. Spiritu revelatum."

decision was annulled by the Pope, in 253, under threat of excommunication. St. Dionysius the Great of Alexandria prevented a schism,[33] but Firmilian stuck to his opinion, and in reply to St. Cyprian's inquiry said: "We join custom to truth and oppose to the custom of Rome that of the truth."[34] The very fact that both Cyprian and Firmilian confessedly acted in opposition to an ancient tradition shows that the Roman practice was of Apostolic origin. "This most wholesome custom," says St. Augustine, "according to the Blessed Cyprian, began to be what is called amended by his predecessor Agrippinus, but . . . we ought to believe that it rather began to be corrupted than to receive correction at the hands of Agrippinus."[35] And Vincent of Lerins says: "The antiquity was retained, the novelty was exploded."[36] The doubts that arose on various later occasions had nothing to do with the principle itself, but merely concerned its practical application. Often it was not easy to determine whether this or that particular sect used the proper formula in baptizing. Thus St. Basil (d. 379) was in doubt about the Encratites and the Pepuzians. St. Augustine, in his controversy with the Donatists, confidently appealed to tradition. He drew a clearer distinction between character and grace than St. Cyprian had done, and declared that, while a Sacrament may be validly administered by heretical ministers, yet its effects might not be visible among their sects.[37]

33 Cfr. Eusebius, *Hist. Eccles.*, VII, 2.

34 *Inter Ep. Cypr.*, 75, n. 19 (ed. Hartel, II, 822): "*Ceterum nos veritati et consuetudinem iungimus et consuetudini Romanorum consuetudinem sed veritatis opponimus.*"

35 *De Bapt. c. Donat.*, II, 7, 11: "*Hanc ergo saluberrimam consue-*

tudinem per Agrippinum praedecessorem suum dicit S. Cyprianus quasi coepisse corrigi, sed . . . verius creditur per Agrippinum corrumpi coepisse, non corrigi."

36 *Commonit.*, I, 6: "*Retenta est scil. antiquitas, explosa novitas.*"

37 Cfr. St. Augustine, *Contra Donat.*, VI, 1: "*Non ob aliud*

b) The theological reason for the validity of Baptism when conferred by a heretical minister, is to be sought in the maxim so constantly urged by St. Augustine: "It is Christ who baptizes." [38] Let it not be objected that no one can give what he does not himself possess (*nemo dat quod non habet*); for he who confers Baptism, whether he be himself baptized or unbaptized, orthodox or heretical, pure or unclean, does not confer his own Baptism but the Baptism of Christ. [39]

What we have said of Baptism applies also to the remaining Sacraments, especially to Confirmation and Holy Orders. The practice of the Church with regard to them is the same and based on the same reasons. Only the Sacrament of Penance, is, as a rule, considered invalid if administered in heretical sects, even such as have validly ordained bishops and priests; not, however, as we have already remarked, because these ministers have not the power to absolve, but because, except in cases of urgent necessity, they lack ecclesiastical jurisdiction. Even the most orthodox Catholic confessor cannot give absolution if he lacks jurisdiction and is generally known

visum est quibusdam, etiam egregiis viris, antistitibus Christi, inter quos praecipue b. Cyprianus eminebat, non esse posse apud haereticos vel schismaticos baptismum Christi, nisi quia non distinguebatur sacramentum ab effectu vel usu sacramenti; et quia eius effectus atque usus in liberatione a peccatis et cordis rectitudine apud haereticos non inveniebatur, ipsum quoque sacramentum non illic esse putabatur." For further information we refer the student to Part II of this volume, on Baptism. The historical aspects of the controversy are well treated by J. Ernst, *Die Ketzertaufangelegenheit in der altchristlichen Kirche nach Cyprian*, Mainz 1901; IDEM, *Papst Stephan I. und der Ketzertaufstreit*, Mainz 1905. See also B. Poschmann, *Die Sichtbarkeit der Kirche nach der Lehre des hl. Cyprian*, pp. 49 sqq., 114, Paderborn 1908.

38 "*Christus est qui baptizat.*"

39 Cfr. 1 Cor. I, 13.

to lack it   Where good faith and a *titulus coloratus* may be presumed, the Church supplies the defect.   For this reason confession among the schismatic Greeks or Russians cannot be rejected as invalid.   *Sacramenta propter homines,*— the Sacraments have been instituted for the sake of men, and we may safely assume that the Church, desiring to aid those who are blamelessly in error, supplies the lack of jurisdiction in schismatical ministers.[40]

ARTICLE 3

NECESSITY OF A RIGHT INTENTION

1. PRELIMINARY REMARKS.—Intention (*intentio*) may be defined as an act of the will by which that faculty efficaciously desires to reach an end by employing the necessary means.[41]   Intention is not synonymous with attention, for man can act with a purpose even when his mind is distracted.

a) It is customary to distinguish various kinds of intention by which an act may be prompted.

There is, first, the *actual* intention, operating with the full advertence of the intellect.   When a minister wishes here and now to confer, *e. g.,* the Sacrament of Baptism, he has an actual intention.

Secondly, there is the *virtual* intention.   Its force is borrowed from a previous volition, which is accounted as continuing in some result produced by it.   Thus, if a

40 Cfr. Billot, *De Sacramentis Ecclesiae,* Vol. I, 4th ed., p. 158, Rome 1907.

41 Cfr.   St.   Thomas, _____ *Theol.,* 1a 2ae, qu. 12, art. 1, ad 3: " *Intentio nominat actum voluntatis praesuppositâ ordinatione rationis ordinantis aliquid in finem.*"

minister begins with an actual intention, but is distracted while administering the Sacrament, he has a virtual intention.

Thirdly, an *habitual* intention is one that once actually existed, but of the present continuance of which there is no positive trace. The most that can be said of it is that it has never been retracted. A priest subject to somnambulism, who would administer Baptism in his sleep, might be said to act with an habitual intention.

Fourthly, an *interpretative* intention is an intention that would be conceived if one thought of it, but which for want of thinking of it, is not elicited. It is simply the purpose which it is assumed a man would have had in a given contingency, had he given thought to the matter. There has been and is no actual movement of the will.[42]

An intention of some sort is necessary in the minister for the valid administration of a Sacrament. It need not be actual. Distractions cannot always be avoided. A virtual intention is sufficient. Not so, however, an habitual or interpretative intention, which is really not in existence while the action is performed, and consequently can have no effect upon it.

b) With regard to quality, an intention may be either *direct* or *reflex,* according as the minister realizes the full import of his action or performs it without being fully conscious of its character and effects. Thus, a priest who, in baptizing an infant, explicity desires to cleanse the soul from original sin and to bestow sanctifying grace, acts with a reflex intention. One who simply performs all that is prescribed by the ritual has a direct intention.

Theologians also distinguish an *indirect* intention, by

[42] Cfr. J. F. Delany in the *Catholic Encyclopedia,* Vol. VIII, p. 69;   Thos. Slater, *Moral Theology,* Vol. II, p. 28.

virtue of which a man intends an action not in itself but in its cause (*voluntarium in causa sive indirectum*), as when one under the influence of liquor does something which he had made up his mind to do when sober.   Such an indirect intention is not sufficient in the minister of a Sacrament; if it were, Baptism could be administered, or the Holy Sacrifice of the Mass celebrated, by a priest in the state of intoxication.   A direct intention suffices for the valid administration of the Sacrament.

A species of the direct intention is the so-called *intentio mere externa*. It may be defined as the purpose of performing the external rite of a Sacrament while internally withholding the intention to administer the same.   The term was invented by Ambrosius Catharinus in order to safeguard the objectivity of the Sacraments.   Catharinus, and some other theologians who followed his lead, thought that such an intention of performing the external rite, even if coupled with an internal refusal to do what the Church does, would suffice for the validity of a Sacrament.   To-day this opinion has scarcely any adherents.   The common doctrine now is that a real internal intention, *viz.:* the will to accomplish what Christ instituted the Sacraments to effect, in other words, truly to baptize, absolve, etc., is required.[43]

2. DOGMATIC THESES CONCERNING THE INTENTION OF THE MINISTER.—To administer a Sacrament validly, the minister must have a real intention to do what the Church does (Thesis I).   For this the mere external intention postulated by Catharinus is not sufficient (Thesis II).

43 Delany, *l. c.*

Thesis I: To administer a Sacrament validly, the minister must have the intention at least to do what the Church does.

This proposition embodies an article of faith.
Proof. The *Decretum pro Armenis* defines that the intention to do what the Church does is a necessary requisite for the valid administration of a Sacrament.[44] The Tridentine Council solemnly declares: "If anyone saith that in ministers, when they effect and confer the Sacraments, there is not required the intention at least of doing what the Church does, let him be anathema."[45] To understand the full significance of this declaration it should be noted that the Council does not say, "what the Church *intends*," but merely, "what the Church *does*." Consequently, all that is necessary for the valid administration of the Sacraments is the direct intention, *i. e.* the purpose of performing the rite as is usual among Catholics. To demand in addition a reflex intention, either for the administration of the Sacrament as such, or for the production of the sacramental character and the infusion of grace, would be to make the validity of the Sacrament depend upon the orthodoxy of the minister,—an assumption which we have shown to be false.[46]

44 *V. supra*, p. 162, n. 2.
45 *Conc. Trident.*, Sess. VII, can. 11: "*Si quis dixerit, in ministris, dum sacramenta conficiunt et conferunt, non requiri intentionem sal-tem faciendi quod facit Ecclesia, anathema sit.*" (Denzinger-Bannwart, n. 854).
46 *V. supra*, Art. 2, Thesis II.

a) The Apostle says: "So let men account us as ministers of Christ." [47]   It follows from this that the minister of a Sacrament, being a servant or minister of Christ, must have the intention of exercising the powers delegated to him by the Master.   Now, since the Church acts in the name of her Divine Founder, one who has not the intention of doing at least what the Church does, does not conduct himself as a minister of Christ, nor does he exercise the powers conferred by Him.   Consequently, without the intention of doing what the Church does there can be no Sacrament.

This Biblical argument can be supported by philosophical considerations.   We know from John XX, 23, that by the power of absolving which, in the Sacrament of Penance, he exercises in the name of Christ, a confessor may either forgive or retain sins.   Hence he must, after hearing the penitent, make up his mind either to absolve him or to send him off without absolution. He can do neither the one nor the other without having some kind of an intention.

Matrimony is not only a Sacrament, but it is also a contract requiring the mutual consent of both parties.   There can be no true consent without an intention to get married.

A priest who, in saying Mass, would refuse to subject himself to the will of Christ, in whose name he speaks and acts, would not have the right intention, and consequently would not act as a minister of Christ, and the

---

[47] 1 Cor. IV, 1: "*Sic nos existimet homo ut ministros Christi.*" (Cfr. the Westminster Version).

words of consecration pronounced by him would be void. The same, *mutatis mutandis*, holds true of the other Sacraments.

b) **The teaching of Tradition on this point has undergone a lengthy process of clarification.**

The most ancient testimony that has come down to us is contained in a letter of Pope Cornelius (251–253) to Fabius of Antioch.   The Pontiff relates how the anti-pope Novatian, who was the leader of the rigorist party, enticed three ignorant provincial bishops to Rome, made them drunk, and compelled them to give him episcopal consecration.   The Pope distinctly says that this consecration was invalid.[48]   The reasons plainly are: first, because the consecrating bishops were under the influence of liquor and therefore irresponsible; second, because they acted under compulsion (*cogit*).

There is an old legend that Bishop Alexander received into the Christian fold certain companions of St. Athanasius, whom the boy had baptized at play.[49]   This is probably a mere fable, but if it were true, it would prove that very liberal notions were current in the third century regarding the intention of the minister of a Sacrament, though we can not help wondering why Bishop Alexander did not inquire whether the baptized boys had the intention necessary to receive the Sacrament.

St. Augustine was evidently not quite clear on this matter, for he hesitated to declare that Baptism is invalid if administered in jest or as a farce.   "But where [if] . . . the whole thing were done as a farce, or a comedy, or a jest, I should think that to know whether the Baptism thus

48 Cfr. Eusebius, *Hist. Eccles.*, VI, 43: "*Eos ille a quibusdam sui simillimis, quos ad id comparaverat, inclusos horâ decimâ, temulentos et a crapula oppressos adumbratâ qua-* *dam et inani manuum impositione episcopatum sibi tradere per vim cogit.*"

49 Cfr. Rufinus, *Hist. Eccles.*, I, 14.

conferred should be approved, we ought to pray for the declaration of God's judgment through the medium of some revelation . . ." [50]

In the primitive Church there was a tendency to regard every Sacrament administered according to the prescribed rite as valid, without inquiring into the intention of the minister, which was always presumed to be right. The philosophic discussion concerning the necessity of the right intention as a requisite of validity was reserved to the Schoolmen. Hugh of St. Victor, so far as we know, was the first theologian to insist on this point.[51] William of Auxerre (d. 1223) invented the formula: *"Intentio faciendi quod facit Ecclesia."* This was introduced into the terminology of the schools and more adequately explained by Alexander of Hales, whose teaching was followed by St. Bonaventure,[52] Scotus, and the whole Franciscan school. St. Thomas, following his master Albert, proves the necessity of a right intention on the part of the minister from the proposition that every free instrumental cause must voluntarily accommodate itself to the principal cause,— in this case Christ, the author and chief administrator of the Sacraments. "There is required on the part of the minister that intention by which he subjects himself to the principal agent, *i. e.* intends to do what Christ does and the Church." [53] The entire Thomist school faithfully adhered to this doctrine, which was adopted even by Durandus and the Nominalists

---

[50] Cfr. St. Augustine, *De Baptismo contra Donatistas*, VII, 53, 102: *" Ubi autem . . . totum ludicre et mimice et ioculariter ageretur, utrum approbandus esset `baptismus, qui sic daretur, divinum iudicium . . . implorandum censerem."*

[51] *Summa*, tr. 6, c. 4; *De Sacram.*, II, 6, 13.

[52] *Brevil.*, VI, 5: *" Dispensatio*

sacramentorum est opus hominis ut rationalis, ut ministri Christi, et ut ministri salutis; hinc est quod necesse est quod fiat ex intentione."

[53] Cfr. *Summa Theol.*, 3a, qu. 64, art. 8, ad 1: *" Requiritur eius intentio, qua se subiiciat principali agenti, ut scil. intendat facere quod facit Christus et Ecclesia."*

and finally became the common teaching of Catholic theologians. Innocent III, Martin V, and Eugene IV, by employing the Scholastic formula in official pronouncements, prepared the way for its dogmatization by the Council of Trent.[54]

c) The theological argument for our thesis is based on three facts: (1) the minister of a Sacrament acts as the representative of Christ; (2) without some definite intention the administration of a Sacrament would be an indifferent act; and (3) the contrary proposition leads to absurd consequences.

(1) The minister of a Sacrament, as we have repeatedly pointed out, acts not in his own name but in the name of Christ and as His representative. To do this he must have the intention of doing one thing in preference to another, *viz.:* what Christ wishes him to do. As the will of the Church in the administration of the Sacraments necessarily coincides with that of her Divine Founder, it suffices to have the intention of doing what the Church does.

(2) The *confectio* of a Sacrament, i. e. the combination of matter and form into the sacramental sign, is not necessarily of itself a sacramental act, but indifferent and ambiguous, inasmuch as the minister, being a free agent, may act with any one of a number of different purposes, *e. g.,* to practice, to play a joke, to make a mockery of religious ceremonies, etc. It depends entirely on his free will whether what he does is intended as a

54 Cfr. Schanz, *Die Lehre von den hl. Sakramenten,* pp. 173 sqq., Freiburg 1893.

sacramental rite or not. Hence the necessity of a proper intention.

(3) The contrary teaching of Luther entails utterly absurd consequences. If no intention were required in the administration of the Sacraments, a mother would baptize her baby by bathing it in a tub and invoking the name of the Trinity; a priest reading the words of consecration from the Bible would *nolens volens* consecrate a loaf of bread accidentally lying near him, and so forth.

Thesis II: A merely external intention in the sense of Catharinus is not sufficient for the validity of a Sacrament.

This proposition may be technically qualified as *communis.*

Proof. Catharinus teaches that all that is required for the validity of a Sacrament on the minister's part is that he have the intention of performing the external rite, even though he withhold interior assent.[55] This teaching seems to have been forecast by Aureolus (d. 1322) and Sylvester Prierias (d. 1523), but did not come prominently forward until the seventeenth century, when it was espoused by a number of French and Belgian theologians, notably Contenson, Farvacques, Duhamel, Juenin, Serry, and Drouin.

In the nineteenth century this theory was sporadically defended by L. Haas, Glossner, and Oswald. The last-mentioned writer retracted his earlier teaching in the

[55] *V. supra,* p. 177.

fifth edition of his treatise on the Sacraments, published in 1894. His ablest opponents were Morgott [56] and Franzelin.[57]

The question at issue may be briefly formulated thus: Does a minister who has the intention of performing the external rite, but withholds his interior assent from the mind of the Church, validly confer a Sacrament? Catharinus and his followers answer this question affirmatively.

a) Though their opinion has never been directly and formally condemned, it runs counter to a number of conciliary and papal decisions.

Innocent III demanded of the Waldenses that they subscribe to a profession of faith containing these words in regard to the Holy Mass: "For which celebration three things are necessary, as we believe, namely, a certain person, *i. e.* the priest, . . . those solemn words [of institution], . . . and the honest intention of the one who pronounces them." [58]   Can he who interiorly repudiates what he externally does, be said to have an "honest intention"?   Note, too, that the Pope mentions the "*fidelis intentio*" as something independent of and separable from the act of uttering the words of consecration.   This last-mentioned point is brought out more clearly in the following question, addressed to certain suspected Wiclifites and Hussites by command of Martin V: "Does he believe that a bad priest, employing the proper matter and form, and having the intention of doing what the

56 Fr. Morgott, *Der Spender der hl. Sakramente nach der Lehre des hl. Thomas,* pp. 132 sqq., Freiburg 1886.

57 *De Sacramentis,* thes. 17.

58 " *Ad quod officium tria sunt, ut credimus, necessaria, scil. certa persona, i. e. presbyter . . . et illa solemnia verba* [*institutionis*] *. . . et fidelis intentio proferentis.*" (Denzinger-Bannwart, n. 424).

Church does, truly consecrates, truly absolves, truly baptizes, truly confers the other Sacraments?"[59]   He who
employs the proper matter and form, manifestly has the
external intention postulated by Catharinus and means to
perform the external rite in the prescribed way.   But this
is not sufficient, or else the Pope would not add: "and
having the intention of doing what the Church does."
Eugene IV in his famous *Decretum pro Armenis* (1439),
besides the putting together of matter and form (in which
the *intentio mere externa* of Catharinus is sufficiently
guaranteed), expressly demands the *intentio faciendi quod
facit Ecclesia* as a distinct *conditio sine qua non* of
validity.   Now this intention, in addition to the external
performance of the sacramental rite, coincides with the
internal intention which we defend.   It is evidently this
interior intention that the Council of Trent means when
it commands the minister of a Sacrament to do what
the Church does.[60]   A minister who, while carefully ob-
serving the prescribed rite, would withhold interior assent to the mind of the Church, could have no other intention than to play the hypocrite.   The correctness of
this interpretation may be judged from the Council's
declaration as to the right intention of confessors:
". . . The penitent ought not so to confide in his own
personal faith as to think that — even though there be
. . . no intention on the part of the priest of acting seriously and absolving truly — he is nevertheless . . . absolved, . . . nor would he be otherwise than most care-
less of his own salvation who, knowing that a priest absolved him in jest, should not carefully seek for another

59 ". . . *utrum credat, quod malus
sacerdos cum debita materia et
forma et cum intentione faciendi
quod facit Ecclesia, vere conficiat,*
*vere absolvat, vere baptizet, vere
conferat alia sacramenta.*" (Denzinger-Bannwart, n. 672).
60 *V. supra,* Thesis I.

who would act in earnest." [61]   In this passage the Holy
Synod mentions two separate and distinct intentions:
that of " acting seriously " and that of " absolving truly."
These two intentions are either substantially identical or
they are separate and distinct. If they are identical, the
second phrase is merely an explanation of the first, and
the intention of acting seriously coincides with that of
absolving truly, which latter is evidently an interior intention. If they are not identical, then the intention of
acting seriously (which is precisely Catharinus' *intentio
mere externa*), is not sufficient for valid absolution, because there is further required the intention of absolving
truly.   In either case the merely external intention is insufficient.

The opinion of Catharinus sustained a severe blow [62]
by the condemnation pronounced by Alexander VIII
(1690) against the proposition that " Baptism is valid
if conferred by a minister who observes the whole external rite and form of the Sacrament, but interiorly in
his heart says: I do not intend to do what the Church
does." [63]   This proposition was extracted from the writings of the Belgian theologian Farvacques, who was an
ardent champion of the *intentio mere externa,* and hence
it is perhaps not too much to say that Catharinus' theory
stands condemned.[64]

[61] Cfr. *Conc. Trident.,* Sess. XIV,
cap. 6: *"Non debet poenitens
adeo sibi de sua ipsius fide blandiri,
ut etiamsi . . . sacerdoti animus
serio agendi et vere absolvendi desit,
putet tamen se . . . esse absolutum,
. . . nec is esset nisi salutis suae
negligentissimus, qui sacerdotem
iocose absolventem cognosceret, et
non alium serio agentem sedulo re-
quireret."* (Denzinger-Bannwart, n.
902).

[62] *V.* Benedict XIV, *De Synodo
Dioecesana,* VII, 4, 8.

[63] *" Valet · baptismus collatus a
ministro, qui omnem ritum externum
formamque baptizandi observat, intus
vero in corde suo apud se resolvit:
Non intendo quod facit Ecclesia."*
(Denzinger-Bannwart, n. 1318).

[64] Serry's evasive arguments on
this subject are convincingly refuted
by Tepe, *Instit. Theol.,* IV, 79 sqq.

b) The arguments alleged in favor of the sufficiency of a merely external intention are inconclusive.

The laudable desire manifested by our opponents to safeguard the objective efficacy of the Sacraments against the wiles of unworthy men and to give the faithful as great a certainty as possible of receiving the sacramental graces, must not lead us to overlook the necessity of an interior intention. Two elements, the one objective, the other subjective, enter into the composition of every Sacrament: the external rite and the interior intention. No Sacrament is complete without them. Nor is it safe to extol the former to the prejudice of the latter. It is not pertinent to compare the external rite to a fire[65] which, laid to dry wood, at once kindles it, even when there is no intention of arson on the part of him who brings about the contact. On the other hand, Divine Providence has seen fit to entrust the administration of the Sacraments to human beings. We must therefore be satisfied with such moral certitude as can generally be had.[66]

READINGS:— B. J. Otten, S. J., *A Manual of the History of Dogmas,* Vol. I, St. Louis 1917, pp. 342 sqq.; Vol. II (1918), pp. 290 sqq.

[65] As the followers of Catharinus do.

[66] *V. supra,* Thesis I. Cfr. Pesch, *Praelect. Dogmat.,* Vol. VI, 3rd ed., pp. 119 sqq.; De Augustinis, *De Re Sacramentaria,* I, 2nd ed., pp. 235 sqq.

SECTION 2

THE REQUISITES OF WORTHY ADMINISTRATION

As this subject is fully dealt with in moral and pastoral theology, we shall confine ourselves to a few general remarks.

1. THE STATE OF GRACE.—The minister of a Sacrament represents Jesus Christ, who is all-holy; he performs a sacred rite endowed with sanctifying power, and therefore should be a man of unblemished character. If he solemnly and officially confers a Sacrament in the state of mortal sin, he commits a sacrilege.[1]

Both the natural [2] and the positive divine law prescribe that the priest of God be holy. In the Old Testament Yahweh admonished the sons of Aaron: " Be ye holy, because I the Lord your God am holy," [3] and demanded of the Levites " that they shall be holy to their God, and shall not profane his name: for they offer the burnt offering of the Lord, and the bread of their God, and therefore they shall be holy." [4] With how much greater force does this apply to the Catholic priest, who offers up, not calves and oxen, but the flesh and blood

1 Cfr. St. Thomas, *Summa Theol.,* 3a, qu. 64, art. 6.
2 Cfr. St. Thomas, *Comment. in Sent.,* IV, dist. 24, qu. 1, art. 3, sol.
5: *" Est de iure naturali, ut homo sancta sancte pertractet."*
3 Lev. XIX, 2.
4 Lev. XXI, 6.

of the God-man, and becomes a visible instrument of sanctification in the hands of His invisible Master. Justly does St. Gregory the Great declare: " It is necessary that the hand be pure which is engaged in cleaning away filth, lest it spread contamination by contact." [5] A priest who habitually lives in the state of mortal sin not only provokes the divine vengeance, but, by his bad example and the scandal he gives, helps the devil to ruin those immortal souls which he has been commissioned to save. The great defection in the West probably would never have come about had the clergy of the sixteenth century lived up to their high calling.

2. THE DUTY OF ADMINISTERING THE SACRAMENTS.—He who possesses the power of validly conferring the Sacraments, is in duty bound to do so when he has charge of souls. This applies to bishops, pastors and their representatives, and religious superiors.[6] Besides, a priest may be bound by charity, under penalty of mortal sin, to administer certain Sacraments in case of urgent necessity.

3. THE DUTY OF REFUSING THE SACRAMENTS. —Under certain conditions, which it is the business of moral and pastoral theology to determine, a priest is bound to refuse the Sacraments to unworthy applicants.[7] If there be danger of sacrilege, he must be ready to suffer martyrdom

[5] Ep., I, 25: " Necesse est ut esse munda studeat manus, quae diluere sordes curat, ne tacta quaeque deterius inquinet."

[6] Cfr. Concilium Trident., Sess. XXIII, De Reform., c. 1.

[7] Cfr. Matth. VII, 6; 1 Tim. V, 22.

rather than be unfaithful to his charge, for it is never permitted to do evil, not even to save one's life, and the desecration of a Sacrament is always a great evil.   Nor is it licit to escape danger of death by simulation, either by omitting an essential part of a Sacrament where such omission cannot be externally known and the people have a right to the Sacrament, or by secretly harboring the intention not to administer it; for Innocent XI (1679) has solemnly condemned the proposition that "urgent fear furnishes a just cause for simulating the administration of the Sacraments." [8]   To omit an essential part or all of the Sacrament, or substitute for it something else, is permissible for just cause, provided there be no contempt in so acting and no injury done to either Sacrament or recipient.

[8] " *Urgens metus gravis est causa iusta sacramentorum administrationem simulandi.*" (Denzinger-Bannwart, n. 1179).   On the subject of this Section the student may profitably consult Pesch, *Praelect. Dogmat.*, Vol. VI, 3rd ed., pp. 124 sqq.

CHAPTER V

THE RECIPIENT OF A SACRAMENT

SECTION 1

THE REQUISITES OF VALID RECEPTION

1. THE PERSON OF THE RECIPIENT.—The only fit subject for the reception of the Sacraments is man in the wayfaring state. The angels cannot receive them because they are pure spirits; the brutes, because they are irrational; dead bodies, because they are no human persons; departed souls, because they are incapable of receiving any rite, and because they have reached the *status termini*.

However, not every living man is a fit subject for all the Sacraments. The only Sacrament which an unbaptized person is capable of receiving is Baptism. Women are excluded from Holy Orders, subdeacons and clerics in major orders cannot receive the Sacrament of Matrimony, persons in good health are debarred from Extreme Unction, infants from Penance, Matrimony, and Extreme Unction. All these points will be more fully explained in connection with the several Sacraments.

2. ORTHODOXY NOT A REQUISITE FOR THE VALID RECEPTION OF THE SACRAMENTS.—With the sole exception of Penance, which demands certain supernatural acts (faith, contrition, etc.) either as quasi-matter, or at least as a necessary condition, the possession of the true faith is not an indispensable requisite for the valid reception of the Sacraments on the part of the subject.

a) The proofs of this assertion can be gathered from the controversy that was waged about the question of rebaptizing heretics. St. Augustine says in his famous treatise on Baptism against the Donatists: "It is immaterial, when we are considering the question of the integrity and holiness of the Sacrament, what the recipient of the Sacrament believes, and with what faith he is imbued. It is of the very highest consequence as regards the entrance into salvation, but it is wholly immaterial as regards the question of the Sacrament. For it is quite possible that a man may be possessed of the genuine Sacrament and a corrupted faith." [1] If the validity of the Sacraments depended on the faith of the recipients, Protestantism would be quite consistent in denying their objective efficacy and in basing justification solely on personal belief.

[1] *De Baptismo contra Donatistas,* III, 14, 19: "*Nec interest, quum de sacramenti integritate et sanctitate tractatur, quid credat et quali fide imbutus sit ille, qui accipit sacramentum. Interest quidem plurimum ad salutis viam, sed ad sacramenti quaestionem nihil interest.* *Fieri enim potest, ut homo integrum habeat sacramentum et perversam fidem.*" Cfr. the same author's *Contra Lit. Petil.,* II, 35, 82: "*Baptismi puritas a puritate vel immunditia conscientiae sive dantis sive accipientis prorsus distincta est.*"

If a heretical belief cannot imperil the validity of the Sacraments, neither can the presence or absence of some particular subjective disposition. Hence it is true of recipient and minister alike,[2] that personal unworthiness does not render a Sacrament invalid, though, of course, it may rob it of its proper and ultimate effect, *viz.:* the sanctification of the soul. Absence of the right disposition for the fruitful reception of a Sacrament is called *obex gratiae* (*obex* = a bar or obstacle). Hence, according to the Tridentine Council, the *non positio obicis* (= *remotio indispositionis*) is an indispensable condition of sacramental grace. " If anyone saith that the Sacraments of the New Law . . . do not confer that grace on those who do not place an obstacle thereunto, . . . let him be anathema." [3] Hence, if one places an obstacle to sacramental grace,[4] he receives the Sacrament unworthily, but the Sacrament itself is not invalid ; it is valid but lacking its proper form (*validum et informe*).

b) Can a Sacrament received validly though unworthily (*i. e.* if an obstacle prevents the infusion of divine grace at the time of reception), obtain its effects after the obstacle has been removed? This is the famous question regarding the " reviviscence " of the Sacraments (*reviviscentia sacramentorum*), to which so much attention has been given by theologians.[5] In every case of that kind there is a twofold possibility. Either the recipient is unaware of the obstacle (mortal sin) existing in his soul, and therefore receives the Sacrament in good faith (*obex*

---

2 *V. supra,* Thesis I, pp. 166 sqq.

3 Cfr. *Conc. Trident.,* Sess. VII, can. 6: " *Si quis dixerit, sacramenta Novae Legis . . . gratiam ipsam non ponentibus obicem non conferre, anathema sit.*"

4 The *obex gratiae* is also called *simulata dispositio* or *fictio.*

5 Cfr. the *Catholic Encyclopedia,* Vol. XIII, 304 b.

negativus sive inculpabilis) ; or the obstacle is known and voluntary, and then the Sacrament is received sacrilegiously (*obex positivus sive culpabilis*). The first-mentioned possibility has already been considered in a previous part of this treatise.[6] It remains to inquire whether a person who has received a Sacrament sacrilegiously can recover its effects.

Theologians are agreed [7] that if Baptism be received by an adult in the state of mortal sin, he can obtain the graces of the Sacrament later, when the obstacle has been removed by contrition or by the worthy reception of Penance. " In the case of him who has approached the Sacrament in deceit," says St. Augustine, " there is no second Baptism, but he is purged by faithful discipline and truthful confession, which he could not be without Baptism, so that what was given before, becomes then powerful to work his salvation, when the former deceit is done away by the truthful confession." [8] It is to be remarked, however, that cases of this kind are sometimes quite complicated in practice. If one who has received Baptism *ficte,* as it is technically termed, commits no additional mortal sin after his sacrilegious Baptism, the Sacrament may recover its effects as soon as he has the disposition he ought to have had when he received it, *i. e.* imperfect contrition (*attritio*). But if he renders himself guilty of new mortal sins after Baptism, attrition will not suffice ; he must have perfect contrition (*contritio*) with a firm

6 *V. supra,* pp. 68 sqq.

7 Some have excepted Vasquez (*Disp.,* 159, sect. 1), but that author's teaching on this head is really in accord with the common doctrine.

8 *De Baptismo c. Donat.,* I, 12, 18: " *In illo, qui fictus accesserat,* *fit ut non denuo baptizetur, sed ipsâ piâ correctione et veraci confessione purgetur, quod non posset sine baptismo, ut quod ante datum est, tunc valere incipiat ad salutem, quum illa fictio veraci confessione recesserat."*

purpose of going to confession, because grievous sins committed after Baptism can be remitted only by the power of the keys.[9] If his contrition is not perfect, the unworthily received Sacrament of Baptism can recover its effects only in connection with Penance, which blots out mortal sin *ex opere operato,* and removes the obstacle that prevented the infusion of grace. The same is true of one who, being deceived as to his own disposition, has received Baptism without imperfect contrition, (which, in the adult, is an indispensable requisite for the valid reception of that Sacrament), and then commits additional mortal sins.

The reviviscence is not so certain in the case of the other Sacraments. Theologians unanimously hold that Confirmation and Holy Orders can recover their effects on account of the permanent character which they imprint on the soul. The contrary assumption would lead to the untenable and intolerable conclusion that the sacrilegious reception of Sacraments that cannot be repeated would deprive the recipient forever both of sanctifying grace and the sacramental (actual) graces proper to these Sacraments. In other words, one who has received Confirmation unworthily, even if he repent, could never receive the grace of that Sacrament, which is so necessary for the preservation of the faith, and a priest who had received Holy Orders unworthily, though validly, would never, according to that theory, receive the special graces peculiar to ordination, without which it is impossible to administer the sacerdotal office properly.[10]

---

9 On this point see the treatise on the Sacrament of Penance.

10 Cfr. St. Augustine, *Contra Crescon.,* II, 10: " *Christiana sane sacramenta in vobis agnosco . . .*

Apud vos quidem aliena sunt; sed quum vos correctos recipit, cuius sunt, fiunt ea salubriter vestra, quae perniciose habebatis aliena."

Applying what we have said to Extreme Unction and Matrimony, we may go a step further and affirm that these two Sacraments are likewise capable of being " revived." Matrimony cannot be received twice by the same parties, and Extreme Unction may not be repeated whilst the same danger of death lasts.   Hence these two Sacraments may be said to be at least relatively incapable of repetition, and therefore capable of reviviscence.

The case is different with Penance and the Holy Eucharist.   These two Sacraments, if sacrilegiously received, do not recover their effects when the obstacle is removed.   There can be no " reviviscence " of Penance, because if the penitent is not sufficiently disposed to receive grace at the time he confesses his sins, the Sacrament is not validly received, since the acts of the penitent are a necessary part of the matter of this Sacrament.[11] There can be no " reviviscence " of the Holy Eucharist after the sacred species are consumed, because the fruits of this Sacrament may be supplied through other channels.[12]   To these particular reasons must be added a general one, viz.: that Catholics can receive these two Sacraments as often as they please.[13]

3. THE RIGHT INTENTION A NECESSARY REQUISITE FOR THE VALID RECEPTION OF THE SACRAMENTS ON THE PART OF THE RECIPIENT.—In adults, according to the teaching of the Council of Trent, justification always takes place "through the voluntary reception of grace and the gifts." [14]

11 See the treatise on Penance.

12 See the treatise on the Holy Eucharist.

13 On the whole subject of this subdivision cfr. De Lugo, De Sacramentis in Genere, disp. 9, sect. 6.

14 Conc. Trident., Sess. VI, cap. 7: ". . . per voluntariam susceptionem gratiae et donorum."

Consequently, justification, if effected through the Sacraments, must be voluntary and requires a corresponding intention in the recipient. We have learned in a previous treatise,[15] that the entire process of justification, no matter whether it terminate in the reception of a Sacrament or not, consists of a long chain of preparatory acts performed with the help of grace. Hence every adult who desires to be justified, must have a positive intention to receive the Sacrament. *Pace* Cardinal Cajetan, who stands alone in his opposition to this theory, interior repugnance, or even neutrality, renders the Sacrament invalid.

a) The teaching of Tradition is unanimous on this point.

St. Augustine says: "From insufficiency of age they [infants] can neither believe with the heart unto righteousness, nor make confession with the mouth unto salvation. Therefore, when others take the vows for them, that the celebration of the Sacrament may be complete in their behalf, it is unquestionably of avail for their dedication to God, because they cannot answer for themselves. But if another were to answer for one who could answer for himself, it would not be of the same avail. In accordance with this rule we find in the Gospel what strikes every one as natural when he reads it: 'He is of age, he shall speak for himself.'"[16] Several ancient councils

---

15 *Grace, Actual and Habitual*, pp. 272 sqq.

16 *De Bapt. c. Donat.*, IV, 24: "*Ex aetatis indigentia* [*parvuli*] *nec corde credere ad iustitiam possunt nec ore confiteri ad salutem. Ideo quum alii pro eis respondent, ut impleatur erga eos celebratio sacramenti, valet utique ad eorum consecrationem, quia ipsi respondere*

forbade the administration of the Sacraments, including those that are indispensable for salvation, to subjects indisposed for their worthy reception.[17]   Pope Innocent III, in his decree against the adherents of Pierre de Bruys and other sectaries, emphatically insists upon the necessity of a right intention. He says: "He who never consents, but contradicts with all his might, receives neither the grace nor the character of the Sacrament."[18]   The Roman Ritual and the ordinary practice of the Church are in perfect conformity with this teaching, which St. Thomas, and the Scholastics generally, base (1) on the positive will of Christ, who does not force His benefits upon any one, and (2) on the essential character of the Sacraments as acts of religious worship, which can only be performed deliberately and with a free will.[19]

b) What kind of an intention must the recipient have to receive a Sacrament validly?[20]

The majority of theologians hold that the Holy Eucharist requires for its valid reception no intention whatever. This is a strange opinion, which we cannot share. A Catholic forced to take the Sacred Host against his will could no more be said to receive Holy Communion validly than an unbelieving Jew. True, he would receive a per-

---

non possunt. At si pro eo qui respondere potest, alius respondeat, non itidem valet. Ex qua regula illud in evangelio dictum est, quod omnes, quum legitur, naturaliter movet (Ioa. IX, 21): Aetatem habet, ipse pro se loquatur."

17 E. g., the First Council of Orange; cfr. Labbé, Concil., t. III, p. 1449: "Subito obmutescens, prout status eius est, baptizari aut poenitentiam accipere potest, si voluntatis aut praeteritae testimo-

nium aliorum verbis habet aut praesentis in suo nutu."

18 Cap. "Maiores:" "Ille vero, qui nunquam consentit, sed penitus contradicit, nec rem nec characterem suscipit sacramenti." (Denzinger-Bannwart, n. 411).

19 On some alleged instances of compulsory ordination see Billuart, De Sacram. in Communi, diss. 6, art. 1.

20 On the intention required of the minister, see supra, pp. 175 sqq.

manent Sacrament, but his reception of it would be a merely physical act, and consequently devoid of the true sacramental character and unproductive of grace.

Matrimony requires for its valid reception not merely an habitual or interpretative, but a virtual intention, because the contracting parties mutually administer the Sacrament to each other.[21]

Some theologians demand a virtual intention also for the valid reception of Holy Orders, claiming that such onerous duties as celibacy and the recitation of the Divine Office demand mature deliberation and a deep selfknowledge.

In all other cases it may safely be affirmed that the habitual intention is sufficient, because the Church regards the reception of the Sacraments by insane or unconscious persons as valid if it can be shown that the recipient had previously expressed, and never formally revoked, the intention of receiving them.[22]   In the case of Extreme Unction it is customary to administer the Sacrament on the strength of a purely interpretative intention, because every Catholic may reasonably be presumed to have the wish of dying in conformity with the teaching and practice of the Church.

21 See the treatise on Matrimony in Vol. XI of this series.

22 Cfr. Pope Innocent III, *Cap. " Maiores "*: *" Dormientes autem et amentes, si priusquam amentiam incurrerent aut dormirent, in contradictione persisterent, quia in eis intelligitur contradictionis propositum perdurare, etsi fuerint immersi, characterem non suscipiunt sacramenti; secus autem si prius catechumeni exstitissent et habuissent propositum baptizandi."*

SECTION 2

THE REQUISITES OF WORTHY RECEPTION

1. Preliminary Remarks.—A Sacrament, though validly administered, is not received worthily, *i. e.* does not confer grace, unless the recipient has the right disposition.

A Sacrament (*sacramentum tantum*) and the sacramental grace which it confers (*res tantum, effectus*) are two separate and distinct things. A Sacrament does not fulfil the whole purpose for which it was instituted unless it actually confers grace. (The sacramental characters imprinted by Baptism, Confirmation, and Holy Orders are also interior effects; but they are merely *gratiae gratis datae,* not *gratiae gratum facientes,* and therefore have nothing to do with the disposition of the recipient.) [1] It follows that the worthy reception of a Sacrament requires something more on the part of the recipient than mere valid reception.[2] In determining the requisites of a worthy reception of the Sacraments the Church shows how exalted her moral ideals are.[3] She declares that whoever consciously receives a Sacrament in an unworthy manner, *i. e.* without due preparation, is guilty of a sacrilege.[4] The unworthy recipient commits a greater

[1] *V. supra,* pp. 79 sqq.
[2] *V. supra,* Section 1.
[3] Cfr. *Conc. Trident.,* Sess. XIII, cap. 7.

[4] Cfr. St. Thomas, *Summa Theol.,* 2a 2ae, qu. 90, art. 3.

sin than the unworthy minister, because he prevents the
Sacrament from taking effect.   What St. Paul says of the
unworthy reception of the Eucharist,[5] applies in a manner
to all the Sacraments, inasmuch as the sacrilegious recipient manifests contempt for the Precious Blood of
Christ and compels our Lord, who is the principal minister, to perform a useless act, at least in as far as the
object of immediate sanctification is concerned.   St. Augustine draws a distinction between *habere* and *utiliter
habere*[6] and asks: "What does it avail a man to
be baptized if he is not justified?"[7]   The Church has
always insisted on the necessity of due preparation for the
reception of the Sacraments.

2. SACRAMENTS OF THE LIVING AND SACRA-
MENTS OF THE DEAD.—The requisites of worthy
reception are not the same for all the Sacraments.
The so-called Sacraments of the dead require for
their worthy reception attrition along with its
various dispositive acts (faith, fear, hope, etc.),
whereas the Sacraments of the living demand
nothing less than the state of grace.

a) Sacraments of the dead are those instituted
for the remission of sin or the production of the
state of grace (*iustificatio prima*).   There are
two—Baptism and Penance.   Their worthy reception depends upon the same requisites as justification itself, *viz.:* faith, fear, hope of forgiveness, contrition and a firm purpose of amend-

5 I Cor. XI, 27 sq.
6 *De Bapt. c. Donat.*, **IV**, 17, 24.
7 *De Civitate Dei*, XXI, 27, 3:

"*Quid cuiquam prodest quod baptizatur, si non iustificatur?*"

ment.   Cfr. Mark XVI, 16: "He that believeth
and is baptized, shall be saved."   Acts II, 38:
"Do penance and be baptized every one of you in
the name of Jesus Christ." [8]

The contrition required for Baptism and Penance need not be perfect.   Perfect contrition
(*contritio*), which is a true supernatural sorrow
from a motive of perfect charity, justifies a man
independently of the Sacraments.   Baptism and
Penance can be worthily received by one who has
an imperfect contrition.   Imperfect contrition
(*attritio*) is a true supernatural sorrow from a
motive of incipient charity or fear, coupled with a
firm purpose of amendment.[9]   It removes moral
indisposition (*remotio obicis*) and renders the
sinner worthy of receiving either Baptism or
Penance, thereby enabling these Sacraments to
effect his justification *ex opere operato*.

b) The case is somewhat different with the
Sacraments of the living.   Confirmation, the
Holy Eucharist, Extreme Unction, Matrimony,
and Holy Orders presuppose the state of sanctifying grace, which they merely increase (*iustificatio secunda*).   Hence the only requisite of a
worthy reception of these Sacraments is the state
of grace.   He who is in the state of grace places
no obstacle (*obex*) to the efficacy of these Sacra-

---

8 On justification, cfr. Pohle-
Preuss, *Grace, Actual and Habitual*,
pp. 274 sqq.

9 Cfr. *Conc. Trident.*, Sess. VI,
cap. 7; Sess. XIV, cap. 3.

ments, because he is not guilty of mortal sin. Venial sin may diminish but cannot prevent the effect of these Sacraments.

The sanctifying grace required for these Sacraments can be obtained either by making an act of perfect contrition or by worthily receiving the Sacrament of Penance.[10]   Confession, moreover, is prescribed by a law of the Church for the worthy reception of Communion.[11]   Though no such positive precept exists with regard to the other Sacraments, still confession as a fitting preparation for every one of them cannot be too urgently recommended.

READINGS :— St. Thomas, *Summa Theol.*, 3a, qu. 64; *Billuart, *De Sacramentis in Genere,* diss. 1, art. 2 sqq.; Ambrosius Catharinus, *De Necessaria Intentione in Perficiendis Sacramentis,* Rome 1552; Serry, *De Necessaria Intentione in Sacramentis Conficiendis,* Padua 1727; L. Haas, *Die notwendige Intention des Ministers zur gültigen Verwaltung der hl. Sakramente,* Bamberg 1869; *Franzelin, *De Sacramentis in Genere,* thes. 15 sqq.; P. Schanz, *Die Lehre von den hl. Sakramenten,* § 11, Freiburg 1893; B. J. Otten, S. J., *A Manual of the History of Dogmas,* Vol. I, p. 349. Additional bibliographical information in *Fr. Morgott, *Der Spender der hl. Sakramente nach der Lehre des hl. Thomas,* Freiburg 1886.

Concerning the requisites of worthy reception cfr. Suarez, *Comment. in S. Theol.,* III, disp. 14 sqq.; *De Lugo, *De Sacramentis in Genere,* disp. 9; Tournely, *De Sacramentis in Genere,* qu. 8; Schanz, *op. cit.,* § 12; N. Gihr, *Die hl. Sakramente der kath. Kirche,* Vol. 1, 2nd ed., § 23, Freiburg 1902.

10 Cfr. St. Thomas, *Summa Theol.,* 3a, qu. 79, art. 8.

11 Cfr. *Conc. Trident.,* Sess. XIII, cap. 7: Of course this law " only affects those who have fallen into mortal sin, so that, although venial sin may be confessed and affords sufficient matter for sacramental absolution, yet there is no law, human or divine, which imposes any obligation on the faithful in general to confess venial sins. The divine law does not do this, as the Council of Trent explains (Sess. XIV, c. 5), and the Lateran law only determines the divine law." (Slater, *A Manual of Moral Theology,* Vol. I, p. 566).

PART II

BAPTISM

The Catechism of the Council of Trent defines Baptism as "the Sacrament of regeneration by water in the word." [1]

This definition has been amplified by Catholic theologians as follows: "Baptism is a Sacrament instituted by Christ, in which, by the outward washing of the body with water, with invocation of the Three Persons of the Most Holy Trinity, man is spiritually reborn and sanctified unto life everlasting."

Hence the names: βαπτισμός (from βάπτειν, to immerse), "laver of regeneration;" φώτισμα, i. e. "illumination," "tinctio," etc.[2] Baptismus is sometimes used by the early Fathers to designate not only Baptism proper, but the anointing and laying-on of hands peculiar to the Sacrament of Confirmation. It is not true, however, as Harnack asserts, that Confirmation developed into an independent Sacrament by "a despoliation of the baptismal rite." [3]

---

[1] P. II, cap 2, n. 5: "Sacramentum regenerationis per aquam in verbo."

[2] The term tinctio is frequently used by Tertullian. Cfr. Oswald, Die dogmatische Lehre von den hl. Sakramenten, Vol. I, § 1, Münster 1894.

[3] Dogmengeschichte, Vol. I, 3rd ed., p. 358. See Dölger, Das Sakrament der Firmung, pp. 1 sqq., Vienna 1906.

CHAPTER I

Baptism is a true Sacrament because it was instituted by Jesus Christ as an external sign for the communication of internal grace.

SECTION 1

DIVINE INSTITUTION

The Council of Trent defines: "If any one saith that the Sacraments of the New Law were not all instituted by Jesus Christ our Lord, or that they are more or less than seven, to wit: Baptism, etc., . . . or even that any one of these seven is not truly and properly a Sacrament, let him be anathema." [1]

1. PROOF FROM REVELATION.—Notwithstanding Harnack's assertion that "it cannot be shown that Jesus instituted Baptism," [2] a perfectly conclusive argument for the divine institution of this Sacrament may be construed from Scripture and Tradition.

a) In the Old Testament Baptism was prefigured as a true Sacrament by many important types,—*e. g.,* circumcision, the deluge, the passage of the Chosen People through the Red Sea, etc. [3]

---

1 Sess. VII, *De Sacram.,* can. 1: "*Si quis dixerit, sacramenta Novae Legis non fuisse omnia a Iesu Christo instituta aut esse plura vel pauciora quam septem, vid. baptismum, etc., . . . aut etiam aliquod horum septem non esse vere et* proprie sacramentum, anathema sit.*" (Denzinger-Bannwart, n. 844).

2 *Dogmengeschichte,* Vol. I, 2nd ed., p. 68, n. 3, Freiburg 1894.

3 Cfr. St. Ambrose, *De Myst.,* cap. 3.

Cfr. Ez. XXXVI, 25: "I will pour out upon you clean water, and you shall be cleansed from all your filthiness." [4]

Zach. XIII, 1: "In that day [of the Messianic kingdom] there shall be a fountain open to the house of David, and to the inhabitants of Jerusalem, for the washing of the sinner and of the unclean woman." [5]

When John the Baptist told the priests and Levites who had been sent from Jerusalem to question him, that he was not the Christ, they wonderingly inquired: "Why then dost thou baptize, if thou be not Christ, nor Elias, nor the prophet?" [6] John explained that he baptized not as the future Messias would baptize, *i. e.* "with the Holy Ghost," but merely as a preparation for His coming. "I indeed baptize you in water unto penance, but he that shall soon come after me, is mightier than I, . . . he shall baptize you in the Holy Ghost and fire." [7]

Shortly after Christ began His public life, He came to the Jordan and was baptized by John, [8] thereby, as the Fathers explain, communicating to the baptismal water the power of forgiving sins. In his discourse with Nicodemus, Jesus declared that "unless a man be born again of water and the Holy Ghost, he cannot enter into the kingdom of God." [9] At His command the dis-

---

[4] Ez. XXXVI, 25: "*Effundam super vos aquam mundam et mundabimini ab omnibus inquinamentis vestris.*"

[5] Zach. XIII, 1: "*In die illa erit fons patens domui David et habitantibus Jerusalem in ablutionem peccatoris et menstruatae.*"

[6] John I, 25: "*Quid ergo baptizas, si tu non es Christus neque Elias neque propheta?*"

[7] Matth. III, 11: "*Ego quidem baptizo vos in aqua in poenitentiam; qui autem post me venturus est, fortior me est, . . . ipse vos baptizabit in Spiritu Sancto et igni.*"

[8] Cfr. Matth. III, 13.

[9] John III, 5: "*Nisi quis rena-*

ciples also baptized with water.[10]   Before His
Ascension He commanded them to go into the
whole world, to preach the gospel to all men, and
to baptize. "All power is given to me in heaven
and on earth. Going therefore, teach ye all nations, baptizing them in the name of the Father,
and of the Son, and of the Holy Ghost." [11]

b) How firmly the belief in the divine institution of Baptism was rooted among the faithful
in the primitive Church, is clear from the fact
that, with but few exceptions,[12] all heretical sects
admitted the Sacrament, though some of them
misunderstood its nature or denied its necessity.

This well-nigh universal consensus renders it superfluous to work out a detailed argument from Tradition. We
will merely adduce a passage from Tertullian. Com-
menting on the opposition between the Old and New
Testaments, that writer says: " In days gone by there
was salvation by means of bare faith, before the passion
of the Lord. But now that the faith has been enlarged,
. . . there has been an amplification of the Sacrament,
[namely], the sealing act of Baptism. . . . For the
law of baptizing has been imposed, and the formula prescribed: Go, saith [Jesus], teach all nations, baptizing

---

tus fuerit ex aqua et Spiritu Sancto,
non potest introire in regnum Dei."
   10 Cfr. John III, 26.
   11 Matth. XXVIII, 19: *" Data*
est mihi omnis potestas in coelo et
in terra. Euntes ergo docete omnes
gentes baptizantes eos in nomine
Patris et Filii et Spiritus Sancti."
(Cfr. Mark XVI, 15 sq.). On the
authenticity of this text see Riggen-

bach, *Der trinitarische Taufbefehl*
nach seiner ursprünglichen Textge-
stalt und seiner Authentie, Güters-
loh 1903, and the *Journal of Theo-*
logical Studies, 1905, pp. 481 sqq.

   12 The only exceptions we know
of, are the ancient Gnostics and
Manichæans, certain spiritualistic
sects of the Middle Ages, and the
modern Socinians.

them in the name of the Father, and of the Son, and of the Holy Ghost." [13]

2. WHEN DID CHRIST INSTITUTE BAPTISM?
—While the Fathers and theologians are unanimous regarding the fact of the divine institution of Baptism, they differ as to the precise time when this Sacrament was instituted.

a) Some [14] think that Baptism was instituted on Ascension day, when our Lord said to His disciples: "Going therefore, teach ye all nations, baptizing them in the name of the Father, and of the Son, and of the Holy Ghost." [15] The advocates of this view contend that the institution of a Sacrament is a legislative act, and that no such act with regard to Baptism is on record anywhere in the Gospels outside of Matth. XXVIII, 19. This agrees with the idea that the Church was formally established on Pentecost, and that it was only after its formal establishment that Baptism became necessary as a " door of entrance " into the Church.

It is objected to this view that the Apostles were alike Christians and priests before Christ's Passion and death, and that the power of consecrating bread and wine, which they received at the Last Supper, manifestly supposes that they were baptized. The defenders of the theory just

13 *De Bapt.*, c. 13: " *Retro quidem salus fuit per fidem nudam ante Domini passionem. At ubi fides aucta est credendi, addita est ampliatio sacramenti: obsignatio baptismi. . . . Lex enim tingendi imposita est et forma praescripta: Ite, inquit, docete omnes nationes, tingentes eas in nomine Patris et Filii et Spiritus Sancti.*" Further Patristic texts *infra*, No. 2.

14 Tertullian (*De Bapt.*, c. 11 sqq.), St. Chrysostom (*Hom. in Ioa.*, 28), St. Leo the Great (*Ep.* 16 *ad Sic. Episc.*), Alexander of Hales (*Comment. in Sent.*, IV, dist. 4, qu. 12, m. 3, art. 1), Melchior Cano (*De Locis Theol.*, VIII, 5), Berlage, Oswald, Bisping, Schanz, *et al.*

15 Matth. XXVIII, 19.

outlined reply that a mere act of the will on the part of the God-man was sufficient to make the Apostles Christians, nay priests and bishops, and that the only one who needed Baptism was St. Paul, because he came later. Cfr. Acts IX, 18: "And rising up, he was baptized." [16]

b) Others hold that our Lord instituted the Sacrament of Baptism before His sacred passion, either at the time of His own Baptism by St. John, or in his discourse with Nicodemus.[17] That the act of institution began with Christ's own Baptism as *terminus a quo,* was the opinion of such eminent Fathers as St. Gregory of Nazianzus, St. Augustine, and St. Ambrose.[18] It is also the teaching of St. Thomas. "A Sacrament is then instituted," he says, "when it receives the power of producing its effect. Now Baptism received this power when Christ was baptized. Consequently Baptism, considered as a Sacrament, was truly instituted at that time." [19]

Suarez [20] explains this more fully as follows: What happened when our Lord was baptized in the Jordan was merely the designation of matter and form. The formal institution of the Sacrament required a positive act or command, which must have followed soon after, as we read in the third and fourth chapters of St. John's Gospel that the disciples of Jesus baptized.[21] The Baptism they

16 Act. IX, 18: "*Et surgens baptizatus est.*"

17 That the Sacrament of Baptism was instituted by our Lord in His discourse with Nicodemus, was held by very few theologians, notably St. Bernard and Estius. Modern writers quite generally reject this view because of the private character of that discourse.

18 *In Luc.,* l. II, n. 83: "*Baptizatus est ergo Dominus non mundari volens, sed mundare aquas, ut ablutae per carnem Christi, quae pec-*

catum non novit, baptismatis ius haberent."

19 *Summa Theol.,* 3a, qu. 66, art. 2: "*Tunc videtur aliquod sacramentum institui, quando accipit virtutem producendi suum effectum. Hanc autem virtutem accepit baptismus, quando Christus est baptizatus. Unde tunc vere baptismus institutus fuit quantum ad ipsum sacramentum.*"

20 *De Sacram.,* disp. 19, sect. 2, n. 3.

21 John III, 26; IV, 2.

administered cannot have been a mere Baptism of prose-
lytes, nor yet a Baptism unto penance, like that of the
Precursor, but it must have been that Baptism "in the
Holy Ghost and fire" which John himself had so sharply
distinguished from his own.[22]

According to this theory, therefore, the institution of
the Sacrament of Baptism coincides with the beginning
of our Lord's public career.[23] Scotus says: "The disciples of Christ baptized before the passion; whence it
follows that the Sacrament was instituted before that
event, though the Gospel tells us nothing about the exact
time." [24]

There is an ancient legend that Jesus Himself baptized St. Peter, St. Peter baptized St. Andrew and the
sons of Zebedee, and these in turn baptized the remaining
Apostles, while the seventy disciples received the Sacra-
rament at the hands of Peter and John.[25]

c) Which of the opinions just reviewed is the more
probable one? Both are supported by solid arguments.
Sacramental Baptism may have been instituted by our
Lord before His Passion without those characteristics of
universality and necessity (*necessitas medii*) which attached to it after the Ascension. It was only when He
spoke the words: "*Euntes ergo,*" etc., that He solemnly
promulgated this Sacrament as an indispensable means of
salvation for all men. Hence the two views can easily be

22 Cfr. Matth. III, 11; Mark I,
8; Luke III, 16; John I, 33.

23 Cfr. J. Grimm, *Das Leben
Jesu,* Vol. II, pp. 364 sq., Ratisbon
1878.

24 *Comment. in Sent.,* IV, dist. 3,
qu. 4: "*Discipuli Christi ante passionem Christi baptizabant. Con-
vincitur ergo tempus institutionis
fuisse ante illud tempus, quo dis-*

*cipuli Christi baptizabant, licet hora
institutionis non legatur in Evangelio.*" Similarly Gabriel Biel,
Suarez, Holzklau (*Wirceb.*), and
more recently Chr. Pesch (*Praelect. Dogmat.,* Vol. VI, 3rd ed., p.
156, Freiburg 1908).

25 Cfr. Nicephorus Callistus, *Hist.
Eccles.,* II, 3.

reconciled by assuming that Baptism was instituted for a limited circle and without superseding circumcision, at the beginning of our Saviour's public career, but was not solemnly promulgated nor invested with the characteristics of universality and necessity until after His Ascension. St. Bonaventure, finding a grain of truth in each of these hypotheses, happily blends them as follows: " When was Baptism instituted? With regard to its matter, it was instituted at the time when Christ was baptized in the Jordan; with regard to its form, when He arose from the dead and designated the form (Matth. XXVIII, 19) ; with regard to its effects, when He suffered, because it is from His passion that the virtue of the Sacrament springs; and with regard to its final end and object, when He foretold its necessity and utility by saying (John III, 5) : ' Unless a man be born again,' etc." [26]

[26] *Comment. in Ioa., c. 3, n. 19:* " *Quando institutus est baptismus? Dicendum quod materialiter, quum baptizatus fuit Christus; formaliter, quum resurrexit et formam dedit (Matth. XXVIII, 19); effective, quum passus fuit, quia inde habuit virtutem; sed finaliter, quum eius necessitatem praedixit et utilitatem (Ioa. III, 5): Nisi quis renatus fuerit, etc.*" Cfr. the Innsbruck *Zeitschrift für kath. Theologie,* 1905, pp. 53 sqq.

SECTION 2

MATTER AND FORM

According to Catholic teaching the remote matter of Baptism is natural water; its proximate matter is the act of external washing; while the sacramental form is contained in the words: "I baptize thee in the name of the Father, and of the Son, and of the Holy Ghost."

1. NATURAL WATER THE REMOTE MATTER OF BAPTISM.—By natural water (*aqua naturalis*) is meant a liquid compound of hydrogen and oxygen in the proportion of two to one. This definition excludes artificial compounds such as *eau de Cologne,* as well as water in other than liquid form, *e. g.* steam or ice.[1] That natural water is indispensable for the validity of Baptism has been clearly defined by the Tridentine Council: "If any one saith that true and natural water is not of necessity for Baptism, . . . let him be anathema."[2] This declaration excludes the figurative use of the term "water," as employed by the later Socinians, and denies Luther's assertion that

---

[1] Cfr. the *Catechismus Romanus,* P. II, c. 2, n. 7.

[2] *Conc. Trident.,* Sess. VII, *De Bapt.,* can. 2 (Denzinger-Bannwart, n. 858): "*Si quis dixerit, aquam veram et naturalem non esse de necessitate praecepti, . . . anathema sit.*"

any liquid that can be used to bathe in, is valid
matter for Baptism.[3]

a) The Old Testament types clearly point to natural
water as the element of the future Sacrament of Baptism. Such types are, *e. g.,* the deluge,[4] the passage of
the Israelites through the Red Sea,[5] the stream of water
which Moses drew from the rock in the desert, etc. The
prophetical "*fons patens*" in the passage quoted from
Zacharias [6] obviously refers to the baptismal font of the
New Law. John and the disciples baptized with ordinary
water. Jesus Christ descended into the river Jordan to
receive Baptism. Wherever the New Testament mentions the Sacrament of regeneration, it invariably speaks
of water. Cfr. John III, 5: "Unless a man be born
again of water and the Holy Ghost, he cannot enter into
the kingdom of heaven." When Philip and the eunuch
of Queen Candace "came to a certain water," the latter
exclaimed: "See, here is water: what doth hinder me
from being baptized?"[7]

The Baptism "of fire and the Holy Ghost," of which
the Precursor speaks, does not denote an outward rite but
refers to the spiritual effect of the Sacrament administered
in the name of Christ.[8]

b) The Catholic Church has always conscien-
tiously adhered, both in theory and practice, to the
use of natural water as the only valid element of
Baptism.

---

3 ". . . *quidquid balnei loco esse
possit, illud aptum esse ad baptizandum.*" The passage occurs in his
Table Talk. Cfr. Pallavicini, *Hist.
Conc. Trident.,* IX, 7.

4 1 Pet. III, 20 sqq.

5 1 Cor. X, 2 sqq.

6 Zach. XIII, 1 (*supra,* p. 205, n. 5).

7 Acts VIII, 36: "*Ecce aqua,
quid prohibet me baptizari?*" Cfr.
Acts X, 47; Eph. V, 26.

8 Cfr. Ansaldi, O. P., *De Baptismate in Spiritu Sancto et Igni,*
Milan 1752.

Tertullian exclaims: "O happy Sacrament of our water, by which, cleansed of the faults of pristine blindness, we are made free unto eternal life!"[9]

St. Augustine says: "What is the Baptism of Christ? A bath in the word. Take away the water, and there is no Baptism; take away the word, and there is no Baptism."[10]

The Fathers of the Church were familiar with the ceremony of blessing the baptismal font.[11]

St. Cyprian writes: "Therefore it behooves water to be first cleansed and sanctified by a priest, in order that by his Baptism he may be able to wash away the sins of him who is baptized."[12]

St. Gregory of Nyssa says: "The sanctified water cleanses and illumines a man."[13]

It was because of her firm conviction that water is the necessary element of Baptism that the Church condemned the practice of baptizing with oil, introduced by the Gnostic sect of the Marcosians, or with fire, as affected by the Jacobites and Cathari in the Middle Ages, or with beer, as attempted by certain Norwegians.[14]

c) Speculative theology has discovered a variety of reasons showing the fitness of water to

[9] De Bapt., c. 1, n. 1: "Felix sacramentum aquae nostrae, qua abluti delictis pristinae caecitatis in vitam aeternam liberamur!"

[10] Tract. in Ioa., 15, n. 4: "Quid est baptismus Christi? Lavacrum aquae in verbo. Tolle aquam, non est baptismus; tolle verbum, non est baptismus."

[11] On the antiquity of this ceremony consult Probst, Sakramente und Sakramentalien in den ersten drei Jahrhunderten, pp. 74 sqq., Tübingen 1872.

[12] Ep., 70, 1: "Oportet ergo mundari et sanctificari aquam prius a sacerdote, ut possit baptismo suo peccata hominis, qui baptizatur, abluere."

[13] Or. de Bapt. Christi: ὕδωρ εὐλογούμενον καθαίρει καὶ φωτίζει τὸν ἄνθρωπον.— On certain exaggerated notions current in Patristic days with regard to the efficacy of the water "sanctified" for Baptism, see Pourrat, La Théologie Sacramentaire, pp. 47 sqq., Paris 1910 (English tr., pp. 56 sq.).

[14] Cfr. the letter addressed by Pope Gregory IX to the bishops of

serve as the element of Baptism. We will mention only a few.

a) Baptism, being a Sacrament instituted for the forgiveness of sins, requires an element which symbolizes both the dissolution and removal of moral filth and the healing of the soul. Now water is not only the ordinary and most effective means of cleansing, but it is likewise a medicine and a preservative of health. Pindar's saw ᾽Αριστον μὲν ὕδωρ, embodies the universal conviction of mankind. Water, moreover, is by nature cool and refreshing, and consequently well adapted to serve as a symbol of grace, which extinguishes the fire of concupiscence. It was quite natural, therefore, for the Jews to employ water as an element of purification in their religious ceremonies,[15] and for the Gentiles to use it in their mystic ablutions.[16] Such usages clearly speak for the Catholic doctrine.[17]

β) As the Sacrament of " regeneration,"— whence the term " neophytes " for those recently baptized,— Baptism furthermore requires an element that serves an important purpose in organic nature. Water is indispensable for the growth of plants and animals. Gen. I, 2: " And the spirit of God moved [the Hebrew text has ' brooded '] over the waters." The fact that the foetus of mammals, birds, and reptiles is enclosed in a " water bag " (amnion), led some of the Fathers, *e. g.* St. Chrysostom, to compare the baptismal font with the womb.[18] Then there are creatures that can live only in water, and since Baptism, being " the first and most necessary Sacrament," is as in-

Norway, in Raynald, *Annales Ecles. ad annum* 1241, n. 42.

15 Cfr. Numb. VIII, 7.

16 Cfr. Tertullian, *De Bapt.*, c. 5.

17 On Baptism in pre-Christian times and among non-Christian nations, consult Oswald, *Die dogmatische Lehre von den hl. Sakramenten,* 5th ed., § 1.

18 *V. supra,* pp. 130 sq.

dispensable to the supernatural life of the soul as water is to the natural life of fish, Tertullian appropriately compares the faithful to " little fishes," who are born in water and move in it as their vital element.[19]

The fact that no natural element is so easily available as water also points to the necessity of Baptism for salvation.

2. Washing with Water the Proximate Matter of Baptism.

—Baptism is administered by means of washing, *i. e.* applying the water to the subject. This application must be a true ablution (*ablutio vera*), *i. e.* it must involve a contact that is both physical and successive. In other words, the baptismal water must actually touch the body and flow over it.

This twofold contact can be effected by immersion, effusion, and aspersion. The validity of the present practice of effusion has been indirectly defined against the schismatic Greeks by the Council of Trent: " If any one saith that in the Roman Church, which is the mother and mistress of all churches, there is not the true doctrine concerning the Sacrament of Baptism, let him be anathema." [20]

a) The very name *baptismus* (derived from βάπτειν, *to immerse*), as well as St. Paul's use of the

---

19 *De Bapt.*, c. 1: " *Sed nos pisculi secundum* ἰχθύν *nostrum Iesum Christum in aqua nascimur, nec aliter quam in aqua permanendo salvi sumus.*"

20 Sess. VII, *De Bapt.*, can. 3:

" *Si quis dixerit, in Ecclesia Romana, quae omnium ecclesiarum mater est et magistra, non esse veram de baptismi sacramento doctrinam, anathema sit.*" (Denzinger-Bannwart, n. 859).

term "laver of water,"[21] indicate that Baptism was originally accomplished by immersion.

However, since the Baptism of the three thousand converts on Pentecost Day,[22] and that of the keeper of the prison and his family by Paul and Silas,[23] can hardly be supposed to have taken place by immersion, it is likely that already in the Apostolic age Baptism was sometimes conferred by effusion or aspersion.

b) That washing with water is the *materia proxima* of Baptism cannot be proved from Sacred Scripture, but it can be convincingly demonstrated from Tradition.

Tertullian describes Baptism as " a sprinkling with any kind of water."[24]

St. Augustine declares that Baptism has the power of forgiving sins even if the water "merely sprinkles the child ever so slightly."[25]

A convincing proof for the antiquity of Baptism by effusion is furnished by the so-called "*baptismus clinicorum*" ($\dot{\eta}$ $\kappa\lambda\acute{\iota}\nu\eta$, bed), which was always administered in that way.[26] When a certain Magnus professed to have scruples of conscience regarding this mode of administering the Sacrament, St. Cyprian assured him that it was perfectly valid.[27]

---

21 Eph. V, 26: $\tau\hat{\omega}$ $\lambda o\upsilon\tau\rho\hat{\omega}$ $\tau o\hat{\upsilon}$ $\mathring{\upsilon}\delta a\tau o\varsigma$.

22 Acts II, 41.

23 Acts XVI, 33.

24 *De Bapt.*, c. 6: "*una aspergio cuiuslibet aquae.*"

25 *Tract. in Ioa.*, 80, n. 3: " *Hoc verbum fidei tantum valet in Ecclesia Dei, ut per ipsum . . . tingen-* tem etiam tantillum mundet infantem.*"

26 Cfr. Eusebius, *Hist. Eccl.*, VI, 43; Martène, *De Antiquis Ecclesiae Ritibus*, I, 1, 14.

27 *Ep.*, 69, n. 12, ed. Hartel, II, 761: " *Nec quemquam movere debet quod aspergi vel perfundi videntur aegri, quum gratiam dominicam con-*

Baptism by effusion was regarded as equally valid with
Baptism by immersion long before the time of St. Cyprian. The famous Didache (*Doctrina XII Apostolorum*), rediscovered in 1883 and ascribed to the time of
the Emperor Nerva (d. 98), says: "Baptize in the name
of the Father, and of the Son, and of the Holy Ghost, in
running water; but if thou hast no running water, baptize in other water, and if thou canst not in cold, then in
warm. But if thou hast neither, pour water three times
on the head in the name of the Father, and of the Son,
and of the Holy Ghost (ἔκχεον εἰς τὴν κεφαλὴν τρὶς ὕδωρ εἰς
ὄνομα πατρὸς καὶ υἱοῦ καὶ ἁγίου πνεύματος)." [28]

c) A few observations on the history of the
various methods of administering Baptism may
prove useful.

a) During the first twelve centuries Baptism was generally administered by immersion. Three times in suc-
cession the candidate was plunged entirely in water by
the baptizing bishop or priest, assisted by deacons, or, in the
case of adult females, by deaconesses. Numerous ancient
baptisteries (*fontes sacri*, κολυμβῆθραι) in various parts of
the western world attest the antiquity of this custom.
The Greeks (Russians, Bulgarians, etc.) have retained
Baptism by immersion, though they no longer practice it
in its pure form, but dip the child in warm water up to

sequantur, quando Scriptura sancta
per Ezechielem prophetam dicat:
'Aspergam super vos aquam mundam.' Unde apparet, aspersionem
quoque aquae instar salutaris lavacri
obtinere."

28 *Doctrina XII Apost.*, c. 7, ed.
Funk, p. 23, Tübingen 1887; English tr. by Kirsopp Lake, *The Apostolic Fathers* in the Loeb Classical
Library, pp. 320 sq., London 1912.

On a painting in the catacombs which
illustrates this passage cfr. De
Rossi, *Roma Sotteranea*, Vol. I, p.
334, Rome 1867. Rogers (*Baptism
and Christian Archaeology*, London
1903) is evidently mistaken when he
asserts that immersion is the oldest
form of Baptism. Cfr. Ermoni, *Le
Baptême dans l'Eglise Primitive*,
Paris 1904.

the neck and then pour water over his head.[29] Despite
the complaint of Marcus Eugenicus of Ephesus, the Ori-
entals at the Council of Florence (1439) raised no objection to the Latin mode of baptizing, though to-day they
regard it as invalid.[30]

Baptism by immersion was still the rule in Western
Christendom at the time of St. Thomas, for he says in
the third part of the *Summa:* "Although it is safer to
baptize by immersion,·because this is the more ordinary
fashion, yet Baptism can be conferred by sprinkling or
also by pouring . . ."[31]

In Spain, which had been overrun by the Arian Visi-
goths, a single immersion was substituted for the three
formerly employed, in order to illustrate Catholic belief
in the unity of the Godhead in three Persons. St. Martin
of Bracara (d. 580) decried this practice as Sabellian,[32]
but it was approved by Pope Gregory the Great (d. 604)
and formally prescribed by the Fourth Council of Toledo
(632).

β) Baptism by effusion gradually came into use in
the thirteenth century, and finally replaced Baptism
by immersion entirely in the West. St. Charles Borro-
meo still prescribed the ancient form of trine immersion for the churches of the Ambrosian rite, and this
form continued to be widely used in Europe up to the
sixteenth century. The reasons for the universal adoption of the change probably were the difficulties arising

---

[29] Cfr. Denzinger, *Rit. Orient.*,
Vol. I, p. 235, 287, Würzburg 1863;
Goar, *Euchologium s. Rituale Graecorum, in bapt. off. not.* 24, Paris
1647.

[30] Cfr. *Synod. Lat.* IV, c. 4
(1215), in Denzinger-Bannwart, n.
435.

[31] *Summa Theol.*, 3a, qu. 66, art.

7: "*Quamvis tutius sit baptizare
per modum immersionis, quia hoc
habet communior usus, potest tamen
fieri baptismus per modum asper-
sionis vel etiam per modum infu-
sionis.*"

[32] Cfr. Bardenhewer-Shahan, *Patrology,* p. 659, St. Louis 1908.

in cold countries and in regard to the immersion of women. When Europe had become entirely Christian, and there were no longer any adult pagans, the institute of deaconesses ceased to exist.

The method of baptizing by aspersion has never acquired practical importance, and the discussion of its validity is therefore purely academic.[33]

3. THE SACRAMENTAL FORM, OR THE FORMULA OF BAPTISM.—The form of Baptism consists in the words accompanying the ablution. There are two essential parts: (1) the verbal designation of the baptismal act, and (2) the express invocation of the three Persons of the Most Holy Trinity.

The *Decretum pro Armenis* of Eugene IV says: "The form is: 'I baptize thee in the name of the Father, and of the Son, and of the Holy Ghost,' . . . because when the act is expressed, which is performed by the minister with the invocation of the Holy Trinity, the Sacrament is accomplished." [34]

a) The necessity of a baptismal formula is indicated by St. Paul in his Epistle to the Ephesians:

33 For further information on the various ways of baptizing and their history the student may consult the treatise on "*Die Entstehung der heutigen Taufform,*" in Funk's *Kirchengeschichtliche Abhandlungen und Untersuchungen,,* Vol. I, pp. 478 sqq., Paderborn 1897; also A. Staerk, *Der Taufritus in der griechisch-russischen Kirche,* sein apostolischer Ursprung und seine Entwicklung, Freiburg 1903.

34 "*Forma autem est: ' Ego te baptizo in nomine Patris et Filii et Spiritus Sancti' . . .; quoniam si exprimitur actus, qui per ipsum exercetur ministrum cum SS. Trinitatis invocatione, perficitur sacramentum.*" (Denzinger-Bannwart, n. 696).

". . . cleansing it by the laver of water in the word of life." [35]

The words of our Lord: ". . . baptizing them in the name of the Father, and of the Son, and of the Holy Ghost," [36] have always been understood by the Church not merely as a command to baptize, but as embodying the formula of Baptism. This is the unanimous teaching of Tradition. Tertullian writes: "The law of baptizing has been imposed, and the formula prescribed: 'Go,' He saith, 'teach the nations,' etc." [37] St. Cyprian says: "Christ Himself commanded the nations to be baptized in the full and undivided Trinity." [38] St. Ambrose instructs his catechumens that "Unless a man is baptized in the name of the Father, and of the Son, and of the Holy Ghost, he cannot receive remission of his sins nor the gift of spiritual grace." [39] St. Augustine asks: "Who is there who does not know that there is no Baptism of Christ, if the words of the Gospel, in which consists the outward visible sign, are lacking?" [40] St. Basil denies the validity of Baptism if conferred merely "in the name of the Lord," because, he says, "as we believe in the Father, and the Son, and the Holy Ghost, so, too, we are baptized in the name of the Father, and of the Son, and of the Holy Ghost." [41] St. Chrysostom, in his explanation

[35] Eph. V, 26: ". . . mundans lavacro aquae in verbo vitae."

[36] Matth. XXVIII, 19: ". . . baptizantes eos in nomine Patris et Filii et Spiritus Sancti."

[37] De Bapt., c. 13: "Lex tingendi imposita est et forma praescripta: Ite, inquit, docete nationes, etc."

[38] Ep. 73 ad Iubai., n. 18, ed. Hartel, II, 791: "Ipse Christus gentes baptizari iubet in plena et adunata Trinitate."

[39] De Myst., c. 4, n. 20: "Nisi baptizatus fuerit in nomine Patris et Filii et Spiritus Sancti, remissionem non potest accipere peccatorum nec spiritualis gratiae munus haurire."

[40] De Bapt., VI, 25, 47: "Quis nesciat non esse baptismum Christi, si verba evangelica, quibus symbolum constat, illic defuerint?"

[41] De Spiritu Sancto, c. 12.

of Eph. V, 26, observes: "In the laver of water he cleanses him from his impurity. In the word, he says. In what word? In the name of the Father, and of the Son, and of the Holy Ghost." [42]

b) In connection with this subject theologians are wont to discuss two incidental problems, *viz.*: What was the meaning of Baptism "in the name of Jesus," of which we read in the Acts of the Apostles? and: In how far may the prescribed baptismal formula be altered without affecting the validity of the Sacrament?

α) Did the Apostles baptize validly when they baptized "in the name of Jesus"? [43] Opinions differ on this question. Peter Lombard says: "He who baptizes in the name of Christ, baptizes in the name of the Trinity, which is thereby understood;" but he cautiously adds: "It is, however, safer to name the Three Persons expressly." [44] The majority of theologians dissent from this view. They hold that the Apostles employed the formula "In the name of Jesus" by virtue of an extraordinary privilege. St. Thomas says: "It was by a special revelation from Christ that in the primitive Church the Apostles baptized in the name of Christ, in order that the name of Christ, which was hateful to Jews and Gentiles, might become an object of veneration, in that the Holy Ghost was given in Baptism at the invocation of that name." [45] Since the Tridentine Council the more general

---

42 *Hom. in Ep. ad Eph.*, 20. Cfr. St. John Damascene, *De Fide Orth.*, IV, 9.

43 Cfr. Gal. III, 27; Acts II, 38; VIII, 12; X, 48.

44 *Sent.*, IV, dist. 3: "*Qui ergo baptizat in nomine Christi, baptizat in nomine Trinitatis, quae ibi intelligitur. Tutius est tamen, tres personas ibi nominare.*"

45 *Summa Theol.*, 3a, qu. 66, art. 6: "*Dicendum quod ex speciali Christi revelatione Apostoli in primitiva Ecclesia in nomine Christi*

opinion [46] is that Baptism in the name of Jesus, in contra-distinction to the " Baptism of penance " which the Precursor administered,[47] received its name not from the external rite but from its institution by Christ; in other words that in baptizing in the name of Christ the Apostles meant to baptize by His authority. This is not a new theory, but was held by many of the early Fathers.[48] Though the Roman Catechism [49] attempts to justify the view that " there was a time when, by the inspiration of the Holy Ghost, the Apostles baptized in the name of our Lord Jesus Christ only," we do not deem it prudent, without stringent proofs to admit such a radical distinction between the baptismal practice of Apostolic and that of post-Apostolic times. It is true that Pope Nicholas I (d. 867) seems to have admitted the validity of Baptism in the name of Christ,[50] but his letter to the Bulgarians, in which he expresses this opinion, is not an *ex cathedra* decision; [51] and even if it were, the fact would prove nothing, because in the case of the Bulgarians the question at issue was not the formula of Baptism but the qualifications required in the minister.[52]

baptizabant, ut nomen Christi, quod erat odiosum Iudaeis et gentibus, honorabile redderetur per hoc, quod ad eius invocationem Spiritus Sanctus dabatur in baptismo." This opinion is shared by St. Bede, Albertus Magnus, St. Bonaventure, Scotus, Cajetan, Toletus, Orsi, *et al.*

46 Among those who espouse this teaching are Melchior Cano, Dom. Soto, Cardinal Bellarmine, Suarez, Vasquez, Tournely, and nearly all modern theologians.

47 Cfr. Acts XIX, 1 sqq.

48 Among others, St. Cyprian (*Ep.* 73 *ad Iubai.*, n. 17, ed. Hartel, II, 791), St. Augustine (*Contra Maxim.*, II, 17, 1), St. Fulgentius (*C.*

Fabian., fragm. 37), Origen (*In Ep. ad Rom.*, l. 5; Migne, *P. G.*, XIV, 1039), St. Basil (*De Spiritu S.*, c. 12), St. Chrysostom (*Hom. in 2 Cor.*, XXX, 13, 13).

49 P. II, c. 2, n. 15 sq.

50 " *A quodam Iudaeo . . . multos in patria vestra baptizatos asseritis et quid de iis sit agendum consulitis. Hi profecto, si in nomine S. Trinitatis vel tantum in Christi nomine . . . baptizati sunt, constat eos non esse denuo baptizandos."* (Denzinger-Bannwart, n. 335).

51 See Hergenröther's *Antijanus*, p. 55, Freiburg 1869.

52 For further information on this

β) Alterations in the formula of Baptism may or may not affect its substance. Substantial changes render the Sacrament invalid; purely accidental changes do not. It would be a substantial change, for instance, to omit all reference to the act performed, or to neglect to invoke the Three Persons of the Trinity. Hence we may distinguish three groups of formulas: (1) such as are certainly invalid, (2) such as are undoubtedly valid, and (3) such as are doubtful.

(1) Alexander III decided that it would render Baptism invalid to omit the words: "I baptize thee," and simply to say: "In the name of the Father," etc.[53] As all Three Divine Persons must be expressly mentioned, it would likewise be invalid to baptize "in the name of the Most Holy Trinity." The Montanist formula: "I baptize thee in the name of the Father, and of the Son, and — of Montanus and Priscilla," was plainly invalid. But even when all Three Persons are expressly named, Baptism would still be invalid if the minister would introduce a phrase embodying an anti-Trinitarian heresy,[54] e. g., "I baptize thee in the names of the Father, and of the Son, and of the Holy Ghost."[55]

(2) Any baptismal formula that meets the two requirements mentioned, is valid, even though it show accidental variations from the approved text, as does, for instance, the Greek formula: Βαπτίζεται ὁ δοῦλος τοῦ Θεοῦ (ὁ δεῖνας) εἰς τὸ ὄνομα τοῦ πατρὸς καὶ τοῦ υἱοῦ καὶ τοῦ ἁγίου πνεύματος, the validity of which is expressly admitted

subject cfr. Cano, de Locis Theol., VI, 8; Orsi, De Baptismo in Nomine Iesu, Florence 1743; Heitmüller, Im Namen Jesu, 1905; H. Koch, Die Tauflehre des Liber de Rebaptismate, Braunsberg 1907; J. Tixeront, Apologetical Studies, St. Louis 1917, pp. 34 sqq.

[53] C. "Si quis," 1 Extrav., De

Bapt.: "Si quis puerum ter in aqua merserit in nomine Patris et Filii et Spiritus Sancti, . . . et non dixerit: 'Ego te baptizo,' puer non est baptizatus."

[54] Tritheism, Arianism, etc.

[55] "Baptizo te in nominibus Patris et Filii et Spiritus Sancti."

in the *Decretum pro Armenis*.[56] Valid, though illicit, are all those formulas in which some non-essential word or phrase is either added to or omitted from the prescribed text; *e. g.*: "*Baptizo* (*abluo, tingo*) *te in nomine*," etc., or: "*Baptizo te credentem in nomine Patris et Filii et Spiritus Sancti, ut habeas vitam aeternam.*" Alterations made in ignorance of the language employed, and without heretical intent, do not render Baptism invalid, provided that, according to popular estimation, the objective meaning of the formula is preserved. This was decided by Pope Zachary in a case submitted to him by St. Boniface, where an ignorant cleric had mispronounced the usual formula as follows: "*Ego te baptizo in nomine patria et filia et spiritu sancta.*"[57] The Slavic formula: "*Ja te krstim*" (*krstim* derived from *krstiti* = make Christian; *Krst* = Christ) was approved by the Holy See in 1894, on the ground that the verb *krsti* also means to wash off.[58] This can hardly be said to apply to our English word "christen."

(3) Doubtful, though presumably valid, are those formulas in which it is difficult to decide whether the alterations that have been introduced relate to essential or to purely accidental portions, as, *e. g.*: "I baptize thee in the Father, and in the Son, and in the Holy Ghost." The formula: "I baptize thee in the name of the Father, and in the name of the Son, and in the name of the Holy

---

[56] "*Non tamen negamus, quin et per illa verba: 'Baptizatur talis servus Christi in nomine Patris et Filii et Spiritus Sancti,' verum perficiatur sacramentum.*" (Denzinger-Bannwart, n. 696). The variant "*Baptizetur*" in the above text is probably incorrect, because the Greeks do not say βαπτιζέσθω, but βαπτίζεται. Cfr. Goar, *Euchol.*, p. 355; Probst, *Sakramente und Sakramentalien in den ersten drei Jahrhunderten*, pp. 148 sqq., Tübingen 1872.

[57] Cfr. Mansi, *Conc.*, t. XII, p. 325.

[58] See the Innsbruck *Zeitschrift für kath. Theologie*, 1901, p. 318.

Ghost," was considered doubtful by St. Alphonsus, but on Jan. 13, 1882, the Congregation of the Holy Office decided that the use of this formula does not render Baptism invalid, because the heresy of Tritheism is not necessarily implied therein.

SECTION 3

SACRAMENTAL EFFECTS

Baptism has for its general effect the regeneration of the soul,[1] and hence belongs to the " Sacraments of the dead."

Its specific effects are three, *viz.:* (1) the grace of justification (*iustificatio prima*); (2) forgiveness of all the penalties of sin; and (3) the sacramental character.

1. FIRST EFFECT: THE GRACE OF JUSTIFICATION.—Justification comprises the remission of sin and the sanctification of the soul. Baptism, as a means of justification, must therefore forgive sin and infuse sanctifying grace. Such is indeed the defined teaching of the Church. "If any one denies," says the Council of Trent, "that, by the grace of our Lord Jesus Christ, which is conferred in Baptism, the guilt of original sin is remitted, or even asserts that the whole of that which has the true and proper nature of sin, is not taken away, . . . let him be anathema." [2] And in the *Decretum pro Armenis* Eugene IV de-

---

[1] Cfr. Tit. III, 5: " *lavacrum regenerationis.*"

[2] Sess. V, can. 5: " *Si quis per Iesu Christi Domini nostri gratiam, quae in baptismate confertur, reatum originalis peccati remitti negat aut etiam asserit non tolli totum id, quod veram et propriam peccati rationem habet, . . . anathema sit.*" (Denzinger-Bannwart, n. 792).

clares: "The effect of this Sacrament [Baptism] is the remission of every sin, original and actual."[3]

a) For the Scriptural proof of this dogma we refer to our treatises on *God the Author of Nature and the Supernatural,* pp. 238 sqq., and *Grace, Actual and Habitual,* pp. 328 sqq., and also to the general introduction to the Sacraments, *supra,* pp. 188 sqq.

b) In this connection theologians are wont to discuss several problems intimately related to sacramental justification.

α) Though Baptism completely blots out the guilt of original sin (*reatus culpae*), there still remains concupiscence (*fomes peccati, concupiscentia*), which, however, no longer partakes of the nature of guilt, but is merely a consequence of original sin.[4] This teaching was emphasized by St. Augustine.[5]

Besides forgiving sin and producing sanctifying grace, with all its formal effects — justice, supernatural beauty, the friendship of God, and His adoptive sonship [6]— Baptism also effects the supernatural concomitants of sanctifying grace, *viz.*: the three divine virtues of faith, hope, and charity, the infused moral virtues, and the seven gifts of the Holy Ghost, including His personal indwell-

3 "*Huius sacramenti effectus est remissio omnis culpae originalis et actualis.*" (Denzinger-Bannwart, n. 696).

4 Cfr. *Conc. Trident.,* Sess. V, can. 5.

5 *Contra Duas Epist. Pelag.,* III, 3: "*Baptismus abluit peccata omnia, prorsus omnia factorum, dictorum, cogitatorum sive originalia sive addita [i. e. actualia] . . .; sed non aufert infirmitatem [i. e. fomitem], cui regeneratus resistit, quando bonum agonem luctatur.*"

6 Cfr. Pohle-Preuss, *Grace, Actual and Habitual,* pp. 356 sqq.

ing in the soul, which is the crown and climax of the process of justification.[7] The Fathers extol these prerogatives in glowing terms. St. Gregory of Nazianzus, *e. g.*, says: " Baptism is the splendor of the soul, life's amendment, the uplifting of conscience to God, a means of getting rid of our weakness, the laying aside of the flesh, the attainment of the spirit, the participation of the Word, the drowning of sin, the communication of light, the dispersion of darkness." [8]

β) The very excellence of these effects,— not to speak of the sacramental character which Baptism imprints,[9] — compels us to draw an essential distinction between the Baptism of Christ and that administered by John the Baptist. The existence of such a distinction is expressly affirmed by the Tridentine Council: " If any one saith that the Baptism of John had the same force as the Baptism of Christ, let him be anathema." [10] The Baptism of John was merely an exhortation to do penance and to prepare for the coming of the Messias, and consequently cannot have had the same power as the Baptism of Christ. This explains why St. Paul, upon meeting the twelve disciples of John at Ephesus, commanded them to be rebaptized in the name of Jesus before he imposed his hands on them and called down the Holy Ghost. " John," he explained, " baptized the people with the Baptism of penance, saying that they should believe in him who was to come after him, that is to say, in Jesus." [11] The teaching of the Fathers agrees perfectly with this. We pass

---

[7] *Ibid.,* pp. 362 sqq.

[8] *Or. de Bapt.,* 40, n. 4 (Migne, *P. G.,* XXXVI, 362).

[9] *V. infra,* No. 3, pp. 234 sqq.

[10] Sess. VII, *De Bapt.,* can. 1: " Si quis dixerit, baptismum Ioannis habuisse eandem vim cum baptismo Christi, anathema sit." (Denzinger-Bannwart, n. 857).

[11] Acts XIX, 4: " *Ioannes baptizavit baptismo poenitentiae* (βάπτισμα μετανοίας) *populum, dicens: In eum qui venturus esset post ipsum ut crederent, hoc est in Iesum.*"

over Tertullian,[12] St. Ambrose,[13] St. Chrysostom,[14] St. Gregory the Great,[15] and others, and content ourselves with quoting a passage from St. Augustine. "I ask, therefore," he says in his treatise *De Baptismo contra Donatistas*, "if sins were remitted by the Baptism of John, what more could the Baptism of Christ confer on those whom the Apostle Paul desired to be baptized with the Baptism of Christ after they had received the Baptism of John?"[16] The difference must have consisted in this that the Baptism of John did not produce its effects *ex opere operato*, but through the disposition of the recipient (*ex opere operantis*), as St. Thomas explains with his usual clearness: "The Baptism of John did not confer grace, but only prepared for grace; and this in three ways: first, by John's teaching, which led men to faith in Christ, secondly, by accustoming men to the rite of Christ's Baptism; thirdly, by penance, preparing men to receive the effect of Christ's Baptism."[17] In other words, "the Baptism of John was not in itself a Sacrament, properly so called, but a kind of sacramental, preparatory to the Baptism of Christ."[18]

2. SECOND EFFECT: THE REMISSION OF PUNISHMENTS DUE TO SIN.—Sin and its punishment

12 *De Bapt.*, c. 10.

13 *In Luc.*, c. 3.

14 *Hom. in Matth.*, 12, 2.

15 *Hom.*, I, 7, 3.

16 *De Bapt. c. Donat.*, V, 10: "*Quaero itaque, si baptismo Ioannis peccata dimittebantur, quid amplius praestare potuit baptismus Christi iis, quos Apostolus Paulus post baptismum Ioannis Christi baptismo voluit baptizari?*"

17 *Summa Theol.*, 3a, qu. 38, art. 3: "*Baptismus Ioannis gratiam non conferebat, sed solum ad gratiam praeparabat tripliciter: uno quidem modo per doctrinam Ioannis inducentem homines ad fidem Christi; alio modo assuefaciendo homines ad ritum baptismi Christi; tertio modo per poenitentiam praeparando homines ad suscipiendum effectum baptismi Christi.*"

18 *Ibid.*, art. 1, ad 1: "*Baptismus Ioannis non erat per se sacramentum, sed quoddam sacramentale disponens ad baptismum Christi.*" Cfr. Bellarmine, *De Bapt.*, c. 19 sqq.

are really distinct,[19] and the remission not only of sin but of all the penalties due to it, is an effect peculiar to Baptism alone. According to the constant teaching of the Church, the Sacrament of Baptism remits not only the eternal penalties of sin,—the remission of which seems to be an essential part of the forgiveness of sin itself,—but likewise all temporal punishments, so that, were one to die immediately after receiving Baptism, he would go straightway to Heaven.[20] "In those who are born again," says the Council of Trent, "there is nothing that God hates, because there is no condemnation to those who are truly buried together with Christ by Baptism into death; . . . so that there is nothing whatever to retard their entrance into Heaven." [21]

a) This dogma cannot be conclusively proved from Sacred Scripture,[22] but if we carefully consider the language used by St. Paul in comparing Baptism with the death and burial of our Lord, we can hardly doubt that the Apostle means to teach that Baptism remits not only all sins but also all the penalties due to them. Cfr. Rom. VI,

19 This point will be dealt with in the treatise on the Sacrament of Penance.

20 Cfr. *Decretum pro Armenis:* " *Morientes, antequam culpam aliquam committant, statim ad regnum coelorum et Dei visionem perveniunt.*" (Denzinger-Bannwart, n. 696).

21 Sess. V, can. 5: " *In renatis enim nihil odit Deus, quia nihil est damnationis iis, qui vere consepulti sunt cum Christo per baptisma in mortem . . ., ita ut nihil prorsus eos ab ingressu coeli remoretur.*" (Denzinger-Bannwart, n. 792).

22 The texts cited by the Tridentine Fathers (*l. c.*) do not express the remission of the punishment of sins as clearly as that of the sins themselves.

4: "For we are buried together with him by baptism into death; that as Christ is risen from the dead by the glory of the Father, so we also may walk in newness of life." [23] The Roman Catechism comments on this text as follows: "Of Baptism alone has it been said by the Apostle, that by it we die and are buried with Christ. Hence holy Church has always understood that to impose those offices of piety which are usually called by the holy Fathers works of satisfaction, on him who is to be purified by Baptism, cannot be done without the gravest injury to this Sacrament." [24]

b) Tertullian speaks the mind of the Latin Fathers when he says: "The guilt being removed, the penalty is removed also. Thus man is restored to God according to the likeness of him [*i. e.* Adam] who in days gone by had been [created] to the image of God." [25]   And St. Athanasius expresses the universal belief of the Greeks when he declares: "Baptism is called a laver, because in it we wash off our sins; it is

---

23 Rom. VI, 4: "*Consepulti enim sumus cum illo per baptismum in mortem: ut quomodo Christus surrexit a mortuis per gloriam Patris, ita et nos in novitate vitae ambulemus.*"

24 P. II, cap. 2, n. 44: "*De solo tamen baptismo dictum est ab Apostolo, nos per ipsum commori et sepeliri, ex quo s. Ecclesia semper*

intellexit sine iniuria sacramenti fieri non posse, ut ei qui baptismo expiandus sit, . . . opera satisfactionis imponantur."

25 *De Bapt.,* c. 5: "*Exempto reatu eximitur et poena; ita restituitur homo Deo ad similitudinem eius qui retro ad imaginem Dei fuerat.*" (Migne, *P. L.,* I, 1206).

called grace, because through it are remitted the punishments due to sins." [26]

c) From this teaching Catholic theologians consistently infer that such penalties as remain after Baptism (*e. g.* sickness and death) no longer partake of the nature of punishment, but are purely medicinal. In the technical terminology of the Schoolmen, they are not *poenae* but *poenalitates*.[27] This explains why no works of satisfaction are imposed on adults at Baptism. True, in the olden time the *baptizandi* were compelled to fast, as Tertullian reminds us; [28] but this was done only to aid them in subduing concupiscence, to accustom them to pious practices, to obtain special graces, and for similar purposes.

By the " temporal punishments of sin " we do not, of course, mean those which a secular judge is bound by law to inflict upon convicted offenders. Nevertheless St. Thomas [29] recommends Christian rulers, " for the honor of the Sacrament," to remit capital punishment to convicted pagans who ask for Baptism, and the Roman Catechism repeats the recommendation.[30]

3. THIRD EFFECT: THE BAPTISMAL CHARACTER.—Like Confirmation and Holy Orders, Baptism imprints in the soul of the recipient an indelible mark, which renders repetition impossible. The Tridentine Council defines: "If any one saith that in the three Sacraments, to wit, Baptism, Confirmation, and Order, there is not imprinted in the soul a character, that is a certain

26 *Ep.* 4 *ad Serap.*

27 Cfr. St. Thomas, *Summa Theol.*, 1a 2ae, qu. 85, art. 5.

28 *De Bapt.*, c. 20.

29 *Summa Theol.*, 3a, qu. 69, art. 2, ad 3.

30 *Cat. Rom.*, P. II, cap. 2, n. 45.

spiritual and indelible sign, on account of which they cannot be repeated; let him be anathema." [31]

a) For the Scriptural argument in support of this dogma, see *supra,* pp. 76 sqq.

b) From the theological point of view the following considerations are pertinent.

α) That Baptism cannot be repeated, is owing to the fact that it is a rebirth of the soul [32] and in a mystic manner exercises the same functions as Christ's death on the cross.[33] Referring to the former, St. Augustine observes: " The womb does not repeat its births," [34] and with the latter analogy in mind St. Chrysostom says: " As there is no second crucifixion for Christ, so there can be no such a thing as rebaptism." [35]

Rebaptism has always been condemned by the Church as sacrilegious. St. Augustine shows its intrinsic absurdity by comparing it to an *" impositio Christi super Christum."* [36] The older Fathers furnish plenty of material for this argument. Clement of Alexandria, for example, quotes the following remarkable passage from the eclogues of Theodotus the Valentinian: " As even the dumb animals show by a mark to whom they belong, and each can be recognized by that mark, thus the faithful soul that has received the seal of truth [37] bears the stigmata of

---

31 Sess. VII, *De Sacram.,* can. 9: *" Si quis dixerit, in tribus sacramentis, baptismo scil., confirmatione et ordine non imprimi characterem in anima, h. e. signum quoddam spirituale et indelebile, unde ea reiterari non possunt, anathema sit."* (Denzinger-Bannwart, n. 852).

32 Cfr. John III, 5; Tit. III, 5.

33 Cfr. Rom. VI, 1 sqq.

34 *Tract. in Ioa.,* 11: *" Uterus non partus repetit."*

35 *Hom. in Ep. ad Hebr.,* 9, n. 3; "Ὥσπερ οὖν οὐκ ἔστι δεύτερον σταυρωθῆναι τὸν Χριστόν, οὕτως οὐδὲ δεύτερον βαπτισθῆναι.

36 *In Ps.,* 39, n. 1: *" Baptismus ille tamquam character infixus est: ornabat militem, convincit desertorem. Quid enim facis [rebaptizans]? Christum imponis super Christum."* (Migne, *P. L.,* XXXVI, 433).

37 τὸ τῆς ἀληθείας σφράγισμα.

Christ." [38] St. Basil eulogizes the Sacrament as follows: "Baptism is the ransom paid for prisoners, the remission of debts, the death of sin, the rebirth of the soul, a shining garment, an indelible seal,[39] a vehicle [to convey men] to Heaven, a medium of the kingdom [of God], a free gift of sonship." [40]

β) The general purpose of the sacramental character has been sufficiently explained *supra,* pp. 88 sqq. In addition to what we have said there, we will briefly comment on what may be termed the secondary effects of the baptismal character.

In the first place the baptismal character, as a *signum configurativum,* incorporates the recipient into Christ's own family, bestows upon him the Saviour's coat-of-arms, and thus renders him a Christian, *i. e.* one who is like unto Christ. Cfr. Gal. III, 27: "As many of you as have been baptized in Christ, have put on Christ." [41]

By Baptism, furthermore, one becomes a member of our Lord's "mystic body," *i. e.* the true Church. "Baptism," says the *Decretum pro Armenis,* "is the door to the spiritual life, for by it we are made members of Christ and [part] of the body of the Church." [42] This is but another way of expressing St. Paul's thought, 1 Cor. XII, 13, 27: "We were all baptized into one body. . . . Now you are

38 Migne, *P. G.,* IX, 698.

39 σφραγὶς ἀνεπιχείρητος.

40 *Hom. de Bapt.,* 13, n. 5 (Migne, *P. G.,* XXXI, 434). For a speculative discussion of the baptismal character, *v. supra,* pp. 84 sqq.

41 Gal. III, 27: "*Quicunque enim in Christo baptizati estis, Christum induistis.*"

42 "*Primum omnium sacramentorum locum tenet s. baptisma, quod vitae spiritualis ianua est; per ipsum enim membra Christi ac de corpore efficimur Ecclesiae.*" (Denzinger-Bannwart, n. 696).

[together] the body of Christ, and severally his members." [43] In this respect the baptismal character is a *signum distinctivum,* marking off those who are baptized from those who are not. Only the former are "members" of the *corpus Ecclesiae,* while the latter may at most belong to the *anima Ecclesiae.*

By making them members of the Church, the baptismal character, as a *signum obligativum,* subjects all baptized Christians to her jurisdiction, obliges them to keep their baptismal vow and to observe the ecclesiastical precepts. In return, it guarantees them the graces they require for their respective state of life [44] as well as all the benefits, privileges, and means of sanctification which the Church is pleased to bestow upon her children, particularly the right to receive the other Sacraments. [45]

---

[43] 1 Cor. XII, 13, 27: "*Omnes nos in unum corpus baptizati sumus . . . Vos autem estis corpus Christi et membra de membro.*" (We use the Westminster Version). Cfr. J. MacRory, *The Epistles of St. Paul to the Corinthians,* Dublin 1915, pp. 192 sq.

[44] Cfr. St. Thomas, *Summa Theol.,* 3a, qu. 69, art. 5.

[45] St. Thomas, *Comment. in Sent.,* IV, dist. 24, qu. 1: "*Qui characterem baptismalem non habet, nullum alterum sacramentum suscipere potest.*"— On the character as a *signum dispositivum, v. supra,* pp. 93 sq.

CHAPTER II

THE NECESSITY OF BAPTISM

Baptism is necessary for salvation, but, under certain conditions, the place of Baptism by water (*baptismus fluminis*) may be supplied by Baptism of desire (*baptismus flaminis*) or by Baptism of blood (*baptismus sanguinis*). We shall explain the Catholic teaching on this point in three theses.

Thesis I: Baptism is necessary for salvation.

This proposition embodies an article of faith.

Proof. We have, in a previous treatise,[1] distinguished between two kinds of necessity: necessity of means (*necessitas medii*) and necessity of precept (*necessitas praecepti*).

Since Baptism is necessary for infants no less than for adults, it follows that all men need it as a means of salvation (*necessitas medii*), and that for adults it is also of precept (*necessitas praecepti*). However, since the Baptism of water may sometimes be supplied by the Baptism of desire or the Baptism of blood, Baptism of water is not absolutely necessary as a means of salvation but merely in a hypothetical way. That Baptism is necessary for salvation is an expressly defined dogma, for the Council of Trent declares: "If any one saith that Baptism is

---

[1] Pohle-Preuss, *Grace, Actual and Habitual,* pp. 281 sqq.

free, that is, not necessary unto salvation, let him be anathema." [2]

a) This can be conclusively proved from Holy Scripture. Our Lord's command: "Teach ye all nations, baptizing them," [3] plainly imposes on all men the duty to receive Baptism, as is evidenced by a parallel passage in St. Mark: "Go ye into the whole world, and preach the Gospel to every creature; he that believeth and is baptized, shall be saved: but he that believeth not shall be condemned." [4] Here we have Christ's plain and express declaration that while unbelief is sufficient to incur damnation, faith does not ensure salvation unless it is accompanied by Baptism.

That Baptism is necessary as a means of salvation (*necessitate medii*) follows from John III, 5: "Unless a man be born again [5] of water and the Holy Ghost, he cannot enter into the kingdom of heaven." Spiritual regeneration is more than a mere keeping of the Commandments; it involves a complete transformation of the soul. As no one can come into this world without being born, so no one can enter Heaven unless he is supernaturally reborn. Hence Baptism is, ordinarily, a necessary means of salvation. [6]

---

2 Sess. VII, *De Bapt.*, can. 5: "*Si quis dixerit, baptismum liberum esse, hoc est non necessarium ad salutem, anathema sit.*" (Denzinger-Bannwart, n. 861).

3 Matth. XXVIII, 19.
4 Mark XVI, 15 sq.
5 ἐὰν μή τις γεννηθῇ.
6 *V.* Theses II and III, *infra.*

b) This teaching is upheld by Tradition.

The African bishops assembled at the Council of Carthage (416), in a letter to Innocent I, complain of the cruelty of the Pelagians, who condemn their children to eternal death by refusing them Baptism.[7]

Tertullian writes: " The precept is laid down that without Baptism salvation is attainable by none, chiefly on the ground of that declaration of the Lord, who says: Unless a man be born of water, he hath not eternal life." [8]

St. Basil, at a somewhat later date, says: " If you have not passed through the water, you will not be freed from the cruel tyranny of the devil." [9]

This belief of the primitive Church was embodied, as it were, in the catechumenate, an institution which lasted well into the Middle Ages. " Catechumeni " [10] was a name applied to adults who were under instruction with a view to receiving Baptism. Until recently they were believed to have been divided into three classes, viz.: audientes (ἀκροώμενοι) ; genuflectentes (γόνυ κλίνοντες) ; and competentes (φωτιζόμενοι). This theory was based upon a misunderstood canon of a council of Neocaesarea (between 314 and 325). Other theologians thought that there were two classes, catechumeni and competentes or electi. But this distinction is equally untenable, because St. Cyril of Jerusalem and other Fathers number the

---

[7] " Parvulos etiam baptizandos negant ac sic eos mortifera ista doctrina in aeternum necant."

[8] De Bapt., c. 12: " Praescribitur nemini sine baptismo competere salutem ex illa maxime pronuntiatione Domini, qui ait: Nisi natus quis ex aqua fuerit, non habet vitam aeternam."

[9] Hom. in Bapt., n. 2.— Cfr. A. Seitz, Die Heilsnotwendigkeit der Kirche nach der altchristlichen Literatur bis zur Zeit des hl. Augustinus, pp. 280 sqq., Freiburg 1903. On Infant Baptism, v. infra, Ch. IV, Sect. 2, pp. 268 sqq.

[10] Κατηχούμενοι, from κατηχεῖν, to instruct orally. On the catechumenate see T. B. Scannell, s. v. " Catechumen," in Vol. III of the Catholic Encyclopedia.

competentes, or candidates for Baptism, among the faithful (*fideles,* πιστοί). To the late Professor Funk belongs the credit of having shown that the catechumens were all in one class.[11] But even though we now discard the three (or two) stages of preparation, this does not alter the fact that the ecclesiastical authorities were at great pains properly to instruct converts, so as to make them well-informed and loyal Catholics. The catechumens had to pass seven consecutive examinations (*septem scrutinia*) before they were admitted to Baptism. Besides, for a whole week after Baptism they wore white garments, which they put off on Low Sunday (*Dominica in albis, scil. deponendis*). Had not the Church been so firmly convinced of the importance and necessity of Baptism, she would certainly not have surrounded this Sacrament with so many imposing ceremonies nor spent so much time and labor in preparing candidates for its reception. The very existence of the catechumenate in the primitive Church proves that Baptism was always regarded as a matter of spiritual life and death.[12]

c) It is a moot question among theologians at what time Baptism became a necessary means of salvation.

Even if it were true, as some older writers hold, that express belief in the Messias and the Trinity was a necessary condition of salvation already in the Old Testament, Baptism certainly was not, either as a means or in con-

11 F. X. Funk, *Kirchengeschichtliche Abhandlungen und Untersuchungen,* Vol. I, pp. 209 sqq., Paderborn 1897.

12 Cfr. J. Mayer, *Geschichte des Katechumenates und der Katechese in den ersten sechs Jahrhunderten,* Kempten 1868; P. Göbel, *Geschichte der Katechese im Abendlande vom Verfalle des Katechumenates bis zum Ende des Mittelalters,* Kempten 1880; T. B. Scannell in the *Catholic Encyclopedia, l.c.*

sequence of a positive precept.[13]   For those living under
the New Law the necessity of Baptism, according to the
Tridentine Council,[14] began with " the promulgation of
the Gospel."   When was the Gospel promulgated?   Was
it promulgated for all nations on the day of our Lord's
Ascension, or did its precepts go into effect only when they
were actually preached to each?   Were we to adopt the
latter assumption, we should have to admit that the necessity of Baptism, and consequently the duty of receiving
the Sacrament, was limited both with regard to time and
place, *e. g.* that the law did not go into effect in Palestine
until the Gospel had been sufficiently promulgated throughout that country, which required some thiry years or more.
To be entirely consistent we should have to admit further
that Baptism did not become necessary for salvation in
the farther parts of the Roman Empire until about the
close of the third century, in the Western hemisphere until the sixteenth century, in Central Africa or the Congo
Free State until the beginning of the twentieth.   This
would practically mean that millions of pagans after the
time of Christ were in precisely the same position as the
entire human race before the atonement, and that their
children could be saved by a mere " Sacrament of nature." [15]   Though this way of reasoning appears quite
legitimate in the light of the Tridentine declaration, it is
open to serious theological objections.   In the first place,
we must not arbitrarily limit the validity of our Saviour's
baptismal mandate.   Secondly, we cannot assume that for
more than a thousand years the children of pagan na-

---

13 On the justification of adults
and children under the Old Testament and among the pre-Christian
Gentiles, *v. supra*, p. 19 sqq.

14 Sess. VI, cap. 4: ". . . *quae
quidem translatio [i. e. iustificatio]*

*post Evangelium promulgatum sine
lavacro regenerationis aut eius voto
fieri non potest."* (Denzinger-Bannwart, n. 796).

15 *V. supra*, p. 18 sqq.

tions were better off in the matter of salvation than innumerable infants of Christian parentage, who were unable to avail themselves of the " Sacrament of nature."
Third, the assumption under review practically renders
illusory the necessity of Baptism through a period extending over many centuries. To obviate these difficulties we prefer the more probable opinion that the law making Baptism necessary for salvation was promulgated on
Ascension day or, if you will, on Pentecost, simultaneously
for the whole world, and at once became binding upon all
nations.[16]

**Thesis II: In adults the place of Baptism by
water can be supplied in case of urgent necessity by
the so-called Baptism of desire.**

This proposition may be qualified as *"doctrina
catholica."*

Proof. The Baptism of desire (*baptismus
flaminis*) differs from the Baptism of water
(*baptismus fluminis*) in the same way in which
spiritual differs from actual Communion. If the
desire for Baptism is accompanied by perfect contrition, we have the so-called *baptismus flaminis,*
which forthwith justifies the sinner, provided, of
course, that the desire is a true *votum sacramenti,
i. e.,* that it implies a firm resolve to receive the
Sacrament as soon as opportunity offers.

The Tridentine Council pronounces anathema
against those who assert "that the Sacraments
of the New Law are not necessary for salva-

16 Cfr. Bellarmine, *De Bapt.,* c.
5; Billuart, *De Bapt.,* dissert. 1, art.
2, § 2. H. Hurter holds a different
opinion (*Compendium Theol. Dogmat.,* Vol. III, 12th ed., n. 317,
Innsbruck 1909).

tion, but superfluous, and that without them, or
without the desire thereof, men obtain of God
through faith alone the grace of justification." [17]

At a later date the Holy See formally condemned a
proposition extracted from the writings of Bajus, which
says that " Perfect and sincere charity can exist both in
catechumens and in penitents without the remission of
sins." [18]   Hence the Church teaches that perfect charity
does remit sin, even in catechumens or in penitents, *i. e.*
before the reception of the Sacrament, yet not without
the Sacrament, as we have seen in Thesis I.   Nothing
remains, therefore, but to say that the remission of sins
through perfect charity is due to the fact that such charity implies the desire of the Sacrament.   Indeed the only
Sacraments here concerned are Baptism and Penance.
The Council of Trent [19] explains that primal justification
(from original sin) is impossible without the laver of regeneration or the desire thereof, and [20] that forgiveness
of personal sin must not be expected from perfect charity
without at least the desire of the Sacrament of Penance.

a) That perfect contrition effects immediate
justification is apparent from the case of David,[21]
that of Zachaeus,[22] and our Lord's own words to
one of the robbers crucified with Him on Cal-

17 Sess. VII, *De Sacram.*, can. 4:
" *Si quis dixerit, sacramenta Novae
Legis non esse ad salutem necessaria, sed superflua, et sine eis aut
eorum voto per solam fidem homines
a Deo gratiam iustificationis adi-
pisci, . . . anathema   sit.*" (Denzinger-Bannwart, n. 847).

18 Prop. 31: " *Caritas   perfecta
et   sincera . . . tam   in   catechu-*

*menis quam in poenitentibus potest
esse sine remissione peccatorum.*"
(Denzinger-Bannwart, n. 1031).

19 Sess. VI, cap. 4. (Note 14,
p. 242, *supra*).

20 Sess. XIV, cap. 4. Cfr. the
dogmatic treatise on the Sacrament
of Penance.

21 Cfr. Ps. 50.

22 Cfr. Luke XIX, 9.

vary: "This day thou shalt be with me in paradise." [23]

The Prophet Ezechiel assured the Old Testament Jews in the name of Jehovah: "If the wicked do penance for all his sins, . . . he shall live, and shall not die." [24] In the New Testament our Lord Himself says of the penitent Magdalen: "Many sins are forgiven her, because she hath loved much." [25] Since, however, God has ordained Baptism as a necessary means of salvation,[26] perfect contrition, in order to obtain forgiveness of sins, must include the desire of the Sacrament. Cfr. John XIV, 23: "If any one love me, he will keep my word, and my Father will love him, and we will come to him, and will make our abode with him." [27]

b) According to primitive Tradition, the Baptism of desire, when based on charity, effects justification, though not without some ideal relation to the Baptism of water.

The anonymous author of the treatise *De Rebaptismate,* which was composed about 256 against the practice championed by St. Cyprian,[28] calls attention to the fact that the centurion Cornelius and his family were justified without the Sacrament,[29] and adds: " No doubt men can be baptized without water, in the Holy Ghost, as you observe that these were baptized, before they were baptized

---

23 Luke XXIII, 43.

24 Ez. XVIII, 21: " *Si autem impius egerit poenitentiam ab omnibus peccatis suis, . . . vitâ vivet et non morietur.*"

25 Luc. VII, 47: " *Remittuntur ei peccata multa, quoniam dilexit multum.*"

26 *V. supra,* Thesis I.

27 Other Scriptural texts in our treatise on the Sacrament of Penance.

28 This treatise was perhaps written by Bishop Ursinus (cfr. Gennad., *De Vir. Illustr.,* c. 27).

29 Acts X, 44 sqq.

with water, . . . since they received the grace of the New Covenant before the bath, which they reached later." [30]

The most striking Patristic pronouncement on the subject is found in St. Ambrose's sermon on the death of the Emperor Valentinian II, who had died as a catechumen. "I hear you express grief," he says, "because he [Valentinian] did not receive the Sacrament of Baptism. Tell me, what else is there in us except the will and petition? But he had long desired to be initiated before he came to Italy, and expressed his intention to be baptized by me as soon as possible, and it was for this reason, more than for any other, that he hastened to me. Has he not, therefore, the grace which he desired? Has he not received that for which he asked? Surely, he received [it] because he asked [for it]." [31]

St. Augustine repeatedly speaks of the power inherent in the desire for Baptism. "I do not hesitate," he says in his treatise *De Baptismo* against the Donatists, "to place the Catholic catechumen, who is burning with the love of God, before the baptized heretic. . . . The centurion Cornelius, before Baptism, was better than Simon [Magus], who had been baptized. For Cornelius, even before Baptism, was filled with the Holy Ghost, while Simon, after Baptism, was puffed up with an unclean spirit." [32] A seemingly contradictory passage occurs in

30 " *Atque hoc non erit dubium, in Spiritu Sancto homines posse sine aqua baptizari, sicut animadvertis baptizatos hos, priusquam aquâ baptizarentur, . . . quandoquidem sine lavacro, quod postea adepti sunt, gratiam repromissionis acceperint.*" (Migne, *P. L.*, III, 1889).

31 *De Obitu Valent.*, n. 51 sq.: " *Audio vos dolere quod non acceperit sacramenta baptismatis. Dicite mihi, quid aliud in nobis est nisi voluntas, nisi petitio? Atqui etiam dudum hoc voti habuit, ut et antequam in Italiam venisset initiaretur, et proxime baptizari se a me velle significavit, et ideo prae ceteris causis me accersendum putavit. Non habet ergo gratiam quam desideravit? Non habet quam poposcit? Certe quia poposcit, accepit.*"

32 *De Bapt. c. Donat.*, IV, 21: " *Nec ergo dubito, catechumenum catholicum divinâ caritate flagrantem*

the same author's Homilies on the Gospel of St. John. "No matter what progress a catechumen may make," it reads, "he still carries the burden of iniquity, which is not taken away until he has been baptized." [33] The two Augustinian passages quoted can, however, be easily reconciled. The command to receive the Baptism of water exists also for the catechumens and ceases to be binding only when there is an impossibility. "I find," says the same author, "that not only martyrdom for the sake of Christ may supply what was wanting of Baptism, but also faith and conversion of heart, if recourse can not be had to the celebration of the mystery of Baptism for want of time." [34] St. Bernard invokes the authority of SS. Ambrose and Augustine in support of his teaching that a man may be saved by the Baptism of desire if death or some other insuperable obstacle prevents him from receiving the Baptism of water.[35] The Popes decided many practical cases of conscience by this rule. Thus Innocent III unhesitatingly declared that a certain deceased priest, who had never been baptized, had undoubtedly obtained forgiveness of original sin and reached Heaven, and that the sacrifice of the Mass might be offered up for the repose of his soul.[36]

haeretico baptizato anteponere. . . . Melior est enim centurio Cornelius nondum baptizatus Simone [Mago] baptizato; iste enim et ante baptismum S. Spiritu impletus est, ille et post baptismum immundo spiritu impletus est." (Migne, P. L., XLIII, 171).

33 Tract. in Ioa., 13, n. 7: "Quantumcunque catechumenus proficiat, adhuc sarcinam iniquitatis portat; non illâ dimittitur, nisi quum venerit ad baptismum."

34 De Bapt. c. Donat., IV, 22: "Invenio, non tantum passionem pro Christo id quod ex baptismo deerat posse supplere, sed etiam fidem conversionemque cordis, si forte ad celebrandum mysterium in angustiis temporum succurri non potest."

35 Ep. 77 ad Hug. Vict., n. 8: "Ab his duabus columnis difficile avellor; cum his, inquam, aut errare aut sapere me fateor, credens et ipse solâ fide [i. e. formatâ] posse hominem salvari cum desiderio percipiendi sacramentum, si tamen pio implendi desiderio mors anticipans seu alia quaecumque vis invincibilis obviaverit." (Migne, Patr. Lat., CLXXXII, 1036).

36 3 Decret., tit. 13, c. 2: "Pres-

The question whether the *votum baptismi* accompanying perfect contrition must be explicit, is to be decided in the same way as the parallel problem whether pagans, in order to be justified, must have an express belief in the Trinity and the Incarnation, or whether an implicit belief in these mysteries is sufficient.[37]   The more common opinion holds that the *votum implicitum* is all that is required.   This " implicit desire " may be defined as " a state of mind in which a man would ardently long for Baptism if he knew that it is necessary for salvation." [38]

Thesis III: Martyrdom (baptismus sanguinis) can also supply the place of Baptism.

Though the Church has never formally pronounced on the subject, the teaching of Scripture and Tradition is sufficiently clear to enable us to regard this thesis as *"doctrina certa."*

Proof.   The Baptism of blood, or martyrdom, is the patient endurance of death, or of extreme violence apt to cause death, for the sake of Jesus Christ.

The theological concept of martyrdom ($\mu\acute{\alpha}\rho\tau\nu$s, *a witness*) includes three separate and distinct elements, *viz.*:

byterum quem sine unda baptismatis diem clausisse significasti, quia in sanctae matris ecclesiae fide et Christi nominis confessione perseveraverit, ab originali peccato solutum et coelestis patriae gaudium esse adeptum asserimus incunctanter."

[37] On this question cfr. Pohle-

Preuss, *Grace, Actual and Habitual,* pp. 182 sqq.

[38] Oswald, *Die Lehre von den hl. Sakramenten der kath. Kirche,* Vol. I, 5th ed., p. 211. Cfr. A. Seitz, *Die Heilsnotwendigkeit der Kirche nach der altchristlichen Literatur bis zur Zeit des hl. Augustinus,* pp. 290 sqq., Freiburg 1903.

(1) Violent death or extremely cruel treatment which would naturally cause death, irrespective of whether the victim actually dies or is saved by a miracle, as was St. John the Evangelist when he escaped unharmed from the cauldron of boiling oil into which he had been thrown by order of the Emperor Domitian. (2) The endurance of death or violence for the sake of Christ, *i. e.* for the Catholic faith or for the practice of any supernatural virtue. Hence the so-called "martyrs" of revolution or heresy are not martyrs in the theological sense of the term. (3) Patient suffering, endured voluntarily and without resistance. This excludes soldiers who fall in battle, even though they fight in defence of the faith.[39]

Since martyrdom effects justification in infants as well as adults, its efficacy must be conceived after the manner of an *opus operatum,* and in adults presupposes a moral preparation or disposition, consisting mainly of faith accompanied by imperfect contrition.[40] It does not, however, require perfect contrition, else there would be no essential distinction between Baptism of blood and Baptism of desire.[41]

a) The supernatural efficacy of martyrdom may be deduced from our Lord's declaration in the Gospel of St. Matthew: "Every one that shall confess me before men, I will also confess him before my Father who is in Heaven," [42] and: "He that findeth his life, shall lose it; and he that shall lose his life for me, shall find it." [43] If a man gives up his life for Jesus, he will surely be re-

39 Cfr. Benedict XIV, *De Serv. Dei Beatif.,* III, 11.

40 Cfr. *Conc. Trid.,* Sess. XIV, cap. 7 (Denzinger-Bannwart, n. 897).

41 *V. supra,* Thesis II.

42 Matth. X, 32.

43 Matth. X, 39. Cfr. Matth. XVI, 25; Luke IX, 24; XVII, 33.

warded. "Greater love than this no man hath, that a man lay down his life for his friends." [44] Consequently, martyrdom must be regarded as equivalent to Baptism for the unbaptized, and as a means of justification for the baptized.

b) The ancient Church explicitly interpreted Christ's teaching in this sense, as is evident from the honors she paid to the martyrs.

Tertullian says: "We have, indeed, likewise a second font, itself one [with the former], of blood to wit. . . . This is the Baptism which both stands in lieu of the fontal bathing when that has not been received, and restores it when lost." [45] St. Cyprian declares that the catechumens who suffer martyrdom for Christ's sake, go to Heaven. "Let them know . . . that the catechumens are not deprived of Baptism, since they are baptized with the most glorious and supreme Baptism of blood." [46] St. Augustine expresses himself in a similar manner: "To all those who die confessing Christ, even though they have not received the laver of regeneration, [martyrdom] will prove as effective for the remission of sins as if they were washed in the baptismal font." [47]

The Greek Church held the same belief. St. Cyril of Jerusalem writes: "If a man does not receive Baptism, he hath not salvation, the martyrs alone excepted, who

---

44 John XV, 13.

45 *De Bapt.*, c. 16: "*Est quidem nobis etiam secundum lavacrum, unum et ipsum, sanguinis scil. . . . Hic est baptismus, qui lavacrum et non acceptum repraesentat et perditum reddit.*"

46 *Ep.* 73 *ad Iubaian.*, n. 21, ed. Hartel, II, 735: "*Sciant . . . catechumenos . . . non privari bap-*tismi *sacramento, utpote qui baptizentur gloriosissimo et maximo sanguinis baptismo.*"

47 *De Civ. Dei*, XIII, 7: "*Quicumque etiam non recepto regenerationis lavacro pro Christi confessione moriuntur, tantum eis valet ad dimittenda peccata, quantum si abluerentur fonte baptismatis.*"

attain to Heaven without water." [48]   And St. Chrysostom: "As those baptized in water, so also those who suffer martyrdom, are washed clean, [the latter] in their own blood." [49]

The primitive Church venerated in a special manner all those who suffered martyrdom for the faith, the unbaptized as well as the baptized.   Among the earliest martyrs to whom public honors were paid, are St. Emerentiana, a foster-sister of St. Agnes, and the Holy Innocents, of whom St. Cyprian, following St. Irenaeus,[50] says that though they were too young to fight for Christ, they were old enough to gain the crown of martyrdom.[51]

c) The Baptism of blood is more perfect than the Baptism of desire, and, in a certain sense, even excels Baptism by water.

a) It is more perfect than the Baptism of desire, both in essence and effect, because it justifies infants as well as adults *quasi ex opere operato,* whereas the Baptism of desire is efficacious *ex opere operantis,* and in adults only. Martyrdom, however, is not a Sacrament because it is no ecclesiastical rite and has not been instituted as an ordinary means of grace.   It is superior to the Baptism of desire in this respect, that, like ordinary Baptism, it not only forgives sins and sanctifies the sinner, but remits all temporal punishments.   St. Augustine says: " It would be an affront to pray for a martyr; we should [rather] commend ourselves to his prayers." [52]   Hence

---

48 *Catech.,* 3, n. 10 (Migne, *P. G.,* XXXIII, 439).

49 *Hom. in Martyr. Lucian.,* n. 2 (Migne, *P. G.,* L, 522). Other apposite texts in Seitz, *Die Heilsnotwendigkeit der Kirche,* pp. 287 sqq.

50 *Adv. Haeres.,* III, 16, 4. On

the veneration of the martyrs in the early Church cfr. Pohle-Preuss, *Mariology,* pp. 144 sqq., 150.

51 *Ep.* 56 *ad Thibarit.:* " *Aetas necdum habilis ad pugnam idonea exstitit ad coronam.*"

52 *Serm.,* 159, c. 1: " *Iniuria est*

the famous dictum of Pope Innocent III: "He who prays for a martyr insults him."[53] St. Thomas teaches: "Suffering endured for Christ's sake . . . cleanses [the soul] of all guilt, both venial and mortal, unless the will be found actually attached to sin."[54]

β) Martyrdom is inferior to Baptism in so far as it is not a Sacrament, and consequently neither imprints a character nor confers the right of receiving the other Sacraments. It excels Baptism in that it not only remits all sins, together with the temporal punishments due to them, but likewise confers the so-called aureole.[55] It is superior to Baptism also in this that it more perfectly represents the passion and death of Christ. Cfr. Mark X, 38: "Can you drink of the chalice that I drink of, or be baptized with the baptism wherewith I am baptized?"—"Let him who is deemed worthy of martyrdom," say the Apostolic Constitutions,[56] "rejoice in the Lord for obtaining such a great crown. . . . Though he be a catechumen, let him depart without sadness; for the suffering he endures for Christ will be to him more effective than Baptism."[57] St. Bonaventure explains this as follows: "The reason why [martyrdom] has greater efficacy is that in the Baptism of blood there is an ampler and a fuller imitation and profession of the Passion of Christ than in the Baptism of water. . . . In the

pro martyre orare, cuius nos debemus orationibus commendari."

[53] "Iniuriam facit martyri, qui orat pro eo." Cap. "Cum Marthae," De Celebr. Missae.

[54] Summa Theol., 3a, qu. 87, art. 1, ad 2: "Passio pro Christo suscepta . . . purgat ab omni culpa et veniali et mortali, nisi actualiter voluntatem peccato invenerit inhaerentem."

[55] See Eschatology. On the three-

fold aureola (martyrum, virginum, doctorum) v. St. Thomas, Summa Theol., 3a, qu. 96.

[56] Probably composed in the beginning of the fourth century.

[57] Const. Apost., V, 6: "Qui martyrio dignus est habitus, laetitiâ in Domino efferatur, quod tantam coronam nactus fuerit. . . . Quamvis catechumenus sit, sine tristitia excedat: passio enim pro Christo perlata erit ei sincerior baptismus."

Baptism of water death is signified; in the Baptism of blood it is incurred." [58]

[58] *Comment. in Sent.*, IV, dist. 4, p. 2, art. 1, qu. 2, ad 2: *" Ratio autem quare efficaciam habet maiorem est, quoniam in baptismo sanguinis amplior et plenior est imitatio et professio passionis Christi quam in baptismo aquae. . . . In baptismo aquae mors significatur, hic autem suscipitur."* For a fuller treatment of this topic cfr. Gihr, *Die hl. Sakramente der kath. Kirche,* Vol. I, 2nd ed., pp. 271 sqq.

CHAPTER III

Catholic theology makes a distinction between solemn Baptism (*baptismus solemnis*) and private Baptism, which is also called Baptism of necessity (*baptismus necessitatis*). Any one can administer private Baptism, whereas solemn Baptism requires a specially qualified minister. The ordinary minister (*minister ordinarius*) of solemn Baptism is the bishop or priest. A deacon may administer the Sacrament solemnly only with the express permission of a bishop or priest, and consequently is called the extraordinary minister (*minister extraordinarius*) of the Sacrament.

SECTION I

THE MINISTER OF SOLEMN BAPTISM

1. THE ORDINARY MINISTER OF SOLEMN BAPTISM.—Baptism is called solemn when it is administered with all the prescribed ecclesiastical ceremonies. These ceremonies are not essential to the validity of the Sacrament and are omitted when it is conferred privately.[1]

The ordinary minister of solemn Baptism is any validly ordained priest, who has the requisite ecclesiastical jurisdiction, that is to say, the bishop or any pastor or other priest duly authorized by either bishop or pastor to administer the Sacrament. "The [ordinary] minister of this Sacrament [Baptism]," says the *Decretum pro Armenis,* "is the priest, to whose office it belongs to baptize." [2]

a) Our Lord's official mandate to baptize all nations [3] was addressed to the Apostles and their successors, *i. e.* the bishops, who, in turn, gave it

---

1 On the ceremonies of solemn Baptism cfr. Bellarmine, *De Bapt.,* c. 24-27; Chr. Pesch, *Praelect. Dogmat.,* Vol. VI, 3rd ed., pp. 212 sqq., Freiburg 1908; N. Gihr, *Die hl. Sakramente der kath. Kirche,* Vol. I, 2nd ed., §39, Freiburg 1902.

2 " *Minister* [*ordinarius*] *huius sacramenti est sacerdos, cui ex officio competit baptizare.*" (Denzinger-Bannwart, n. 696).

3 Matth. XXVIII, 19.

to others when it became impossible for them to be the sole ministers of the Sacrament. Cfr. 1 Cor. I, 17: "Christ hath not sent me to baptize, but to preach the gospel."[4]　St. Peter did not himself baptize Cornelius and his family, but "commanded them to be baptized."[5]　From which it may be seen that Holy Scripture, to say the least, is not averse to the *ministerium ordinarium* of the priesthood in respect of Baptism.

b) In the early days the solemn administration of Baptism usually took place at Easter or Pentecost, and was regarded as the exclusive prerogative of the bishop.[6] When Christianity gradually spread to the rural districts, and the dioceses increased in size, simple priests were permitted to confer Baptism by virtue of their office, and the administration of this Sacrament became a prerogative of the pastors. Tertullian says: "Of giving Baptism, the chief priest, who is the bishop, has the right; in the next place the presbyters and deacons, not however, without the bishop's authority, on account of the honor of the Church."[7]　St. Thomas states the reason for this as follows: "Just as it belongs to a priest to consecrate the Eucharist, . . . so it is the proper office of a priest to baptize; since it seems to belong to one

---

[4] 1 Cor. I, 17: "*Non enim misit me Christus baptizare, sed evangelizare.*"

[5] "*Iussit baptizari.*" (Acts X, 48).

[6] The biographer of St. Ambrose, Paulinus, says of him (*De Vita S. Ambros., apud* Migne, *P. L.*, XIV, 27 sqq.): "*Erat in rebus divinis implendis fortissimus, ut quod soli-tus erat circa baptizandos solus implere, quinque postea episcopi vix implerent.*"

[7] *De Bapt.*, c. 17: "*Dandi quidem baptismum habet ius summus sacerdos, qui est episcopus; dehinc presbyteri et diaconi, non tamen sine episcopi auctoritate propter Ecclesiae honorem.*"

and the same person to produce the whole and to arrange
the part in the whole." [8]

2. THE EXTRAORDINARY MINISTER OF SOLEMN
BAPTISM.—The extraordinary ministry of the
deacon in regard to Baptism comprises two essential elements: (a) the right to administer solemn
Baptism, which is never granted to laymen, nor
to clerics in minor orders; and (b) the special
permission of bishop or pastor, given for an important reason.

The right (a) is required to establish the order of the
diaconate, while without the latter condition (b) bishops
and priests would have no prerogative in matters of Baptism over deacons. With regard to the first-mentioned
point the *Pontificale Romanum* observes: "It belongs to
the deacon to minister at the altar, to baptize, and to
preach." [9] With regard to the last-mentioned point, the
Catechism of the Council of Trent says: "Next to bishops and priests come deacons, for whom, as numerous decrees of the holy Fathers attest, it is not lawful to administer this Sacrament without the leave of the bishop
or priest." [10]

The extraordinary character of the prerogative of deacons to confer Baptism is illustrated by

[8] *Summa Theol.*, 3a, qu. 67, art.
2: " *Sicut ad sacerdotem pertinet
consecrare Eucharistiam*, . . . *ita ad
proprium officium pertinet baptizare;
eiusdem enim videtur esse operari
totum et partem in toto disponere.*"
Cf. Billuart, *De Bapt.*, diss. 2, art. 1.
[9] *De Ordine Diac.*: " *Diaconum*

*oportet ministrare ad altare, bap-
tizare, et praedicare.*"
[10] P. II, c. 2, n. 23: " *Secundum ministrorum locum obtinent diaconi, quibus sine episcopi aut sacer-
dotis concessu non licere hoc sacramentum administrare plurima sanctorum Patrum decreta testantur.*"

the example of the deacon Philip, who, as the Acts of the Apostles tell us, baptized the eunuch of Queen Candace [11] and a great number of other men and women in Samaria.[12] Nevertheless the Church has always insisted that, apart from cases of urgent necessity, deacons may not confer solemn Baptism except with the permission of a bishop or priest.

Thus Pope Gelasius I (d. 496) admonished the bishops of Lucania: " Deacons must not presume to baptize without the permission of a bishop or priest, except in the absence of the aforesaid officials, if there be extreme necessity." [13] A similar passage occurs in the writings of St. Isidore (d. 636).[14]

11 Cfr. Acts VIII, 38.

12 Cfr. Acts VIII, 12.

13 *Ep. ad Episc. Lucan.*, n. 7: " *Diaconi absque episcopo vel presbytero baptizare non audeant, nisi praedictis fortasse officiis longius constitutis necessitas extrema compellat.*" (Migne, *P. L.*, LIX, 51).

14 *De Offic.*, II, 25, 9: " *Constat baptisma solis sacerdotibus esse tractandum eiusque ministerium nec ipsis diaconis explere esse licitum absque episcopo vel presbytero, nisi his pro-cul absentibus ultima languoris necessitas cogat.*" (Migne, *P. L.*, LXXXIII, 822).— For a more detailed treatment consult Suarez, *De Bapt.*, disp. 23, sect. 2.— On the sponsors (*patrini*, ἀνάδοχοι) cfr. Pesch, *Praelect. Dogmat.*, Vol. VI, 3rd ed., pp. 210 sqq.— On the ceremonies of Baptism and their " parallels " in the ethnic religions of antiquity see Cabrol, *Dictionnaire, s. v.* " Baptême."

SECTION 2

WHO HAS THE POWER TO CONFER BAPTISM IN CASES OF EMERGENCY

In case of urgent necessity any human being, irrespective of sex or faith, can validly baptize. This teaching is based on the fact that Baptism is necessary for salvation.[1] It is not a mere question of ecclesiastical discipline but a dogma, and can be rightly understood only in the light of Christ's implicit command, as interpreted by Tradition. The Fourth Council of the Lateran (1215) declared: " The Sacrament of Baptism, . . . properly conferred, no matter by whom (*a quocunque rite collatum*), is useful for salvation." [2] The phrase " *a quocunque* " was explained by the Council of Florence (1439) as follows: " In case of necessity, not only a priest or a deacon, but a lay man or woman, nay even a pagan and a heretic, can [validly] baptize, provided only that he observes the form prescribed by the Church and has the intention of doing what the Church does." [3] To set forth the process of clarification through which this teaching has passed, it will be best to proceed chronologically.

---

[1] *V. supra*, Ch. II, pp. 238 sqq.

[2] *Caput " Firmiter ": " Sacramentum vero baptismi . . . a quocunque rite collatum, proficit ad salutem."* (Denzinger-Bannwart, n. 430).

[3] *Decretum pro Armenis: " In casu necessitatis non solum sacerdos vel diaconus, sed etiam laicus vel mulier, imo etiam paganus et haereticus baptizare [licite] potest, dummodo formam servet Ecclesiae et facere intendat quod facit Ecclesia."* (Denzinger-Bannwart, n. 696).

1. Baptism Administered by Catholic Laymen.

—At a very early date it was believed that Catholic laymen (*homines laici*) could validly baptize in cases of urgent necessity, and that even where no such necessity existed, lay Baptism was valid, though illicit.

Tertullian says: "Besides these, even laymen have the right [to baptize]; for what is equally received can be equally given." [4]

Several centuries later St. Jerome taught: "If necessity urges, we know that even laymen are allowed [to baptize]; for as one has received, he may also give." [5] The argument embodied in this citation is, however, inconclusive and misleading. For if it were true that "what one has received, he may also give," it would be equally true that "one cannot give what he has not received," and Baptism would be invalid when administered by non-baptized persons, which is contrary to the teaching of the Church.

Augustine goes into the subject of lay Baptism at considerable length. He says among other things: "If it is done where no urgent necessity compels, it is a usurpation of another's [*i. e.* the priest's] office. But when necessity urges, it is either no sin at all, or only a venial sin; but though it is usurped without any necessity, and conferred by no matter whom on no matter whom, what is given cannot be said to have not been given, though it may truly be said that it is illicitly given." [6]

---

[4] *De Bapt.*, c. 17: "*Alioquin et laicis ius est; quod enim ex aequo [i. e. indiscriminatim] accipitur, ex aequo dari potest.*"

[5] *Dial. adv. Lucif.*, n. 9: "*Si necessitas cogit, scimus etiam laicis li-cere [baptizare]; ut enim accepit quis, et dare potest.*" (Migne, *P. L.*, XXIII, 165).

[6] *Contr. Ep. Parmen.*, II, 13, 29: "*Nullâ cogente necessitate si fiat, alieni muneris [i. e. sacerdotis]*"

The Oriental Fathers were more reserved in regard to this question. St. Basil seems to have regarded lay Baptism as invalid.[7] In process of time, however, the Greek Church admitted its validity, though only on condition that the baptizing layman be himself baptized, *i. e.* a Christian. In this form lay Baptism was incorporated into the canon law of the East. In 1672, a schismatic council held at Jerusalem decreed: "The minister of this [Sacrament] is the priest alone, but, in case of real and urgent necessity, any man [may baptize], provided only he be a Christian believer."[8]

2. BAPTISM ADMINISTERED BY HERETICS.—

Tertullian denied that Baptism can be validly conferred by a heretic.[9] The question was hotly debated in the famous controversy between St. Cyprian (d. 258) and Pope Stephen I, who finally decided that repenting heretics must not be rebaptized but reconciled through the Sacrament of Penance.[10]

The First Ecumenical Council (325) forbade the rebaptism of heretics. When the controversy broke out anew, in the time of the Donatist schism, St. Augustine

usurpatio est. Si autem necessitas urgeat, aut nullum aut veniale delictum est; sed etsi nullâ necessitate usurpetur, et a quolibet cuilibet detur, quod datum fuerit, non potest dici non datum, quamvis recte dici possit illicite datum." (Migne, *P. L.*, LXIII, 71).

[7] *Ep. ad Amphiloch.*, I, c. 1 (A. D. 374).

[8] Hardouin, *Concil.*, XI, 250: *"Huius minister sacerdos solus, quin et urgente verâ necessitate qui-*

vis homo, modo tamen fidelis." Cfr. Gass, *Symbolik der griechischen Kirche*, p. 242, Berlin 1872.— On the teaching of other Oriental sects, see Denzinger, *Ritus Orientalium*, Vol. I, p. 21, Würzburg 1863.

[9] *De Bapt.*, c. 15.

[10] *"Si quis ergo a quacunque haeresi venient ad nos, nihil innovetur nisi quod traditum est, ut manus illis imponatur in poenitentiam."* (Denzinger-Bannwart, n. 46).

vigorously defended the Nicene teaching. Lastly, the Council of Trent defined: "If any one saith that the Baptism which is given by heretics, . . . is not a true Baptism, let him be anathema." [11]

3. BAPTISM ADMINISTERED BY UNBELIEVERS.

—It is more difficult to understand how unbelievers (pagans, Jews, Mohammedans, etc.) can validly baptize, and hence we need not wonder that this point was long contested.

The false inference drawn from the argument used to defend the validity of Baptism when administered by laymen,[12] *viz.:* that no one can give what he does not himself possess, proved a serious obstacle to the correct understanding of the Sacrament and its administration. Even St. Augustine was puzzled.[13] Here, again, it was the Holy See which gave the final decision. St. Isidore observes: "The Roman Pontiff does not judge the man who baptizes, but [holds that] the Holy Ghost supplies the grace of Baptism, even though it be a pagan who baptizes." [14] The Council of Compiègne (757) confirmed the validity of a heretical Baptism with express reference to a decision of Pope Sergius (687–701). Nicholas I (d. 867) decided a case of conscience brought before him in the same sense. The *Decretum pro Armenis* re-

---

11 Sess. VII, *De Bapt.*, can. 4: "*Si quis dixerit, baptismum qui etiam datur ab haereticis, . . . non esse verum baptisma, anathema sit.*" Cfr. J. Ernst, *Die Ketzertauf-angelegenheit in der altchristlichen Kirche nach Cyprian*, Mainz 1901.

12 *V. supra*, No. 1.

13 Cfr. *Ep. ad Parmen.*, II, 13: "*Haec quidem alia quaestio, utrum et ab his qui numquam fuerunt Christiani, baptismus possit dari; nec tamen inde aliquid affirmandum est sine auctoritate tanti concilii, quantum tantae rei sufficit.*"

14 *De Offic.*, II, 25, 9: "*Romanus Pontifex non hominem iudicat qui baptizat, sed Spiritum Dei subministrare gratiam baptismi, licet paganus sit qui baptizat.*"

affirmed the doctrine, and thus it has remained up to the present day.

It may be noted that the power of unbelievers to baptize was virtually included in the ancient Christian maxim that "Baptism can be given by any one," and that the doctrine only needed to be worked out.

4. BAPTISM ADMINISTERED BY WOMEN.—The validity of Baptism administered by women came to be recognized last of all and rather late.

Tertullian [15] and Epiphanius [16] vigorously denounced certain women who claimed the right to baptize. It should be noted, however, that these women (Quintilla, the Collyridians, etc.) posed as priestesses, and presumed not only to baptize in cases of necessity, but to administer solemn Baptism.[17] Probably the invectives of Tertullian, Epiphanius, and later writers were directed more against the presumption and disobedience of which these women were guilty than against the validity of Baptism administered by women in general. In view of St. Paul's command that women should "keep silence in the churches," [18] it is not likely that Baptism was often administered by women in the primitive Church. To-day midwives give it quite frequently in cases of necessity. The first clear decision on the matter was issued in the eleventh century by Pope Urban II.[19] In principle, Urban's teaching was already contained in the ancient prac-

---

15 *De Bapt.*, c. 17.

16 *Haer.*, 79, n. 3.

17 Cfr. De Augustinis, *De Re Sacramentaria*, 2nd ed., Vol. I, pp. 393 sq.

18 1 Cor. XIV, 34: "*Mulieres in ecclesiis taceant.*"

19 *Decret. Grat.*, causa 30, qu. 3, c. 4: "*Super quibus consuluit nos tua dilectio, hoc videtur nobis ex sententia respondendum, ut et baptismus sit, si instante necessitate femina puerum in nomine Trinitatis baptizaverit.*"

tice of lay Baptism,[20] because there is no hierarchic distinction between lay men and women. But it was not defined dogmatically until 1439, when the *Decretum pro Armenis* [21] recognized Baptism given by women as valid and permitted it in cases of urgent necessity. The dogma is convincingly demonstrated by St. Thomas in the third part of the *Summa.*[22]

[20] *V. supra,* No. 1.

[21] *V. supra,* p. 259, note 3.

[22] *Summa Theol.,* 3a, qu. 67, art. 4.— On the whole argument of this Section the student may profitably consult P. Schanz, *Die Lehre von den hl. Sakramenten der kath. Kirche,* §18, Freiburg 1893.

CHAPTER IV

THE RECIPIENT OF BAPTISM

SECTION 1

THE REQUISITES OF VALID RECEPTION

The requisites of valid reception in the case of Baptism are mainly three: (1) The recipient must be a human being, (2) He must be in the wayfaring state (*status viae*), and (3) He must not have been previously baptized.

1. THE RECIPIENT MUST BE A HUMAN BEING. —Baptism was instituted for the purpose of blotting out original sin, and therefore its effects are limited to the descendants of Adam. The baptismal mandate (Matth. XXVIII, 19; Mark XVI, 15) is intended only for the human race. A brute beast is as incapable of receiving Baptism as a pure spirit, and hence the story of the "baptized lion" in the so-called *Acta Pauli* is sufficient to brand that document as spurious.[1]

The general rule is that every living being born of a human female can receive Bap-

---

[1] Cfr. Holzhey, *Die Thekla-Akten, ihre Verbreitung und Beurteilung in der Kirche*, Munich 1905.

tism. In case of doubt whether the recipient is a human being, the Sacrament should be administered conditionally.[2]

2. THE RECIPIENT MUST BE IN THE WAYFARING STATE.—Since Christ instituted His Sacraments for this world, not for the next, it is self-evident that they can be received only *in statu viae*. This applies particularly to Baptism. It is a somewhat difficult question to decide, however, just where in a given case the wayfaring state begins and where it ends.

(a) The *terminus a quo,* generally speaking, is the moment of birth.

" He who has never been born cannot be born again," says St. Augustine.[3] Consequently a child hidden in the maternal womb is incapable of receiving Baptism, and to baptize the mother in its stead would obviously be invalid. This explains the custom of treating still-born children as unbaptized and refusing them ecclesiastical burial. Quite another question is this: Is it necessary for a fœtus to be fully developed in order to be capable of Baptism, or does the wayfaring state begin at the moment when the soul is infused into the body? As the human fœtus is a person independent of the mother, its existence plainly begins with the infusion of the intellectual soul. Hence it is reasonable and customary to baptize the fœtus in case of premature birth as well as a full-grown child not yet brought to light when

2 On abnormalities, see Capellmann, *Pastoralmedizin,* 16th ed., pp. 124 sqq.; A. J. Schulte, *On the Administration of Baptism,* pp. 14 sq., Phila. 1915.

3 *De Pecc. Mer. et Remiss.,* II, 27, 43: " *Qui natus non fuerit, renasci non potest.*"

there is danger of death, and to rebaptize conditionally only when it has been impossible to reach the head.[4]

b) The *status viae* ends with death. To baptize a corpse would be both illicit and invalid; Benedict XIV has expressly forbidden it.

It belongs to competent medical authority to decide whether or not in a given case death has set in. There is a curious passage in St. Paul's First Epistle to the Corinthians, which has been cited in favor of baptizing the dead and therefore requires a word of explanation. The Apostle says: "Otherwise what shall they do that are baptized for the dead, if the dead rise not again at all? Why are they then baptized for them?"[5] This passage is obscure and anything but relevant to the point. If the Corinthians were accustomed to baptize living persons in place of the dead, St. Paul surely did not mean to approve the practice, but merely cited it as an *argumentum ad hominem* to prove the dogma of the resurrection. In that hypothesis there would be question of baptizing not the dead, but living substitutes for the benefit of the dead.[6] Most likely, however, the text refers to a symbolic intercession, consisting of works of penance voluntarily assumed by living relatives or friends for the spiritual benefit of the departed.[7]

3. THE RECIPIENT MUST BE UNBAPTIZED.— This requisite follows logically from the unity of Baptism and the fact that it cannot be repeated.[8]

4 Cfr. J. E. Pruner, *Lehrbuch der Pastoraltheologie*, Vol. I, 2nd ed., pp. 151 sqq., Paderborn 1904.

5 1 Cor. XV, 29: "*Alioquin quid facient qui baptizantur pro mortuis* (ὑπὲρ τῶν νεκρῶν), *si omnino mortui non resurgunt? Ut quid et baptizantur pro illis* (βαπτίζονται ὑπὲρ αὐτῶν)?"

6 Cfr. on this obscure Pauline text Al. Schäfer, *Erklärung der beiden Briefe an die Korinther*, pp. 321 sqq., Münster 1903.

7 Cfr. the new Westminster Version, *i. h. l.*, and MacRory's commentary, pp. 238 sqq.

8 On the intention of the *baptizandus* as a requisite of validity *v. supra*, pp. 196 sqq.

SECTION 2

INFANT BAPTISM

1. THE VALIDITY OF INFANT BAPTISM.—In regard to the Baptism of infants, and in general of those who have not yet reached the use of reason (*paedobaptismus*), there arises a twofold question: (1) Can infants validly receive the Sacrament? and (2) Should it be administered to children before they have attained the years of discretion?

a) In the first three centuries of the Christian era the Church tolerated, without, however, in any way approving, the practice of delaying Baptism to an advanced age, sometimes even to the hour of death.[9] In 1439, the Council of Florence forbade the postponement of Baptism even for forty or eighty days. Since the Tridentine Council it is a strict ecclesiastical precept that infants must be baptized as soon as possible after birth.

The chief opponents of infant Baptism are the Anabaptists (or re-baptizers: ἀνά) in Germany; the Antipedobaptists (ἀντί, παῖς, βαπτίζω) in England, a name which is now commonly shortened into Baptists; and the Mennonites.[10]

---

9 Cfr. *Conc. Trident.*, Sess. VII, *De Bapt.*, can. 12. (Denzinger-Bannwart, n. 868).

10 " The Baptists," says Fr. Hunter (*Outlines*, Vol. III, p. 118), "who use immersion, are specially careful in the application of the matter and form and there is little room for doubt as to the validity of their Baptisms; it is, therefore, the more

268

b) The Second Council of Mileve (416) anathematized all "who deny that new-born infants should be baptized immediately after birth."[11] The Tridentine Council declared: "If anyone saith that little children, because they have not actual faith, are not, after having received Baptism, to be reckoned among the faithful, and that for this cause they are to be rebaptized when they have attained to years of discretion, or that it is better that the Baptism of such be omitted than that, while not believing by their own act, they should be baptized in the faith alone of the Church, let him be anathema."[12] Hence it is an article of faith that the Baptism of infants is valid, because it incorporates them into the body of the Church, and may not be repeated after they have attained the use of reason.[13]

2. THE DOGMA PROVED FROM REVELATION.—As the validity of infant Baptism is neither posi-

unfortunate that they refuse to administer the Sacrament to infants." — On the Mennonites see N. A. Weber in the *Cath. Encyclopedia*, Vol. X, page 190.— On Baptism among modern Protestants generally, consult A. Seeberg, *Die Taufe im Neuen Testament*, 1905; Rendtorff, *Die Taufe im Urchristentum im Lichte der neueren Forschungen*, 1905; Roberts, *Christian Baptism, Its Significance and its Subjects*, London 1905.

11 Can. 2: "*Quicunque parvulos recentes ab uteris matrum baptizandos negat, . . . anathema sit.*" (Denzinger-Bannwart, n. 102).

12 Sess. VII, *De Bapt.*, can. 13: "*Si quis dixerit, parvulos eo quod actum credendi non habent suscepto baptismo inter fideles computandos non esse ac propterea, quum ad annos discretionis pervenerint, esse rebaptizandos, aut praestare omitti eorum baptisma quam eos non actu proprio credentes baptizari in sola fide Ecclesiae, anathema sit.*" (Denzinger-Bannwart, n. 869).

13 Cfr. the Catholic teaching on original sin, as explained in Pohle-Preuss, *God the Author of Nature and the Supernatural*, pp. 232 sqq.

tively asserted nor practically exemplified in Holy
Writ, it is impossible to demonstrate this dogma
conclusively from Scripture. It can, however, be
so convincingly proved from Tradition that the
great mass of Protestants prefer to contradict
their own system by tacitly admitting the Catholic
principle of Tradition, rather than surrender the
ancient and universal practice of infant Baptism.[14]

a) Though, as we have already remarked, infant Baptism cannot be demonstrated from the Bible, the Catholic
dogma of its validity, far from being unscriptural, is in
perfect conformity with the spirit of God's written Revelation. In the first place, when, as was frequently the
case (cfr. Acts XVI, 15; I Cor. I, 16), whole families
were baptized, it is likely that sometimes there were little
children among them. The Catholic dogma, moreover,
fully agrees with the Scriptural teaching on the nature
and necessity of Baptism. From our Lord's dictum that
the kingdom of heaven is for little children, and His
solemn declaration that " unless a man be born again of
water and the Holy Ghost, he cannot enter into the kingdom of God," [15] we may legitimately conclude that infants
not only may but must be " born again," *i. e.* baptized. It

14 Thus the catechism, which forms
part of the Book of Common Prayer
of the Anglican Church, explains
that faith is required of persons to
be baptized, and that infants who
have no faith are baptized because
their godparents promise that they
shall have the faith hereafter, a
promise which they themselves are
in due time bound to perform.
" How this view secures the requisite faith in case the child die before reaching the years of discretion," observes Fr. Hunter (*Outlines,* Vol. III, p. 221), " is not
explained, nor is it made clear
whether Baptism may be valid in
the absence of godparents; and
many other similar doubts may be
raised as to the meaning."

15 Matth. XIX, 14; John III, 5.

should be noted, too, that the Jewish rite of circumcision, which was preëminently the type of Christian Baptism,[16] would have foreshadowed that Sacrament but very imperfectly, to say the least, if the children of the New Testament were deprived of the means of obtaining forgiveness of original sin,— a privilege which was granted to the children of the Old Testament Jews.

b) Tradition was already crystallized at the time of St. Augustine, who triumphantly opposed the practice of infant Baptism to the Pelagian denial of original sin.[17] Hence we can limit the Patristic argument to the pre-Augustinian period. Augustine himself states the belief and practice of that period as follows: "The infants are brought to church, and if they cannot go there on their own feet, they run with the feet of others. . . . Let no one among you, therefore, murmur strange doctrines. This the Church has always had, this she has always held; this she received from the faith of the ancients; this she preserves tenaciously to the end." [18]

St. Cyprian (d. 258), speaking in his own name and in that of his fellow-bishops at the Council of Carthage (253), said to Fidus: " No one agrees with you in your opinion as to what should be done, but we all, on the

16 *V. supra*, pp. 22 sqq.

17 Cfr. Pohle-Preuss, *God the Author of Nature and the Supernatural*, p. 253.

18 *Serm.*, 176, n. 2: " *Et ipsi [parvuli] portantur ad ecclesiam, et si pedibus illuc currere non possunt, alienis pedibus currunt. . . . Nemo ergo vobis susurret alienas doctrinas. Hoc Ecclesia semper habuit, semper tenuit; hoc a maiorum fide accepit; hoc usque in finem perseveranter custodit.*" (Migne, *P. L.*, XXXVIII, 950).

contrary, judge that to no one born of man was the mercy and the grace of God to be denied." [19]   St. Augustine explains this utterance as follows: "The Blessed Cyprian, not forming any new decree, but maintaining the assured faith of the Church, in order to correct those who held that an infant should not be baptized before the eighth day, gives it as his own judgment and that of his fellow-bishops, that a child can be validly baptized as soon as born." [20]

In the East, at about the same time, Origen says: "The Church hath received it as a tradition from the Apostles that infants, too, ought to be baptized." [21]

Long before either St. Cyprian or Origen, St. Irenaeus of Lyons (b. about 140) wrote: "Christ came to save all through Himself,— all, I say, who through Him are born again in God: infants and little children and boys and young men and old men." [22]

Recent discoveries in the Roman catacombs prove that infant Baptism was common in the primitive Church. Thus a certain Murtius Verinus placed on the tomb of his children the inscription: "Verina received [Baptism] at the age of ten months, Florina at the age of twelve months." Above another tomb we read: "Here

19 *Ep.* 64, n. 2, ed. Hartel, II, 718: "*In hoc quod tu putabas esse faciendum nemo consentit, sed universi potius iudicavimus nulli hominum nato misericordiam Dei et gratiam denegandam.*"

20 *Ep.* 166 *ad Hier.*, n. 23: "*Beatus Cyprianus, non aliquod decretum condens novum, sed Ecclesiae fidem firmissimam servans, ad corrigendum eos qui putabant ante octavum diem nativitatis non esse parvulum baptizandum, . . . mox natum rite baptizari posse cum suis*

episcopis censuit." (Migne, *P. L.*, XXXIII, 731).

21 *In Ep. ad Rom.*, V, n. 9 (Migne, *P. G.*, XIV, 1047).

22 *Adv. Haer.*, II, 22, 4: "*Omnes venit* [*Christus*] *per semetipsum salvare, omnes inquam, qui per ipsum renascuntur in Deum: infantes et parvulos et pueros et iuvenes et seniores.*" (Migne, *P. G.*, VII, 784). Cfr. A. Seitz, *Die Heilsnotwendigkeit der Kirche nach der altchristlichen Literatur bis zur Zeit des hl. Augustinus*, pp. 298 sqq., Freiburg 1903.

rests Achillia, a newly-baptized [infant]; she was one year and five months old, died February 23rd." [23]

3. A DOGMATIC COROLLARY.—The dogma of the validity of infant Baptism imposes on those who have been baptized in infancy the strict duty of keeping the baptismal vow made for them by their sponsors. Erasmus' demand that baptized children should be left free to ratify that vow or to repudiate it when they attain to the years of discretion, was rejected by the Tridentine Council with the declaration: "If any one saith that those who have been thus baptized when children, are to be asked when they have grown up, whether they will ratify what their sponsors promised in their names when they were baptized, and that, in case they answer that they will not, they are to be left to their own will, . . . let him be anathema." [24]

To admit the contention of Erasmus, which is unblushingly put into practice by modern Rationalists, is like unfurling the banner of revolution within the sacred precincts of the Church.

23 Cfr. A. Weber, *Die römischen Katakomben*, 3rd ed., p. 60, Ratisbon 1906.— On the subject of infant Baptism the student may profitably consult Cardinal Bellarmine, *De Baptismo*, c. 8-11; Risi, *De Baptismo Parvulorum in Primitiva Ecclesia*, Rome 1870; W. Wall, *History of Infant Baptism*, 2 vols., London 1900.

24 Sess. VII, *De Bapt.*, can. 14: "*Si quis dixerit, huiusmodi parvulos baptizatos, quum adoleverint, interrogandos esse, an ratum habere velint, quod patrini eorum nomine, dum baptizarentur, polliciti sunt, et ubi se nolle responderint, suo esse arbitrio relinquendos, . . . anathema sit.*" (Denzinger-Bannwart, n. 870).

To allow a baptized child, when he attains the use of reason, to choose freely between the true and a false religion, to decide whether he will keep the holy law of God or repudiate it at pleasure, betrays rank indifferentism. One sometimes hears the objection: "How can a promise given without my knowledge and consent by some other person, bind my conscience, so long as I have not expressly recognized and accepted the duty it imposes?" We answer that the baptismal vow derives its binding force not from the circumstance that it is made by the sponsors in the name of the baptized child, but from the fact that Baptism, by its very nature as well as by a positive divine ordinance, initiates the recipient into the Catholic religion and, by virtue of the baptismal character which it imprints on the soul, constitutes him a subject of Christ and the Church. By Baptism a man is, as it were, born into the society of the faithful and thereby immediately subjected to the law of Christ, just as the children of the Israelites became subject to the Mosaic law by circumcision. As man by the fact of being born a rational being, is bound to observe the moral law of nature and the positive laws of his country, no matter whether he approves of them or not, so, through the fact of his being born again of water and the Holy Ghost, he is incorporated into the Church and becomes subject to her laws. And as one need not ratify his physical birth by an act of formal and express approval, so a Christian has no right to make his supernatural rebirth conditional upon his subsequent consent. The customary renewal of the baptismal vow at solemn first Communion has for its object, not to permit the children to decide whether they will or will not ratify the promise made for them by their sponsors, but to give them an opportunity of freely promising to do what they are bound to do in any event.

READINGS: — The Scholastic commentators on Peter Lombard's *Liber Sententiarum*, IV, dist. 3, and on St. Thomas, *Summa Theol.*, 3a, qu. 66; especially Billuart, *Tract. de Baptismo* (ed. Lequette, Vol. VI, pp. 253 sqq.).— Bellarmine, *De Sacramento Baptismi* (*Opera Omnia*, ed. J. Fèvre, Vol. III, pp. 513 sqq., Paris 1870).—*Tournely, *De Baptismo* (in Migne, *Curs. Theol. Complet.*, Vol. XXI).— Bertieri, *De Sacramentis in Genere, Baptismo et Confirmatione*, Vienna 1774.— Zimmermann, *De Baptismi Origine eiusque Usu Hodierno*, 1815.— Höfling, *Das Sakrament der Taufe*, 2 vols., 1846, 1848.— M. J. Ryan, *De Doctrina S. Ioannis circa Baptismum*, Rochester 1908.—*J. Corblet, *Histoire Dogmatique, Liturgique et Archéologique du Sacrement de Baptême*, 2 vols., Paris 1881.— *Probst, *Sakramente und Sakramentalien in den ersten drei Jahrhunderten*, Tübingen 1872; De Augustinis, *De Re Sacramentaria*, Vol. I, 2nd ed., Rome 1899; P. Schanz, *Die Lehre von den hl. Sakramenten der kath. Kirche*, § 14 sqq., Freiburg 1893; L. Billot, *De Ecclesiae Sacramentis*, Vol. I, 4th ed., Rome 1907; Oswald, *Die dogmatische Lehre von den hl. Sakramenten*, Vol. I, 5th ed., Münster 1894; Chr. Pesch, *Praelectiones Dogmaticae*, Vol. VI, 3rd ed., Freiburg 1908; Tepe, *Institutiones Theologicae*, Vol. IV, Paris 1896; J. B. Sasse, *De Sacramentis Ecclesiae*, Vol. I, Freiburg 1897; P. Einig, *Tractatus de Sacramentis*, Treves 1900; *Heinrich-Gutberlet, *Dogmatische Theologie*, Vol. IX, Mainz 1901; Nik. Gihr, *Die hl. Sakramente der kath. Kirche*, Vol. I, 2nd ed., Freiburg 1902; Cabrol, *Dictionnaire d'Archéologie Chrétienne et de Liturgie, s. v. " Baptême,"* Paris 1903 sqq.; Fr. Dölger, *Der Exorzismus im altchristlichen Taufritual. Eine religionsgeschichtliche Studie*, Paderborn 1909; W. Koch, *Die Taufe im Neuen Testament*, Münster 1910; S. J. Hunter, *Outlines of Dogmatic Theology*, Vol. III, pp. 214-233, London 1894; Wilhelm-Scannell, *A Manual of Catholic Theology*, Vol. II, pp. 378-392, 2nd ed., London 1901; W. Humphrey, *The One Mediator*, pp. 81 sqq., London 1890; A. Devine, *The Sacraments Explained*, pp. 134 sqq., 3rd ed., London 1905; B. J. Otten, S. J., *A Manual of the History of Dogmas*, Vol. I, pp. 38 sqq., 89 sqq., 146, 167, 178, 196, 205, 351, 369; Vol. II, pp. 298 sqq.

PART III

CONFIRMATION

The Sacrament of Confirmation owes its name to the fact that it was always regarded as a making fast or sure ($\beta\epsilon\beta\alpha\acute{\iota}\omega\sigma\iota\varsigma$, *confirmatio*), a perfecting or completing ($\tau\epsilon\lambda\epsilon\acute{\iota}\omega\sigma\iota\varsigma$, *consummatio*) in relation to Baptism. In ancient times these two Sacraments were generally administered together.

From its effects Confirmation is known as the " Sacrament of the Holy Ghost " (*sacramentum Spiritus Sancti*) and also as the " Sacrament of the Seal " (*signaculum, sigillum*, $\sigma\phi\rho\alpha\gamma\acute{\iota}\varsigma$, from $\sigma\phi\rho\alpha\gamma\acute{\iota}\zeta\epsilon\iota\nu$, *to confirm*). It should be noted, however, that in the first two centuries of the Christian era the words $\sigma\phi\rho\alpha\gamma\acute{\iota}\varsigma$ and $\tau\acute{\epsilon}\lambda\epsilon\iota o\nu$ were frequently applied to Baptism.

From the external rite Confirmation was formerly also called " the laying-on of hands " (*impositio manuum*, $\dot{\epsilon}\pi\acute{\iota}\theta\epsilon\sigma\iota\varsigma$ $\chi\epsilon\iota\rho\tilde{\omega}\nu$) or " anointing with chrism " (*unctio, chrismatio*, $\chi\rho\tilde{\iota}\sigma\mu\alpha$, $\mu\acute{\upsilon}\rho o\nu$). To-day these names are no longer in use, but the Sacrament is commonly known as " *Confirmatio* " in the Latin and $\tau\grave{o}$ $\mu\acute{\upsilon}\rho o\nu$ in the Greek Church.

Confirmation may be defined as a Sacrament in which those already baptized, through the imposition of hands, anointment, and the prayer of the bishop, receive the power of the Holy Ghost, by which they are enabled to believe firmly and to profess the faith boldly. The Council of Trent contented itself with three short canons on the subject,[1] which are appended to those dealing with Baptism. Confirmation both internally and externally bears so close a relation to Baptism that we may safely treat it along the same lines.

[1] Sess. VII, *De Confirm.*, can. 1-3.

CHAPTER I

CONFIRMATION A TRUE SACRAMENT

SECTION 1

DIVINE INSTITUTION

1. HERETICAL PERVERSIONS VS. THE TEACHING OF THE CHURCH.—No ancient or medieval sect ever denied the Sacrament of Confirmation.

a) The Novatians underrated its necessity for salvation.[2] The Albigenses (and possibly the Waldenses) denied its divine institution. The Wiclifites and Hussites entertained wrong notions with regard to the requisites of validity in the minister. But it remained for Luther, Melanchthon, Calvin, and the rest of the so-called Protestant reformers to reject Confirmation altogether, or at least to regard it as " an idle ceremony," " a kind of catechism," " a renewal of the baptismal vow," and so forth. The worst offender was Calvin, who referred to this sublime rite as " the abortive larva of a sacrament," " a false promise of the devil," and in other abusive terms.[3] Calvin's example was followed by Dallæus, Basnage, and Antonio de Dominis, apostate archbishop of Spalato (1561–1624).

---

2 Cfr. Theodoret, *Haer. Fabul.*, III, 5: ". . . iis quos baptizabant, chrisma non praebent."

3 *Instit.* IV, 9: " *abortivam sacramenti larvam,*" " *baptismi contumeliam,*" " *falsam diaboli pollicita-*

278

b) The Council of Trent declares that Confirmation is one of the Seven Sacraments of the Church,[4] and that it is a true Sacrament, distinct from Baptism. "If any one saith that the Confirmation of those who have been baptized is an idle ceremony, and not rather a true and proper Sacrament, or that of old it was nothing more than a kind of catechism whereby they who were near adolescence gave an account of their faith in the face of the Church, let him be anathema."[5]

2. THE ARGUMENT FROM REVELATION.—Since it cannot be shown directly from the Bible when and how Christ instituted Confirmation, we have to fall back upon an indirect argument, which will, however, prove conclusive in the light of ecclesiastical Tradition.

a) Holy Scripture furnishes the following data:

a) Christ promised before His Passion [6] that those who believed in Him should receive the Holy Ghost. This promise He repeated after the Resurrection. Luke XXIV, 49: "I send the promise of my Father upon you; but stay you in the city, till you be endued with power from on high."[7] The fulfilment came on Pentecost, when

tionem," "oleum diaboli mendacio pollutum," "oleum putidum," etc.
4 Sess. VII, De Sacram., can. 1.
5 Sess. VII, De Confirm., can. 1: "Si quis dixerit, confirmationem baptizatorum otiosam cerimoniam esse et non potius verum et proprium sacramentum, aut olim nihil aliud fuisse quam catechesin quandam, . . . anathema sit." (Denzinger-Bannwart, n. 871).
6 Cfr. John XIV, 16.
7 Luc. XXIV, 49: "Et ego

"they were all filled with the Holy Ghost." [8] The results were wonderful beyond expectation. Inspired by the Holy Ghost, the disciples spoke in divers tongues, wrought miracles, fearlessly professed their faith in Christ, and suffered martyrdom for His sake.

β) The mission of the Holy Ghost was not limited to the Apostles and disciples. It was intended for all the faithful without exception. Cfr. John VII, 37 sq.: "On the last and great day of the festivity, Jesus stood and cried, saying: If any man thirst, let him come to me, and drink. He that believeth in me, as the scripture saith, Out of his belly shall flow rivers of living water." St. John adds by way of explanation: "Now this he said of the Spirit [9] which they should receive who believed in him; [10] for as yet the Spirit was not given, because Jesus was not yet glorified." [11]

A universal outpouring of the Holy Ghost in the Messianic age had been foreshadowed by the prophets. Cfr. Is. XLIV, 3; LIX, 21; Ez. XI, 19; XXXVI, 25 sq.; XXXIX, 29; Joel II, 28. The pentecostal gift was understood by St. Peter as a grace intended for all, for he says: "Do penance, and be baptized every one of you [12] in the name of Jesus Christ, for the remission of your sins: and you shall receive the gift of the Holy Ghost. [13] For the promise [14] is to you, and to your children, and to all that are far off, whomsoever the Lord our God shall call."

---

mitto promissum Patris mei (τὴν ἐπαγγελίαν τοῦ πατρός μου) in vos; vos autem sedete in civitate quoadusque induamini virtute ex alto."

8 Acts II, 4: "Et repleti sunt omnes Spiritu Sancto."

9 περὶ τοῦ πνεύματος.

10 οἱ πιστεύοντες εἰς αὐτόν = omnes Christifideles.

11 John VII, 39.

12 ἕκαστος ὑμῶν. The passage is Acts II, 38 sq.

13 τὴν δωρεὰν τοῦ ἁγίου πνεύματος.

14 ἡ ἐπαγγελία.

γ) The only question that remains to be answered is: Was the Holy Ghost to be communicated to the faithful by means of a special outward rite distinct from Baptism? The answer may be gathered from the following Scriptural texts. Acts VIII, 14 sqq.: "When the Apostles, who were in Jerusalem, had heard that Samaria had received the word of God, they sent unto them Peter and John, who, when they were come, prayed for them, that they might receive the Holy Ghost; for He was not as yet come upon any of them, but they were only baptized in the name of the Lord Jesus. Then they laid their hands upon them, and they received the Holy Ghost.[15] And when Simon [Magus] saw, that by the imposition of the hands of the Apostles, the Holy Ghost was given,[16] he offered them money," etc. From this passage we may infer: (1) that the Apostles imparted the Holy Ghost by the laying-on of hands, *i. e.* by means of a sacramental rite; (2) that this rite was distinct from Baptism, the people of Samaria having been previously baptized by Philip; (3) that the power to perform this ceremony was reserved to the Apostles, *i. e.* bishops, else why should Peter and John, during a time of persecution, have risked their lives to go to Samaria? (4) That the imposition of hands

---

[15] τότε ἐπετίθεσαν τὰς χεῖρας ἐπ' αὐτοὺς καὶ ἐλάμβανον πνεῦμα ἅγιον.

[16] ὅτι διὰ τῆς ἐπιθέσεως τῶν χειρῶν τῶν ἀποστόλων δίδοται τὸ πνεῦμα τὸ ἅγιον.

was regarded as a necessary complement of, and consequently as a true Sacrament distinct from, Baptism.[17]

The Protestant objection that the imposition of hands had for its sole purpose the conferring of certain extraordinary gifts (*charismata*), such as speaking with divers tongues, prophesying, etc., is refuted by the fact that those gifts were sometimes bestowed without any external rite [18] and that they neither invariably nor necessarily accompanied Confirmation.[19]

b) **Ecclesiastical Tradition is perfectly clear on this subject.** Belief in the divine institution of Confirmation was firmly established in St. Augustine's time, and hence it will suffice to demonstrate its existence during the preceding period.[20]

α) St. Jerome (d. 420), who was so ardent a champion of the rights of the priesthood, speaks of episcopal Confirmation tours as customary in his time [21] and proves their propriety from Scripture and Tradition. " You ask, where is it written? In the Acts of the Apostles. But even if Sacred Scripture supplied no authority [for the custom], the consensus of the whole world would give it the force of a precept." [22] Pope St. Innocent the

---

17 On the scriptural argument drawn from Acts XIX, 1 sqq., see Pohle-Preuss, *The Divine Trinity*, pp. 101 sqq. Cfr. Fr. Dölger, *Das Sakrament der Firmung*, pp. 27 sqq., Vienna 1906.

18 Cfr. Acts X, 44 sqq.

19 Cfr. 1 Cor. XII, 30.

20 On the teaching of St. Augustine *v. supra*, pp. 79 sqq. Of the Saint's writings see especially *Tract.*

in I Ep. Ioan., 6, n. 10; *In Ps.*, 26, n. 2.

21 *Dial. adv. Lucif.*, n. 9: *" Non quidem abnuo, hanc esse ecclesiarum consuetudinem, ut ad eos qui longe a maioribus per presbyteros et diaconos baptizati sunt, episcopus ad invocationem Spiritus Sancti manus impositurus excurrat."*

22 *Ibid.*: *" Exigis, ubi scriptum sit? In actibus Apostolorum.*

First (402–414) issued detailed instructions with regard to the administration of the Sacrament. "As regards the sealing of infants," he says, "it is clear that it may not lawfully be done by any one but a bishop. For presbyters, though they be priests of the second rank, have not attained to the summit of the pontificate. That this pontifical right belongs to bishops only,— to wit, that they may seal or deliver the Spirit, the Paraclete,— is demonstrated not merely by ecclesiastical usage, but also by that portion of the Acts of the Apostles wherein it is declared that Peter and John were sent to give the Holy Ghost to those who had already been baptized. For when presbyters baptize, whether with or without the presence of a bishop, they may anoint the baptized with chrism, provided it be previously consecrated by a bishop, but not sign the forehead with that oil, which is a right reserved to bishops only, when they give the Spirit, the Paraclete. The words, however, I cannot name, for fear of seeming to betray rather than to reply to the point on which you have consulted me." [23]

St. Cyprian (d. 258) writes: "The Samaritans had already obtained legitimate ecclesiastical Baptism, and

Etiamsi S. Scripturae auctoritas non subesset, totius orbis in hanc partem consensus instar praecepti obtineret."

23 *Ep.* (25) *" Si instituta ecclesiastica," ad Decent. Episc. Eugubin.: "De consignandis vero infantibus manifestum est, non ab alio quam ab episcopo fieri licere. Nam presbyteri, licet secundi sint sacerdotes, pontificatus tamen apicem non habent. Hoc autem pontificium solis deberi episcopis, ut vel consignent, vel Paracletum Spiritum tradant, non solum consuetudo ecclesiastica demonstrat, verum etiam et illa lectio Actuum Apostolorum, quae asserit Petrum et Ioannem esse directos, qui iam baptizatis traderent Spiritum Sanctum. Nam presbyteris sive extra episcopum, sive praesente episcopo quum baptizant, chrismate baptizatos ungere licet, sed quod ab episcopo fuerit consecratum, non tamen frontem ex eodem oleo signare, quod solis debetur episcopis, quum tradunt Spiritum Paracletum. Verba vero dicere non possum, ne magis prodere videar, quam ad consultationem respondere."* (Denzinger-Bannwart, n. 98).

hence it was not fitting that they should be baptized anew; Peter and John merely supplied what was wanting, *viz.:* that prayer being made for them and hands imposed, the Holy Ghost should be invoked and poured forth upon them; which also is now done among us; so that they who are baptized in the Church are presented to the bishops of the Church, and by our prayer and the imposition of hands, receive the Holy Ghost and are perfected by the seal of the Lord." [24]

At about the same time, Pope St. Cornelius (251–253) refers to Confirmation in his judgment against the notorious Novatian, who, after having been baptized on his sick-bed, " did not receive the other things, nor was he signed with the seal of the Lord by the bishop; and not having received this seal, how could he receive the Holy Ghost ? " [25]

Tertullian was familiar with the rite of Confirmation, for he says in his treatise *De Baptismo:* " Then, emerging from the laver, we are anointed with a blessed unction. . . . The unction runs bodily over us, but profits spiritually. . . . Then the hand is laid upon us through the blessing, calling upon and inviting the Holy Ghost." [26]

24 *Ep.* 73 *ad Iubaian.,* n. 9, ed. Hartel, II, 785: " *Samaritani quia legitimum et ecclesiasticum baptismum consecuti fuerant, baptizari eos ultra non oportebat; sed tantummodo quod deerat, id a Petro et Ioanne factum est, ut oratione pro iis habitâ et manu impositâ invocaretur et infunderetur super eos Spiritus Sanctus, quod nunc quoque apud nos geritur, ut qui in Ecclesia baptizantur, praepositis ecclesiae offerantur et per nostram orationem et manuum impositionem Spiritum Sanctum consequantur et signaculo dominico consummentur.*"

25 *Ep. ad Fabium,* quoted by Eusebius, *Hist. Eccles.,* VI, 43: " *Morbo tandem elapsus neque cetera acquisivit neque Domini sigillo ab episcopo obsignatus fuit; hoc autem signaculo minime percepto quomodo Spiritum Sanctum potuit accipere?*"

26 *De Bapt.,* c. 7: " *Exinde egressi de lavacro perungimur benedictâ unctione . . . Sic et in nobis carnaliter currit unctio, sed spiritualiter proficit.*" *Ibid.,* c. 8: " *Dehinc manus imponitur per benedictionem advocans et invitans Spiritum Sanctum.*"

According to the recent researches of Dölger,[27] Confirmation in the time of Tertullian and St. Cyprian was administered immediately after Baptism. The neophyte was anointed from head to foot, clothed in white, and led before the bishop, who, laying his hand upon him, invoked the Holy Ghost and made the sign of the cross (*signaculum*) on his forehead.

Pope Sylvester I (d. 335) separated the two anointments, permitting the priest to perform the former and reserving the latter (on the forehead) to the bishop. Tertullian [28] protests against a mock confirmation practiced by the votaries of the Mithraic cult, which ceremony, Cumont [29] thinks, consisted in branding the candidate with a red-hot iron, possibly accompanied by some sort of unction.

β) In the Greek Church, St. John Chrysostom, who was a contemporary of St. Augustine, writes: " Philip was one of the seven, the second [in rank] after Stephen. Hence, when he baptized, he did not communicate to the neophytes the Holy Ghost, because he had not the power to do so. This gift was peculiar to the twelve, a prerogative of the Apostles; whence we see [even now] that the coryphaei [bishops] and none other do this." [30]

St. Basil (d. 379) barely hints at the existence of Confirmation: " We bless the water of Baptism and the oil of unction — by what written authority? Is it not rather in virtue of a secret and hidden tradition? " [31]

St. Cyril of Jerusalem (d. 386) is the great Eastern authority on the subject. In his famous *Catecheses Mystagogicae,* delivered to the newly baptized Christians

27 *Das Sakrament der Firmung,* pp. 65 sqq.

28 *De Praescript.,* c. 40.

29 *Die Mysterien des Mithra,* p. 117, Leipzig 1898.

30 *Hom. in Act.,* 18, n. 3 (Migne, P. G., LX, 144).

31 *De Spir. S.,* c. 27.

in Easter week, he extols Confirmation in such glowing terms that the Lutheran theologian Chemnitz jestingly refers to this Sacrament as "*chrisma Cyrillianum.*" In the third *Catechesis,* which is entirely devoted to Confirmation, we read: "To you also, after you had come up from the pool of the sacred streams, was given the chrism, the emblem [antitype] of that wherewith Christ was anointed; and this is the Holy Ghost. . . . Beware of regarding this as a plain and common ointment. For as the bread of the Eucharist, after the invocation of the Holy Ghost, is no longer common bread, but the body of Christ, so this holy ointment, after the invocation, is no longer plain ointment, nor, so to say, common, but the chrism of Christ, which by the presence of the godhead causes in us the Holy Ghost. This symbolically anoints thy forehead and thy other senses; and the body indeed is anointed with visible ointment ($\tau\tilde{\wp}\ \mu\acute{\upsilon}\rho\wp$), but the soul is sanctified by the holy and life-giving Spirit."[32]

It is extremely probable that St. Theophilus of Antioch (d. about 180) had the Sacrament of Confirmation in mind when he wrote: "Assuredly we have received the name of Christians for no other reason than because we were overspread with divine oil."[33]

An indirect proof for the existence of this Sacrament in the first half of the second century is furnished by the fact that the practice of the laying-on of hands and the anointing of baptized persons was in vogue among the Gnostics, who must have gotten it from the Catholic Church.[34]

32 *Cat. Myst.,* 3, cap. 3 (Migne, *P. G.,* XXXIII, 1090). Cfr. J. Marquardt, *S. Cyrillus Hierosolymitanus Baptismi, Chrismatis, Eucharistiae Mysteriorum Interpres,* Leipzig 1882.

33 *Ad Autolyc.,* c. 1, n. 12 (Migne, *P. G.,* VI, 1042).

34 Cfr. Dölger, *Das Sakrament der Firmung,* pp. 4 sqq.

Speaking generally it may be said that " anointing and the imposition of hands in the Catholic Church did not originate towards the close of the second century, but can be traced by a well-established tradition back to the time of the Apostles." [35]

The argument from prescription becomes irrefutable in the light of the teaching and practice of the schismatic Greeks and the ancient sectaries, who, with the sole exception of the Nestorians, recognized Confirmation as a Sacrament.[36]

[35] *Op. cit.,* p. 8.— The argument from Tradition is fully developed up to the twelfth century by Vitasse in Migne's *Theol. Cursus Compl.,* Vol. XXI, pp. 556 sqq. See also Bellarmine, *De Confirm.,* c. 5 sqq.

[36] Cfr. Dölger, *op. cit.,* pp. 9 sqq., 42 sqq.

SECTION 2

MATTER AND FORM

As there is nothing dogmatically defined with regard to this phase of our subject, we must rely entirely on theological arguments. Catholic writers are at variance as to what constitutes the essential matter of Confirmation.

1. THE MATERIA PROXIMA.—The reason why we do not begin with an attempt to determine the *materia remota* of Confirmation is this: If it were true, as some contend, that the essential matter of this Sacrament consists in the imposition of hands, there would be no *materia remota.*

Concerning the *materia proxima* there are four different theories.

a) Most of the older canonists and theologians [1] regard the *impositio manuum* (χειροθεσία) as the sole matter of Confirmation.

Their chief argument is that Holy Scripture [2] always describes Confirmation as a laying-on of hands, never as an unction (*chrismatio*). However, Staerk,[3] basing his conclusions on 2 Cor. I, 21 sq., contends that the Apostolic

---

[1] Notably Aureolus (*Comment. in Sent.,* IV, dist. 79, qu. 1), Isaac Habert, Petavius, Sirmond (Migne, *Theol. Curs. Compl.,* XXI, p. 769).

[2] Acts VIII, 14 sqq., XIX, 1 sqq.

[3] *Der Taufritus,* p. 159, Freiburg 1903.

formula of Confirmation ran something like this: "*Chrismate sancto, complemento Spiritus Sancti signatur servus Christi.*" Dölger thinks that possibly " the Apostles conferred Confirmation by that imposition of hands, and that the anointment with chrism, as the external sign, was introduced at their behest only towards the close of the Apostolic age." [4] The assertion that Tertullian, Cyprian, and Jerome knew nothing of the *chrismatio,* is rendered doubtful by the express testimony of so many other Patristic writers.

b) St. Thomas, Bellarmine, Gregory of Valentia, Estius, Maldonatus, Nepefny, and a few other theologians contend that the anointing with chrism (*chrismatio*) is the sole matter of Confirmation.

They base their argument on the *Decretum pro Armenis,* which says: "The second Sacrament is Confirmation, of which the matter is chrism, made of oil . . . and balsam . . . blessed by the bishop." [5] This is also the teaching of the Roman Catechism: "That such [*i. e.* a mixture of oil and balsam] is the matter of this Sacrament, holy Church and her councils have always taught, and the same has been handed down to us by St. Denis and by many other Fathers of the gravest authority, particularly by Pope Fabian, who testifies that the Apostles received the composition of chrism from the Lord and transmitted it to us." [6] This explanation is, however,

4 *Das Sakrament der Firmung,* p. 190.

5 " *Secundum sacramentum est confirmatio, cuius materia est chrisma confectum ex oleo . . . et balsamo . . . per episcopum benedicto.*" (Denzinger-Bannwart, n. 697).

6 *Cat. Rom.,* P. II, c. 3, n. 7: " *Quod autem ea [scil. mixtura ex oleo et balsamo] sit huius sacramenti materia, cum S. Ecclesia et Concilia perpetuo docuerunt, tum a S. Dionysio et complurimis aliis gravissimis Patribus traditum est imprimisque a*

open to serious objections. The St. Denis who is quoted as a witness, is none other than the Pseudo-Areopagite, who was not a " disciple of the Apostles," as the Schoolmen believed, but a Christian pupil of the famous neo-Platonist philosopher Proclus, who flourished in the latter part of the fifth and the beginning of the sixth century. The dictum attributed to Pope Fabian (236–250) is spurious. The Tridentine Council evaded the theological point here at issue and contented itself with defending the use of chrism against the attacks of the Protestant reformers. It declared: " If any one saith that they who ascribe any virtue to the sacred chrism of Confirmation offer an outrage to the Holy Ghost, let him be anathema." [7] This is not tantamount to a dogmatic definition that the sacred chrism is an essential element of Confirmation; for the canon quoted would remain valid even if the anointment with sacred chrism were merely a symbolic ceremony instead of a true sacramental rite. The *chrismatio* itself was most fully developed in the Orient, where the laying-on of hands gradually fell into entire desuetude, whereas the Latin Church continued to emphasize the importance of both rites. Professor Nepefny's contention [8] that the " ancient Greeks " never laid on hands in conferring the Sacrament of Confirmation, is disproved by the Egyptian Church Ordinance,[9] the newly discovered Testament of Our Lord Jesus Christ,[10] and the Arabic *Canones*

Fabiano Pontifice, qui Apostolos chrismatis confectionem a Domino accepisse nobisque reliquisse testatus est."

[7] *Conc. Trident.*, Sess. VII, *De Confirm.*, can. 2: " *Si quis dixerit, iniurios esse Spiritui Sancto eos, qui sacro confirmationis chrismati virtutem aliquam tribuunt, anathe-* *ma sit."* (Denzinger-Bannwart, n. 872).

[8] *Die Firmung*, pp. 124 sqq., Passau 1869.

[9] Ed. Achelis, pp. 98 sq., Leipzig 1891.

[10] *Testamentum Domini Nostri Iesu Christi*, ed. Rahmani, pp. 129 sq., Mainz 1899.

Hippolyti,[11] three documents which, according to Funk's exhaustive researches,[12] all grew out of the pseudo-Apostolic Constitutions. The Egyptian Church Ordinance and the *Testamentum Domini Nostri Iesu Christi,* both productions of the fifth century, speak of a two-fold laying-on of hands, one with and the other without the *chrismatio.*[13]

c) A third group of theologians, combining the two opinions just reviewed, hold that the imposition of hands and anointment with chrism conjointly constitute the matter of Confirmation. This opinion has a solid basis in ecclesiastical Tradition.

Since, however, the Latin rite of Confirmation comprises two distinct impositions of the hands — the extension of them (χειροτονία) over all the candidates with which the ceremony begins, and the individual laying-on of hands (χειροθεσία) which takes place in the act of anointing,— most of the representatives of this group [14] regard the latter rite as the essential matter of Confirmation. The individual laying-on of hands, they say, and the anointing of the forehead with chrism, together constitute but one rite.   This opinion is confirmed by the practice of the Greek Church, which employs but one *impositio manuum,* namely, that which takes place simultaneously with the anointment.   The Oriental practice was expressly approved by Benedict XIV in his Encyclical "*Ex quo*

11 Ed. Haneberg, pp. 76 sq., München 1870.

12 *Das Testament unseres Herrn und die verwandten Schriften,* Mainz 1901.

13 Cfr. Dölger, *Das Sakrament der Firmung,* pp. 81 sqq.

14 Tournely is one of the few exceptions.

primum" (March 1, 1756). He says: "No one is permitted to assert that the Greek Church has not the Sacrament of Confirmation. For if any one would hold this opinion, he would be manifestly contradicted by the ancient Oriental discipline." [15] His declaration gains weight from the common consent of present-day Latin theologians that the *extensio manuum* is not essential to the Sacrament, and from the decision of the Propaganda (1840) that Confirmation must not be repeated if that part of the ceremony has been accidentally omitted.

d) According to Morinus, Tapper, and some others, either the imposition of hands or the anointing suffices to make the Sacrament valid.

These writers exemplify their theory by reference to the Holy Eucharist, which, they say, may be validly received under either species or under both. As no solid argument can be adduced in support of this view, we may disregard it.

CRITICAL ESTIMATE OF THE FOUR OPINIONS. —Practically, of course, the minister of Confirmation is bound to proceed according to the *Pontificale Romanum*. As for the theoretical question here at issue, it can be best decided by adopting the opinion that the imposition of hands and the anointment with chrism both appertain to the essential matter of the Sacrament.

---

[15] "*Nemini fas est asserere in Ecclesia graeca non adesse sacramentum confirmationis. Si quis enim hanc opinionem tueretur, huic manifesto obstaret vetus orientalis disciplina.*" (§ 51).

The arguments of the first-mentioned group of authors establish the necessity of the *impositio manuum* on the basis of Sacred Scripture; those of the second, prove the indispensability of the anointment from the teaching of the Fathers and the practice of the ancient Church; and as the Greek Church knows no other χειροθεσία besides that which in the Latin Church takes place simultaneously with the anointing, it follows that the *impositio manuum cum chrismatione coniuncta* constitutes the essential matter of the Sacrament. This is the express teaching of Innocent III [16] and it is re-echoed in the profession of faith of the Greek Emperor Michael Palæologus, read before the Second Council of Lyons (1274).[17] In the light of this teaching we can easily understand why the Fathers often employed the terms *confirmatio, unctio,* and *manus impositio* synonymously, and that this diversity of usage argues no divergency in teaching.[18]

2. THE MATERIA REMOTA.—If the anointing and the imposition of hands conjointly are the *materia proxima* of Confirmation, the chrism (*chrisma,* μύρον) employed in the last-mentioned portion of the rite must manifestly be its *materia remota.*

a) Chrism is a mixture of olive oil (*oleum olivarum*) and balsam (*balsamum*). In the Greek Church it also contains an admixture of odoriferous herbs and a small

---

[16] *Decret.,* l. I, tit. 15, c. 1, § 7: " *Per frontis chrismationem manus impositio designatur.*"

[17] " *Aliud est sacramentum confirmationis, quod per manuum impositionem episcopi conferunt chris-* mando renatos." (Denzinger-Bannwart, n. 465).

[18] Cfr. on the subject of these different opinions Heinrich-Gutberlet, *Dogmatische Theologie,* Vol. IX, §516, and Dölger, *Das Sakrament der Firmung,* pp. 93 sqq., 188 sqq.

quantity of wine. The principal ingredient, of course, is the oil, which must be pure oil of olives. When the Armenians were censured by the Council of Tarsus (1177) for substituting oil of sesame, their only excuse was that poverty compelled them to deviate from the traditional practice.[19]

b) Must the chrism, in order to be valid matter for Confirmation, necessarily be mixed with balsam, and consecrated by a bishop? Theologians differ on these two points.

a) The Thomists, with the majority, regard the admixture of balsam as essential, for the reason that the Bible, the Fathers, and the Church in her official language call mere olive oil alone not *chrisma* ($\mu\acute{\upsilon}\rho o\nu$) but *oleum* ($\check{\epsilon}\lambda\alpha\iota o\nu$). Many Scotists and a number of modern theologians [20] contend that the balsam is a requisite of licit but not of valid administration. The use of balsam as an ingredient of the sacred chrism cannot be proved before the sixth century.[21] Earlier writers speak simply of *oleum,* which Pope Innocent I identifies with *chrisma.* Optatus of Mileve applies *oleum* to unconsecrated, and *chrisma* to consecrated oil, without an admixture of balsam. Innocent III did not venture to declare Confirmation administered with mere olive oil alone as invalid. These and other reasons lead Krüll [22] to conclude that the use of balsam originated in the sixth century,[23] and if this be true, the necessity of mixing it with the oil can only be *de praecepto.*

19 "*Ex paupertate huic derogamus traditioni.*" On the symbolical meaning of the chrism see St. Thomas, *Summa Theologica,* 3a, qu. 72, art. 2; N. Gihr, *Die hl. Sakramente der kath. Kirche,* Vol. I, 2nd ed., § 49.

20 Notably Vitasse, Oswald, and Simar.

21 Cfr. the Pseudo-Areopagite, *De Eccl. Hier.,* c. 4, 3, § 4.

22 In Kraus, *Realenzyklopädie der christl. Altertümer,* I, 211.

23 Cfr. Dölger, *Das Sakrament der Firmung,* pp. 96 sqq., 192 sq.

β) Equally undecided is the question whether the sacred chrism must be consecrated by a bishop. Pope Benedict XIV declared it " beyond controversy " that " in the Latin Church the Sacrament of Confirmation is administered with sacred chrism or olive oil mixed with balsam, and blessed by a bishop. . . ." [24] Episcopal consecration of the chrism is regarded as essential by St. Thomas [25] and his school, by Suarez,[26] and the majority of modern theologians, on the ground that many Fathers [27] speak of the " blessed oil of anointment," and that popes and councils have prescribed that the oil used for Confirmation be previously consecrated by a bishop.[28]

Whether a priest may be the extraordinary minister of this blessing, and if so, under what conditions, is another open question. Cajetan and Soto hold that the Pope may delegate a priest for this purpose. Eugene IV is said to have granted the privilege of consecrating the sacred chrism to the Latin missionaries in India. The deacon John, who lived in the sixth century,[29] holds that in case of necessity bishops can delegate their power in this matter to priests.[30] Whether or not these accounts are reliable, one thing is certain: according to

24 *Encycl. " Ex quo primum," d. 1 Mart.* 1756, § 52: " *Quod itaque extra controversiam est, hoc dicatur: nimirum in Ecclesia latina confirmationis sacramentum conferri adhibito sacro chrismate sive oleo olivarum balsamo admixto et ab episcopo benedicto ductoque signo crucis per sacramenti ministrum in fronte suscipientis, dum idem minister formae verba pronuntiat.*"

25 *Summa Th.,* 3a, qu. 72, art. 3.

26 *De Confirm.,* disp. 33, sect. 2.

27 *E. g.,* SS. Basil, Cyril of Jerusalem, and Leo the Great.

28 Cfr. Innocent I's *Ep.* 25 *ad Decent.,* c. 3: " *Presbyteris sive extra episcopum sive praesente episcopo, quum baptizant, chrismate baptizatos ungere licet, sed quod ab episcopo fuerit consecratum, non tamen frontem ex eodem oleo signare, quod solis debetur episcopis, quum tradunt Spiritum Paracletum.*" (*V. supra,* p. 283).

29 Cfr. Migne, *P. L.,* LIX, 403.

30 Cfr. Löffler, " *Die Weihe der hl. Oele,*" in the *Katholik,* Mainz 1885, II, pp. 236 sqq.

all the existing rituals, the sacred chrism may be consecrated by bishops only. In the Orient the privilege is
reserved to the Patriarch or Katholikos. Hence we may
reasonably conclude that chrism consecrated by a bishop
is an indispensable requisite for the validity of Confirmation. Oswald treats the matter altogether too lightly
when he says: " The previous blessing of the elements
is probably a non-essential matter in all the Sacraments." [31] True, Baptism is valid even if the water is not
blessed. But, as Schell remarks, " In the case of Confirmation there is greater need that the element be blessed
than in the case of Baptism, because Confirmation
truly and properly confers the Holy Ghost. . . . This
explains the exalted rites employed in consecrating the
sacred chrism, the reverence with which it is handled,
and the express declaration of the Tridentine Council,
Sess. VII, *De Confirm.,* can. *2.* All this presupposes
a special dignity and power, which the Church attributes to the sacred chrism in virtue of the blessing
bestowed upon it. It is proper, too, that the element
used in the anointing be blessed, since the hands of the
confirming minister must be consecrated, which is not the
case in Baptism." [32]

3. THE SACRAMENTAL FORM OF CONFIRMA-
TION.—Because of the uncertainty enveloping the
matter of Confirmation, the *form,* too, is in dispute.

a) Speaking in the abstract, and taking the rite
as it is customary to-day, the form may be, either

---

[31] *Die dogmatische Lehre von den hl. Sakramenten,* Vol. I, 5th ed., p. 276, Münster 1894.

[32] *Dogmatik,* Vol. III, p. 496,

Paderborn 1892. Cfr. Dölger, *Das Sakrament der Firmung,* pp. 101 sqq., 193 sqq.

a) The prayer *"Omnipotens sempiterne Deus"* pronounced by the bishop at the general imposition of hands; or

β) The words spoken by him when he anoints the forehead of each candidate with chrism, *viz.:* "I sign thee with the sign of the cross and confirm thee with the chrism of salvation, in the name of the Father, and of the Son, and of the Holy Ghost."

Probably since the First Council of Constantinople (381),[33] but surely since the Trullan Council of 692,[34] the Eastern Church has employed this formula: "The sign [or seal] of the gift of the Holy Ghost."[35]

Though it is customary in some dioceses to lock the door after the general imposition of hands, it may be assumed with reasonable certainty that the prayer accompanying that ceremony does not enter into the essential form of the Sacrament, since this preliminary imposition itself does not constitute part of the essential matter. Consequently the true form must be sought in the words pronounced at the anointing. This is, in fact, the teaching of the Council of Florence.[36] The present formula, "I sign thee with the sign of the cross," etc., is no older than the twelfth century.[37] Before

---

[33] Can. 7.

[34] Can. 94.

[35] "Signaculum doni Spiritus Sancti — Σφραγὶς δωρεᾶς πνεύματος ἁγίου."

[36] "Forma autem est: Signo te signo crucis, etc." (Denzinger-Bannwart, n. 697).

[37] Alexander of Hales (S. Th., IV, qu. 9, m. 1) and Albertus Magnus (Comment. in Sent., IV, dist. 7, art. 2) still give different formulas, while St. Thomas (S. Th., 3a, qu. 72, art. 4) and St. Bonaventure know but one, i. e. the one still in use.

that time others were in use. According to Amalarius of Metz (d. about 857), the Latin Church had no uniform formula of Confirmation in the ninth century. The same may be said of the Oriental churches, with the sole exception of the Greek, which has employed its present formula ever since the sixth century.[38]

b) Which particular words constitute the substance of the formula is a purely theoretical question that can easily be decided if we admit the Greek formula to be essentially equivalent to the longer Latin one, and bear in mind what was said in the first part of this treatise about the specific determination of matter and form for all the Sacraments by Jesus Christ.[39] Manifestly the formula of Confirmation must express two concepts, *viz.:* (1) the act of signing or sealing (*signo te* — σφραγίς), and (2) the grace of the Holy Ghost (*confirmo te* — δωρεᾶς πνεύματος ἁγίου). Neither the invocation of the most holy Trinity nor the words *signo crucis* and *chrismate salutis* are essential.[40] So far as we know, all the formulas ever in use embodied these two leading ideas, at least implicitly.[41]

The blow on the cheek (*alapa*) did not become customary until the twelfth century. It was apparently devised in imitation of the blow by which knighthood was conferred in the Middle Ages, to serve as a symbolic exhorta-

---

[38] A collection of Confirmation formulas may be found in Martène, *De Ant. Eccl. Ritib.*, l. I, c. 2, art. 4; the Coptic, Syriac, and Armenian rites are described by Denzinger, *Rit. Orient.*, I, 49 sqq., 209, 220 sqq., Würzburg 1863.

[39] *V. supra*, pp. 107 sqq.

[40] Making the sign of the cross on the forehead of the recipient is part of the *materia* of the Sacrament, and probably essential. Cfr. St. Au-

gustine, *Tract. in Ioa.*, 118, n. 5 (Migne, *P. L.*, XXXIII, 1950).

[41] On the subject of the matter and form of Confirmation cfr. Merlin, S. J., *Traité Historique et Dogmatique sur les Paroles ou les Formes des Sept Sacrements*, ch. 7-8, Paris 1844 (uncritical); Chr. Pesch, *Praelect. Dogmat.*, Vol. VI, 3rd ed., pp. 234 sqq.; Dölger, *Das Sakrament der Firmung*, pp. 199 sqq.

tion to the recipient to follow the example of Christ in suffering patiently [42] and enduring contumely for His sake.[43]

[42] Cfr. Mark XIV, 65; John XIX, 3.

[43] Acts V, 41.— Cfr. N. Gihr, *op. cit.*, Vol. I, 2nd ed., pp. 360 sqq. Dölger thinks that the blow on the cheek is a sign of endearment and that it was gradually substituted for the "kiss of peace" customary in olden times. (*Op. cit.*, p. 155).

SECTION 3

SACRAMENTAL EFFECTS

Confirmation by its very name signifies the consummation of baptismal grace. The effect it produces is twofold: It increases sanctifying grace and imprints the sacramental character.

1. INCREASE OF SANCTIFYING GRACE.—a) Since Confirmation perfects the grace of Baptism, it must be received in the state of sanctifying grace. Hence Confirmation is a Sacrament of the living; it does not produce the state of grace but merely increases it (*augmentum gratiae sanctificantis, iustificatio secunda*).

The Council of Florence defines: "By Confirmation we receive an increase of grace and are strengthened in the faith." [1] This is in conformity with the Patristic teaching that baptized persons become full-fledged Christians (*pleni Christiani*) through Confirmation; not as if Baptism produced only "half-Christians" (*semichristiani*), as Calvin mockingly says, but as by growth children develop into complete and full-grown men.

b) The specific grace of Confirmation (*gratia sacramentalis*) consists in the "power of the Holy

[1] *Decretum pro Armenis: "Per confirmationem augemur in gratia et roboramur in fide."* (Denzinger-Bannwart, n. 695).

Ghost," by which the recipient is enabled to believe firmly and to profess the faith courageously.

" The effect of this Sacrament," says the *Decretum pro Armenis,* " is that in it is given the Holy Ghost for strengthening, as He was given to the Apostles on the day of Pentecost, namely that the Christian may boldly profess the name of Christ." [2]   This was indeed the effect produced by the descent of the Paraclete, as our Lord Himself had foretold and promised. Acts I, 8: " You shall receive the power of the Holy Ghost coming upon you, and you shall be witnesses unto me in Jerusalem, . . . even to the utmost part of the earth." [3]   Though the Apostles received this power without the Sacrament, the faithful generally can obtain it only through Confirmation.

Confirmation imparts the seven gifts of the Holy Ghost, particularly fortitude, which in extreme cases enables the Christian soldier to lay down his life for the faith.[4] As Doctor Schell aptly says: " Confirmation confers and is intended to effect the possession and use of the supernatural state of grace, the courageous practice of faith, hope, and charity through wisdom, understanding, counsel and strength, knowledge, piety, and the fear of God. The ecclesiastical name for all these gifts is *power,* — power to begin as well as to resist, to break down inordinate self-love, thus enabling man with a free spirit

---

2 *Ibid.: " Effectus autem huius sacramenti est, quia in eo datur Spiritus Sanctus ad robur, sicut datus est Apostolis in die Pentecostes, ut vid. Christianus audacter Christi confiteatur nomen."* (Denzinger-Bannwart, n. 697).

3 Acts I, 8: *" Accipietis virtutem supervenientis Spiritus Sancti* (δύναμιν ἐπελθόντος τοῦ ἁγίου πνεύματος) *in vos, et eritis mihi testes* (μάρτυρες) *in Ierusalem . . . usque in ultimum terrae."*

4 Cfr. St. Ambrose, *De Myst.,* c. 7, n. 42: *" Unde repete quia accepisti signaculum spirituale, spiritum sapientiae et intellectus, spiritum concilii et virtutis, spiritum cognitionis atque pietatis, spiritum sanctum timoris: et serva quod accepisti."*

to fear God alone, and to serve Him, proof against sensual pleasure and human respect." [5]

To effect this sublime purpose, Confirmation bestows a right to all those actual graces which are necessary to enable a man to fight for Christ and to defeat the enemies of his salvation. [6]

In the Apostolic Church, Confirmation often bestowed those extraordinary gifts (*gratiae gratis datae*) known as *charismata, e. g.* speaking in divers tongues, prophesying future events, discerning good spirits from evil, etc. [7] The existence of these gifts may be traced in the writings of the sub-Apostolic Fathers, especially St. Ignatius of Antioch, St. Polycarp, St. Justin Martyr, and St. Irenaeus. The *charismata* had ceased in the time of St. Chrysostom, for reasons which St. Augustine indicates as follows: " Who expects in these days that those on whom hands are laid in order that they may receive the Holy Ghost, should forthwith begin to speak with tongues? . . . He [the Holy Ghost] was given in former days to be the credentials of a rudimentary faith, and for the extension of the first beginnings of the Church." [8]

2. The Sacramental Character.—Like Baptism, Confirmation imprints an indelible mark or character on the soul, and therefore cannot be repeated.

Theologians have not been able to agree on the speculative question how this character differs from the one

5 *Dogmatik*, Vol. III, p. 507.

6 On the relation between sanctifying grace and sacramental grace in general, *v. supra*, pp. 70 sqq.

7 Cfr. 1 Cor. XII, 1 sqq.

8 *De Bapt. contr. Donat.*, III, 16, 21: " Quis enim hoc nunc exspectat, ut ii quibus manus ad accipiendum Spiritum Sanctum imponitur, repente incipiant linguis loqui? . . . Antea dabatur ad commendationem rudis fidei et Ecclesiae primordia dilatanda."

imprinted by Baptism. Some, laying special emphasis on the fact that Confirmation is " the consummation of Baptism," argue that the sacramental character bestowed by the one is simply a more perfect development of that imprinted by the other. This opinion is, however, unacceptable because it fails to make sufficient allowance for the independent status of Baptism and for the fact that each Sacrament has its own specific object. The character imprinted by Baptism can undoubtedly exist by itself alone and has no intrinsic need of being complemented by any other. Moreover, its main function is specifically different from that of the character of Confirmation. The one effects spiritual regeneration, while the other causes spiritual growth. Consequently there is a real distinction between the two. This can be made still clearer by applying to both the notion of the fourfold *signum,* explained above.[9] Thus, to mention but one, Confirmation *qua signum configurativum* marks the recipient as a soldier of Christ, whereas Baptism designates him merely as a subject. There is between the two a distinction as real as that between a soldier's uniform and his coat-of-arms.[10]

9 *V. supra,* pp. 89 sqq.

10 Cfr. Suarez, *De Confirm.,* disp. 34, sect. 1.— On the whole subject of the present Section consult Heinrich-Gutberlet, *Dogmatische Theologie,* Vol. IX, § 520.

CHAPTER II

Confirmation is not necessary as a means of salvation, and the precept to receive this Sacrament does not oblige under penalty of mortal sin. Nevertheless, the fact that Confirmation was instituted by Christ is sufficient proof that it must not be lightly neglected.

1. CONFIRMATION IS NOT NECESSARY AS A MEANS OF SALVATION.—If Confirmation were necessary for salvation *necessitate medii,* like Baptism, an unconfirmed person dying in the state of baptismal innocence could not be saved,—which is contrary to the teaching of Trent [1] and to the practice of the Church.

Unconfirmed adults in danger of death are not given the Sacrament of Confirmation, but that of Extreme Unction, for the simple reason that Confirmation was instituted for the battle of life, not for the death struggle. This explains why a dying Christian who has never been confirmed, is not required to have a desire (*votum sacramenti*) for Confirmation,— a sure proof that the Church does not regard Confirmation as a necessary means of salvation.

[1] Sess. V, can. 5 (quoted *supra,* p. 232).

2. CONFIRMATION IS NECESSARY NECESSITATE PRAECEPTI.

—The fact that this Sacrament was instituted by the Saviour as a means of grace for the saving of souls proves that all men are obliged to receive it, if they are able.

If Confirmation were merely useful but not necessary, *necessitate praecepti,* why did Christ institute it as the complement and consummation of Baptism for all men? In the early days the faithful were more deeply convinced of the necessity of receiving this Sacrament than many are to-day. Confirmation used to be administered to children immediately after Baptism, as is still the practice among the Greeks, and numerous conciliary decrees and papal decretals insisted on the obligation of receiving it. Thus the Council of Laodicæa (370) ordained: " It behooves those who are illuminated, to be anointed after Baptism with the supercelestial chrism, and to be made partakers of Christ." [2]

As to the nature of the obligation, theologians are divided. Some [3] regard neglect to receive Confirmation, provided there be no positive contempt, as scarcely even a venial sin. Others [4] take a more rigorous view. St. Peter Damian (d. 1075) insists that the obligation to receive this Sacrament is a serious one. [5] Benedict XIV teaches that it binds under pain of grievous sin. [6] Clement

2 Can. 48: " *Oportet eos, qui illuminantur, post baptisma inungi supercoelesti chrismate et esse Christi participes.*"

3 Billuart, Chr. Pesch, Gihr, etc., and, among the moralists, Laymann, Lehmkuhl, *et al.* They base their teaching on St. Thomas, *Summa Theol.,* 3a, qu. 72, art. 1, ad 3; art. 8, ad 4.

4 *E. g.,* Scotus (*Comment. in*

Sent., IV, dist. 7, qu. 2) and Tournely.

5 *De Eccl. Dedic. Serm.,* 1, c. 2: " *Decretales paginae et S. Patrum instituta decernunt non esse differendam post baptismum sacramenti huius virtutem, ne nos inermes inveniat fraudulentus ille contortor, a quo nemo unquam nocendi inducias extorsit.*"

6 Quoted by St. Alphonsus in his

XIV, in 1774, approved a decree of the S. Congregation of the Propaganda to the effect that "this Sacrament cannot be refused or neglected without incurring the guilt of mortal sin, if there be an opportune occasion of receiving it." [7] These utterances may not constitute a positive ecclesiastical precept, binding under pain of mortal sin; yet it is perhaps not too much to say that Confirmation is indirectly necessary for salvation, and there is a grave obligation to receive it, when possible. Simar justly observes: "The divine institution of this Sacrament is proof sufficient that God wills every member of the Church to receive it if he possibly can (*praeceptum implicitum*). The love that a Christian must have for his own soul makes it appear a grave duty not to neglect so efficacious a means of grace (*necessitas medii indirecta*)." [8] To-day when the faith is threatened by so many serious dangers, its courageous profession against growing unbelief becomes a sacred duty, and the faithful have greater need perhaps than ever, since the days of the martyrs, of the grace imparted by the Sacrament of Confirmation.[9]

Theologia Moralis, 1. VI, n. 182: "*Monendi sunt ab Ordinariis locorum eos gravis peccati reatu teneri, si (quum possunt) ad confirmationem accedere renuunt ac negligunt.*"

7 "*Hoc sacramentum sine gravis peccati reatu respui non potest ac negligi, quum illud suscipiendi opportuna adest occasio.*"

8 *Lehrbuch der Dogmatik*, Vol. I, 4th ed., p. 827, Freiburg 1899: "*Jedoch schon durch die Einsetzung dieses Sakramentes ist der göttliche Wille, dass die Glieder der Kirche dasselbe womöglich empfangen sollen, genügend kundgetan (praeceptum implicitum); auch die christliche Selbstliebe lässt es als eine schwerwiegende Pflicht erscheinen, dass man nicht ohne zwingende Gründe die Erlangung eines so wirksamen Gnadenmittels versäume (necessitas medii indirecta).*"

9 Cfr. Dölger, *Das Sakrament der Firmung*, pp. 179 sqq.

CHAPTER III

THE MINISTER OF CONFIRMATION

The ordinary ministers of the Sacrament of Confirmation are the bishops. In extraordinary cases, simple priests can administer the Sacrament, though only with special powers from the Pope. We shall demonstrate this in two theses.

Thesis I: The ordinary ministers of Confirmation are the bishops.

This is *de fide*.

Proof. The schismatic Greeks, since Photius, maintain that simple priests are the ordinary ministers of Confirmation; but the Tridentine Council expressly condemns this proposition.[1]

a) Sacred Scripture records no instance where the Sacrament of Confirmation was conferred by any one but an Apostle.

St. Peter and St. John faced the dangers of a religious persecution to confirm the converts baptized by Philip the deacon in Samaria. At Ephesus, St. Paul imposed his hands on the twelve disciples of John after they had been

---

1 *Conc. Trident.*, Sess VII, *De Confirm.*, can. 3: " *Si quis dixerit, sanctae confirmationis ordinarium ministrum non esse solum episco-* *pum, sed quemvis simplicem sacerdotem, anathema sit.*" (Denzinger-Bannwart, n. 873).

baptized in the name of the Lord Jesus.[2]   Evidently, then, the administration of Confirmation was an Apostolic, and therefore episcopal, prerogative.

Tradition always so regarded it, as we have previously shown.[3]

b) A conclusive argument may be drawn from the papal instruction to Bishop Decentius of Eugubium (d. 417), in which Innocent the First distinctly says that the administration of the Sacrament of Confirmation is an episcopal prerogative.[4]   A remarkable example is furnished by Pope St. Gregory the Great (d. 604).   When he learned that the priests of Sardinia administered Confirmation as though it were a right attached to the sacerdotal office, Gregory, in a letter to the Bishop of Cagliari, condemned and forbade the practice.[5]   This decision created wide-spread dissatisfaction, and Gregory subsequently wrote another letter in which, while recalling " the ancient discipline of the Church " in support of his previous decree, he benevolently acceded to the wishes of the Sardinian people and allowed the clergy to continue to give Confirmation by special permission of the Holy See.[6]

2 Cfr. Acts VIII, 14 sqq.; Acts XIX, 1 sqq.

3 *V. supra*, pp. 282 sqq. Cfr. Dölger, *Das Sakrament der Firmung*, pp. 24 sqq., 119 sqq., 201 sqq.

4 " *De consignandis vero infantibus manifestum est, non ab alio quam ab episcopo fieri licere; nam presbyteri, licet secundi sint sacerdotes, pontificatus tamen apicem non habent. Hoc autem pontificium solis deberi episcopis, ut vel consignent vel Paracletum Spiritum tradant, non solum consuetudo ecclesiastica demonstrat, verum et illa lectio Actuum Apostolorum, quae asserit Petrum et Ioannem esse directos, qui iam baptizatis traderent Spiritum Sanctum.*" (Denzinger-Bannwart, n. 98).

5 *Epist.*, l. IV, ep. 9: " *Presbyteri baptizatos infantes signare sacro in frontibus chrismate non praesumant, sed presbyteri baptizatos ungant in pectore, ut episcopi postmodum ungere debeant in fronte.*" (Migne, *P. L.*, LXXVII, 677).

6 Cfr. St. Gregory the Great's *Ep.*, l. IV, *ep.* 26 *ad Ianuarium*: " *Pervenit quoque ad nos, quosdam scandalizatos fuisse, quod presbyteros chrismate tangere in fronte eos, qui*

c) The ordinary power of administering Confirmation is limited to the bishops, for two reasons. First, being a Sacrament of lesser importance, Confirmation demands no such universal and general prerogatives as Baptism, which is absolutely necessary to all men for salvation. Secondly, being the Sacrament of "the plenitude of the Spirit," Confirmation requires an administrator who has himself received full power and consecration. To these considerations St. Thomas Aquinas adds a third. "In every work," he says, "the final completion is reserved to the supreme act or power; thus the preparation of the matter belongs to the lower craftsman, the higher gives the form, but the highest of all is he to whom pertains the use, which is the end of things made by art. Thus also the letter which is written by the clerk is signed by his employer. Now the faithful of Christ are a divine work, . . . and this Sacrament of Confirmation is, as it were, the final completion of the Sacrament of Baptism; in the sense that by Baptism a man is built up into a spiritual dwelling, and is written like a spiritual letter; whereas by the Sacrament of Confirmation, like a house already built, he is consecrated as a temple of the Holy Ghost, and as a letter already written, is signed with the sign of the cross. Therefore the conferring of this Sacrament is reserved to the bishops, who possess the supreme power in the Church. . . ." [7]

The famous Jesuit theologian, Francisco Suarez, compares the bishops to the generals of an army, and says that in this capacity they have the sole right to enlist new recruits for Christ. Only when the general (*i. e.* the

---

baptizati sunt, prohibuimus. Et nos quidem secundum veterem Ecclesiae nostrae usum fecimus; sed si omnino hac de re aliqui contristantur, ubi episcopi desunt, ut presbyteri etiam in frontibus baptizatos chrismate tangere debeant, concedimus." (Migne, *l. c.,* 696).

[7] *Summa Theol.,* 3a, qu. 72, art. 11.

bishop) is prevented, may the commander-in-chief (*i. e.* the Pope) delegate simple officers (*i. e.* priests) with the power of conscription.[8]

Does the power of administering Confirmation belong to the bishops by divine or merely by ecclesiastical right? This question has never been officially decided and is in debate among theologians. Trombelli tries to show that the episcopal prerogative of Confirmation rests entirely on the Canon Law.[9] But despite the erudition which this learned writer brings to bear on the subject, his argument is by no means conclusive. The Fathers and early councils were plainly convinced that the episcopal prerogative is based on a divine ordinance, and the Council of Trent raised the proposition that bishops only are the ordinary ministers of Confirmation, to the rank of a dogma,— which it would hardly have done if the canonical precept were not founded on a divine command.

Thesis II: In extraordinary cases simple priests can administer Confirmation, but only with special powers granted by the Pope.

This proposition may be technically qualified as *"sententia certa."*

Proof. Hugh of St. Victor,[10] Durandus,[11] and other Scholastic theologians deny the right of the Supreme Pontiff to grant the special power referred to; but there is now no longer any reason to doubt it. Thomists, Scotists, Bellarmine,[12] Suarez,[13] and De Lugo,[14] all regard Confirmation

8 *De Confirm.*, disp. 36, sect. 1.
9 *De Sacram.*, dissert. 10, Bologna 1773.
10 *De Sacram.*, II, 7, 2.

11 *Comment. in Sent.*, IV, dist. 7, qu. 3 sq.
12 *De Confirm.*, c. 12.
13 *De Confirm.*, disp. 36, sect. 2.
14 *Resp. Mor.*, I, dub. 6.

administered by simple priests with papal authority as valid.

Our thesis cannot be demonstrated directly from Sacred Scripture, and we therefore have to rely on Tradition.

a) In the Greek Church simple priests have administered Confirmation since the early days.

Though St. Chrysostom regards Confirmation as a " prerogative [15] of the coryphaei " (*i. e.* bishops), he is aware of its administration by ordinary priests. Long before the time of Photius, Confirmation by simple priests had been customary in the East, and the Western Church accepted it as valid. The matter came up for debate in the councils of Lyons (1274) and Florence (1439). At Florence the Oriental practice was vigorously defended by the Bishop of Mytilene. Pope Eugene IV declared in his famous *Decretum pro Armenis:* " However, we read that sometimes, by a dispensation granted by the Apostolic See for some reasonable and urgent cause, a simple priest administered this Sacrament with chrism consecrated by a bishop." [16] This declaration did not, it is true, justify the Oriental practice; but it showed that the Holy See was aware of its existence and tolerated it. Benedict XIV expressly acknowledged its validity —" because of at least a tacit privilege conceded by the Apostolic See." [17] This rule still governs the practice of

[15] δῶρον ἐξαίρετου. *V. supra,* p. 285.

[16] " *Legitur tamen aliquando per Apostolicae Sedis dispensationem ex rationabili et urgente admodum causâ simplicem sacerdotem chrismate per episcopum confecto hoc administrasse confirmationis sacramentum.*" (Denzinger-Bannwart, n. 697).

[17] *De Syn. Dioec.,* VII, 9, 3: " *In aliis locis, in quibus chrismatio data a sacerdotibus graecis non est a Sede Apostolica expresse improbata, ea pro valida est habenda ob tacitum saltem privilegium a Sede Apostolica illis concessum, cuius quidem privilegii praesumptionem inducit ipsamet conniventia et tolerantia*

the Roman Church. Confirmation given by schismatic Greek priests is never repeated except in countries or regions from which the Holy See has expressly withdrawn the privilege, *e. g.* Bulgaria, Cyprus, Italy, Sardinia, Sicily, Corsica, and the Maronite districts about the Lebanon.[18]

b) In the Latin Church Confirmation, as a rule, has always been administered by bishops, and only in exceptional cases by priests.

This practice, which is far more in conformity with the dogmatic teaching defined at Trent, gained the upper hand in the West after the thirteenth century, when Baptism and Confirmation gradually became separated by constantly lengthening intervals of time. The administration of Confirmation by priests was and is comparatively rare, but cases have occurred in every century since the time of Gregory the Great, though always with express papal authorization and with chrism consecrated by bishops. Since the Council of Trent the Holy See has at various times granted the right to administer Confirmation to Jesuit missionaries, to the Custodian of the Holy Sepulchre at Jerusalem, the Provost of St. Hedwig's Church in Berlin, and other priests.[19]

c) It is not easy to justify this exceptional practice in view of the fact that the validity of Confirmation has nothing to do with the power of jurisdiction, but depends entirely on the character of ordination.

Romanorum Pontificum, qui praedictum morem Graecorum scienter non contradixerunt nec unquam illum damnarunt."

18 Cfr. Dölger, *Das Sakrament der Firmung,* pp. 123 sqq., 203 sqq.

19 Cfr. Billuart, *De Confirm.,* art. 7, §1; Benedict XIV, *De Syn. Dioec.,* VII, 7.

A deacon, for instance, could not validly administer this Sacrament even with papal permission, whilst, on the other hand, a heretical, schismatic, suspended, or excommunicated bishop can do so even against the express command of the Pope. How, then, is it possible for a simple priest to confirm validly, if the papal permit does not supply the lack of episcopal consecration?

Various attempts have been made to overcome this difficulty.

Some theologians have assumed that the papal delegation is not a mere extrinsic permission but implies an intrinsic perfectioning of the character of ordination by which the delegated priest receives the episcopal character.[20] Others hold with Suarez [21] that the papal authorization merely gives to the delegated priest a higher extrinsic dignity which, together with his sacerdotal character, suffices to enable him to administer the Sacrament validly. Both hypotheses are unsatisfactory. A simpler and more effective solution is that devised by Gregory of Valentia.[22] It was the will of Christ, he says, that both bishops and priests should be empowered to administer Confirmation, the former as ordinary ministers of the Sacrament by virtue of the episcopal consecration, the latter as its extraordinary ministers by virtue of the priesthood, leaving it to the Pope to determine the manner of exercising this latent power.[23]

20 Cfr. *Der Katholik*, Mainz 1894, I, pp. 271 sqq.

21 *De Confirm.*, disp. 36, sect. 2.

22 *De Confirm.*, disp. 5, qu. 2, punct. 1.

23 Cfr. Bellarmine, *De Confirm.*, c. 12.— The reasons why a merely episcopal delegation is insufficient, are set forth by Benedict XIV, *De Syn. Dioec.*, VII, 8.— On the whole subject of this Chapter see Chr. Pesch, *Praelect. Dogmat.*, Vol. VI, 3rd ed., pp. 243 sqq.; Dölger, *Das Sakrament der Firmung*, pp. 206 sqq.

CHAPTER IV

THE RECIPIENT OF CONFIRMATION

To be validly confirmed one must have been previously baptized; to receive the Sacrament worthily, one must be in the state of grace and, if an adult, have at least a rudimentary knowledge of the faith.

1. THE RECIPIENT MUST HAVE BEEN BAPTIZED.—Since the right to receive the other Sacraments is conferred neither by the Baptism of desire nor by the Baptism of blood, Baptism by water is a necessary requisite of valid Confirmation. Cornelius, the centurion, who received the Holy Ghost before he was baptized, received only the grace of Confirmation, not the Sacrament, nor the character which it imprints. According to indications contained in the Acts of the Apostles, and the constant teaching and practice of the Church, every baptized person, whether male or female, young or old, well or ill, is a fit subject for Confirmation.[1]

---

[1] As to whether and in how far the insane or feeble-minded are fit subjects for Confirmation, see J. Familler, *Pastoral-Psychiatrie*, p. 163, Freiburg 1898.

Regarding children, in particular, it is just as certain that they can be validly confirmed as that they can be validly baptized. The Greek Church still adheres to the ancient practice of confirming infants immediately after Baptism. The Latin Church seems to have pretty generally followed the same rule up to the thirteenth century. At the present time the only difference between the two is that while in the Greek Church it is the priests who confirm, in the Latin Church this Sacrament is administered by the bishops. A Council held at Cologne, A. D. 1280, decreed that Confirmation should be deferred until the years of discretion. The Roman Catechism declares that the administration of this Sacrament is inexpedient until children have attained the use of reason (which is between the ages of seven and twelve), because " Confirmation has not been instituted as necessary to salvation, but that by virtue thereof we might be found very well armed and prepared, when called upon to fight for the faith of Christ." [2] Nevertheless, the Church has never made a law, nor is there any explicit custom sanctioned by antiquity, which forbids the confirming of infants. On the contrary, bishops are free to confirm little children, if they so please, as is evident from the *Pontificale Romanum,* which says: " Infants should be held by their sponsors on the right arm before the bishop who wishes to confirm them." [3] Bishops are generally guided in this matter by the custom of the country.

2. THE RECIPIENT MUST NOT HAVE BEEN CONFIRMED BEFORE.—It is of faith [4] that Con-

---

2 *Cat. Rom.,* P. II, c. 3, n. 18.

3 " *Infantes per patrinos ante pontificem confirmare volentem teneantur in brachiis dextris.*"

4 Cfr. *Conc. Trident.,* Sess. VII, *De Sacram.,* can. 9.

firmation imprints an indelible mark (*character indelebilis*) on the soul, and therefore can not be repeated. To reconfirm a person would be as great a crime as to rebaptize him.

St. Cyprian's view that Confirmation administered by a heretical minister is invalid, and may therefore be repeated, was based on his erroneous belief (later condemned by the Church in connection with the Donatist schism) that a Sacrament, in order to be valid, must be administered by one who is a true believer and in the state of sanctifying grace. The attitude of Pope Stephen the First is uncertain. Though he condemned rebaptism, he seems to have countenanced reconfirmation.[5] Aside from a few such uncertain cases, the Church can be shown to have constantly held the belief that Confirmation by a heretical minister is valid. The "laying-on of hands" of which we read in the writings of the Fathers and the acts of councils in connection with the return of heretics to the Church, was not the Sacrament of Confirmation, but something we should now call a "sacramental"—a ceremony of reconciliation, which was sometimes accompanied by an anointment. "The laying-on of hands in reconciliation," says St. Augustine, "is not, like Baptism, incapable of repetition; for what is it more than a prayer offered over a man?"[6] In order to avoid misunderstanding when reading the ancient Fathers and conciliary decrees, it is necessary in each instance to ascertain from the context what is meant by

5 On this controversy cfr. Dölger, *Das Sakrament der Firmung*, pp. 130 sqq.; B. Poschmann, *Die Sichtbarkeit der Kirche nach der Lehre des hl. Cyprian*, pp. 118 sqq., Paderborn 1908.

6 *De Bapt. contr. Donat.*, III, 16: " Manus impositio (scil. reconciliatoria) non sicut baptismus repeti non potest; quid est enim aliud nisi oratio super hominem? " (Migne, P. L., XLIII, 149).

the phrase " laying-on of hands." There was a threefold laying-on of hands in the primitive Church, to wit: (1) the *manus impositio confirmatoria, i. e.* Confirmation, which is a true Sacrament; (2) the *manus impositio ordinatoria, i. e.* ordination, which is also a true Sacrament; and (3) the *manus impositio reconciliatoria, i. e.* the ceremony of readmitting heretics to the Church, which was no Sacrament at all, but merely what is now called a sacramental.[7]

3. THE RECIPIENT MUST BE PROPERLY PREPARED.—To be duly prepared for Confirmation, the candidate must first of all be in the state of sanctifying grace, because Confirmation is a Sacrament of the living.[8]

In addition there is required a knowledge of the rudiments of the faith, more particularly of the Apostles' Creed, the Ten Commandments, and the Seven Sacraments, especially of the Church's teaching in regard to Confirmation itself. To make sure that the would-be recipients possess this knowledge, the bishop usually subjects them to an examination. The Church also insists on the previous reception of the Sacrament of Penance and admonishes the candidates for Confirmation to prepare themselves for the reception of the Holy Ghost by pious prayer and an ardent desire,[9] and, if possible, to receive the Sacrament fasting.[10]

READINGS : — St. Thomas, *Summa Theologica,* 3a, qu. 72, art. 1-12.— Billuart, *De Confirmatione* (ed. Lequette, Vol. VI, pp. 345

7 Cfr. A. J. Binterim, *Die vorzüg-lichsten Denkwürdigkeiten der christ-katholischen Kirche,* V, 2, pp. 299 sqq., 453 sqq., Mainz 1836.

8 *V. supra,* pp. 300 sqq.
9 Cfr. Acts I, 14.
10 Cfr. *Cat. Rom.,* P. II, c. 3, n. 18.

sqq.).— Bellarmine, *De Sacramento Confirmationis,* c. 1-27 (ed. Fèvre, Vol. III, pp. 588 sqq., Paris 1870).

Other literature see under Baptism, p. 275, *supra.*

Monographs: I. A. Orsi, O.Pr., *De Chrismate Confirmatorio,* Rome 1733; M. Gerbert, O.S.B., *De Sacramentis, Praesertim Confirmatione,* S. Blasien 1764; Jos. Bertieri, *De Sacramentis in Genere et de Baptismo et Confirmatione,* Vienna 1774; *Vitasse, De Sacramento Confirmationis Libri VIII* (in Migne's *Theologiae Cursus Completus,* Vol. XXI, pp. 546 sqq.) ; Fr. Brenner, *Geschichtliche Darstellung der Verrichtung und Ausspendung der Firmung,* Bamberg 1820; Welz, *Das Sakrament der Firmung,* Breslau 1847; B. Nepefny, *Die Firmung,* Passau 1869; G. Bickell, *"Das Sakrament der Firmung bei den Nestorianern,"* in the Innsbruck *Zeitschrift für kath. Theologie,* 1877, pp. 85 sqq.; L. Janssens, O.S.B., *La Confirmation, Exposé Dogmatique, Historique et Liturgique,* Lille 1888; M. Heimbucher, *Die heilige Firmung, das Sakrament des Hl. Geistes,* Augsburg 1889; M. Meschler, S.J., *Die Gaben des hl. Pfingstfestes,* 5th ed., Freiburg 1905; A. F. Wirgman, *The Doctrine of Confirmation,* London 1902; *Fr. Dölger, Das Sakrament der Firmung,* Vienna 1906.

T. B. Scannell, art. " Confirmation," in Vol. IV of the *Catholic Encyclopedia.*— F. H. Chase (Anglican), *Confirmation in the Apostolic Age,* London 1909.— A. Devine, C.P., *The Sacraments Explained,* pp. 158 sqq., 3rd ed., London 1905.— W. Humphrey, S.J., *The One Mediator,* pp. 99 sqq., London 1890.— J. R. Gasquet, " The Early History of Baptism and Confirmation," in the *Dublin Review,* 1895, pp. 116 sqq.— L. Duchesne, *Christian Worship,* pp. 292 sqq., London 1903.— P. Pourrat, *Theology of the Sacraments, passim,* 2nd ed., St. Louis 1914.— J. Tixeront, *History of Dogmas,* Vol. I, St. Louis 1910, Vol. II, 1914.— M. O'Dwyer, *Confirmation: A Study in the Development of Sacramental Theology,* Dublin 1915.— B. J. Otten, S. J., *A Manual of the History of Dogmas,* Vol. I, St. Louis 1917, pp. 42, 52, 167, 178, 340 sqq., 342, 347, 350, 472; Vol. II (1918), pp. 305 sqq.

INDEX